T0289783

ROUTLEDGE LIBRARY EDITIONS:
THE ECONOMICS AND BUSINESS OF
TECHNOLOGY

Volume 17

INDUSTRIAL CHANGE IN ADVANCED ECONOMIES

INDUSTRIAL CHANGE IN ADVANCED ECONOMIES

Edited by
F. E. IAN HAMILTON

LONDON AND NEW YORK

First published in 1987 by Croom Helm Ltd

This edition first published in 2018
by Routledge
2 Park Square, Milton Park, Abingdon, Oxon OX14 4RN

and by Routledge
711 Third Avenue, New York, NY 10017

Routledge is an imprint of the Taylor & Francis Group, an informa business

British Library Cataloguing in Publication Data
A catalogue record for this book is available from the British Library

ISBN: 978-1-138-50336-6 (Set)
ISBN: 978-1-351-06690-7 (Set) (ebk)
ISBN: 978-0-8153-7454-1 (Volume 17) (hbk)
ISBN: 978-1-351-24165-6 (Volume 17) (ebk)

Publisher's Note
The publisher has gone to great lengths to ensure the quality of this reprint but points out that some imperfections in the original copies may be apparent.

Disclaimer
The publisher has made every effort to trace copyright holders and would welcome correspondence from those they have been unable to trace.

INDUSTRIAL CHANGE
IN ADVANCED ECONOMIES

Edited by
F.E. IAN HAMILTON

CROOM HELM
London • Sydney • Wolfeboro, New Hampshire

© 1987 F.E. Ian Hamilton
Croom Helm Ltd, Provident House, Burrell Row,
Beckenham, Kent, BR3 1AT
Croom Helm Australia Pty Ltd, Suite 4, 6th Floor,
64-76 Kippax Street, Surry Hills, NSW 2010, Australia

British Library Cataloguing in Publication Data
Industrial change in advanced economies.
   1. Industrialisation
   I. Hamilton, F.E. Ian
   338.09172'2 HD23Z9

   ISBN 0-7099-3828-4

Croom Helm 27 South Main Street,
Wolfeboro, New Hampshire 03894-2069, USA

Library of Congress Cataloging-in-Publication Data

Hamilton, F.E. Ian.
   Industrial change in advanced economies.

   Includes index.
   1. Technological innovations — Economic aspects.
2. Industry — Location. 3. Industrialization.
4. International business enterprises. I. Title.
HC79.T4H35 1987   338.09   86-19661
ISBN 0-7099-3828-4

Printed and bound in Great Britain
by Billing & Sons Limited, Worcester.

CONTENTS

CONTENTS

CONTRIBUTORS

Claes Alvstam obtained his B.Sc. (Econ.) and Dr.Econ. at the University of Göteborg, Sweden, where he is at present Associate Professor of Economic Geography.

Henri Bakis, M.A. (Université de Paris VIII), Docteur de l'Etat (Sorbonne) is a Professor at the Université de Paris and researcher at the Centre National d'Etudes des Telecommunications, Issy-Les-Moulineaux, France.

Balint Balkay, B.A., Ph.D. in Geology (Eötvös University, Budapest), worked for 15 years in the Hungarian Aluminium Corporation and is now Senior Research Fellow, World Economy Institute, Hungarian Academy of Sciences, Budapest XII, Kallo Esperes Utca 15, H-1531 Budapest, P.O. Box 36, Hungary.

Mark Bandman obtained his B.A. and Ph.D. at Moscow State University and is now Head of the Territorial Production Complex Research unit of the Institute of Economics and Industrial Organisation, Siberian Branch of the Soviet Academy of Sciences, Novosibirsk, USSR.

Györgyi Barta obtained her Ph.D. at the Hungarian Academy of Sciences, Budapest, and is now Senior Researcher in the Centre for Regional Studies, Regional Science Department, Hungarian Academy of Sciences, Budapest, Hungary.

Harold T. Cross, B.S., M.A., Ph.D. (Texas), is Assistant Director, Center for Enterprising, Edwin L. Cox School of Business, Southern Methodist University, Dallas, Texas, USA.

Evangelia Dokopoulou received her Diploma in Architecture at Athens Technical University, M.Sc. in Urban and Regional Planning at Oxford Polytechnic and Ph.D. at the London School of Economics. She is Lecturer in EEC Regional Studies, College of Humanities, National Institute for Higher Education, Limerick, Republic of Ireland.

CONTRIBUTORS

Genevieve Duché received her Docteur des Sciences Economiques at the Paul Valéry University I, Montpellier, and is now Maitre de Conferences at the University of Montpellier Paul Valéry III, France.

Kajsa Ellegård obtained her B.A. and Ph.D. at the University of Göteborg, Sweden. She is at present a Research Assistant in Human and Economic Geography in the Universities of Göteborg and Lund, Sweden.

Peter Herdson, B.Sc.(Econ.) (London School of Economics), has responsibility for business intelligence, is involved in planning functions of the Imperial Chemicals Industries (ICI) Paints' World Group of Companies and is based at ICI Paints Division offices at Slough, England.

Koloman Ivanicka, M.A. (Warsaw), Ph.D. (Prague), Dr.Sc. (Czechoslovak Academy of Science), is Professor of Economic Geography and Environmental Studies, Komensky University, Bratislava, Czechoslovakia.

Risto Laulajainen obtained his BBA and DBA at the Helsinki School of Economics and Business Administration and is at present Professor in Economic Geography, Department of Human Geography, Göteborg University, Sweden.

Peter Lewis, B.A. and Ph.D. (Manchester), is now Emeritus Reader in Geography, University of London, and an industrial consultant at Bricklehurst Manor, Wadhurst, Sussex, England.

Kiyoji Murata, B.Sc. (Econ.) and Ph.D. (Chuo University), is Professor of Regional Economics, Chuo University, Tokyo, Japan.

Suzane Savey obtained her Docteur de l'Etat at the Paul Valéry University, Montpellier, France, and is now Professor, Geography and Planning, Université Paul Valéry III.

Eike Schamp, Diplom-Volkswirt, Ph.D. and Habilitation (Cologne), is Professor in Economic Geography, University of Göttingen, Federal Republic of Germany.

Guy P.F. Steed, B.A. (McGill), Ph.D. (University of Washington), is a Science Adviser, Science Council of Canada, Ottawa.

Atsuhiko Takeuchi, Ph.D. (Rissho University, Tokyo), is currently Professor of Economic Geography, Nippon Institute of Technology, Tokyo, Japan.

CONTRIBUTORS

Eirik Vatne, MBA and Ph.D. (Norwegian School of Economics and Business Administration), is Programme Director, Institute of Industrial Economics, Bergen, Norway.

David Wadley, B.A. (Sydney), Ph.D. (A.N.U.), is Senior Lecturer, University of Queensland, St. Lucia, Australia.

Bernard Weinstein, A.B. (Dartmouth), M.A., Ph.D. (Columbia) is Director, Center for Enterprising, Edwin L. Cox School of Business, Southern Methodist University, Dallas, Texas, USA.

ACKNOWLEDGEMENTS

Risto Laulajainen wishes to acknowledge both companies which have kindly supplied him with the data necessary for his chapter. At Atlas Copco AB the primary contact persons were Mr. Gunnar Palm, Assistant Vice President Marketing and Mr. Sven Standar, Editor of Tryckluft; at Ingersoll Rand Corporation, Mr. Stanley M. Parkhill, Editor of Compressed Air Magazine. Professor Laulajainen wishes also to thank Ms. Diana Matteson-Werner for drawing the figures and The Goteborg Business School Foundation for financing the study.

Ian Hamilton is deeply grateful to Godfrey Linge for his earlier assistance in editing Chapter Eight; to Pat Farnsworth, Jackie Jennings and Evangelia Dokopoulou for retyping several chapters; and to Jane Pugh, Alison Aspden and Gary Llewellyn for drawing some of the figures.

PREFACE

Industrial Change in Advanced Economies, together with its companion volume Industrialisation in Developing and Peripheral Regions, contains a selection of revised papers which were originally presented at, or submitted for, the International Geographical Union Commission on Industrial Systems' symposium in Nebian near Montpellier, France, in August 1984.

Key aspects of the Commission's activity have been to stimulate new directions of study and to push forward the frontiers of research on an international comparative basis. This work has frequently been seen to be dominated by researchers from the more advanced industrial economies and from the English-speaking world where studies are built on deep and long traditions of theoretical and empirical study of industrial development, adaptation and location. The following chapters in part reflect that foundation. Yet the book also expresses another objective in the Commission's remit, namely, to foster the international dissemination of findings - especially by younger teachers and researchers embarking on their careers - from the other industrialised European countries, centrally-managed economies and Japan.

The chapters in this volume are contributed by both younger and established researchers from more than a dozen countries. At least five authors have had experience working in or with the business world. At a time when the changes in the global industrial system are essentially being determined more than for some decades by international business, their counsel can be of real practical significance.

Industrial Change in Advanced Economies examines the salient features and implications of the reorganisation or restructuring of industries and industrial enterprises in the developed world, reflecting their development or harnessing of technological changes - not least to increase their bargaining power with, control over, or use of, labour. Various chapters discuss some of the present-day challenges to policy-making and to the role of the State posed by the apparent speed, scale and character of the changes that are occurring.

The book falls into several fairly well-defined sections. The first three chapters debate the explanations for, and the nature of, industrial reorganisation in both East and West and discuss some of its effects on work and labour, decisions and society. Genevieve Duché and Suzane Savey elaborate on the rising importance of small and medium-sized industrial enterprises in France as an indicator of trends common throughout the developed world; it is seen to reflect the reorganisation of the production system to weaken the bargaining power of labour and to change the relationships between State and capital in the face of contemporary technological opportunities, financial and competitive pressures. To a certain extent, Koloman Ivanicka addresses similar issues in Chapter Two regarding the restructuring of Czechoslovak industry, though he places them in the contexts of both wider changes in the Council for Mutual Economic Assistance countries and the need for a new evolutionary approach to industrial analysis. In the third chapter, Kajsa Ellegård and Claes Alvstam draw on the example of the Swedish firm of Volvo AB to demonstrate the links made in the production system by "the firm" between the changes in the organisation and division of labour at international, national, regional and shopfloor levels.

A second section examines recent trends in the character and location of selected industries and overlaps into a third distinctive part which presents recent work on multinational enterprise. In Chapter Four, Balint Balkay, with 15 years' experience behind him in the Hungarian Aluminium Corporation, discusses the changing forces shaping the world locational patterns of bauxite mining, alumina and aluminium production, emphasising, however, that this is an industry in which technological change is far less important than production economics and industry organisation. He hypothesises that aluminium is a good barometer of the minerals sector in general because in coming years the major transnationals are likely to relinquish their upstream activities, i.e. their backward linkages in mining and primary processing, to local enterprise. Peter Lewis' Chapter Five stresses the inevitability of closures in the West European papermaking industry as more grades of paper become subject to larger economies of scale.

By contrast, Peter Herdson in Chapter Six emphasises how significant technology is in the growth, spread and competitiveness of the multinational paint manufacturers and their market relationships. Attention is focused on specific multinationals by Risto Laulajainen who, in Chapter Seven, uses a longitudinal approach to make a unique comparison of the strategies, development, successes or otherwise of two competing multinational firms in the mature mechanical engineering industry - Ingersoll Rand and Atlas Copco AB - throwing interesting light on the behaviour and imperfections of real world industry. In Chapter Eight, Henri Bakis analyses the operations of IBM France in the context of the firm's worldwide organisation and strategies, illuminating the ways in which a major company can harness modern technology to its maximum advantage and to transcend almost any form of national sovereignty. The multinational theme is continued in Chapters Nine and Ten which, in a complementary manner, examine the oil industry. In the former, Bernard Weinstein and Harold Cross are at pains to show how developments - such as those described in Vatne's chapter - and the global downturn in demand for oil and oil products have had markedly recessionary influences on the economy of the US Gulf Coast "oil patch". They suggest a grassroots industrial policy to cope with the social and economic traumas of adjustment to industrial decline, job loss and the need for local and regional economic restructuring. Eirik Vatne, by contrast, discusses a network organisational approach to the development of a growth oilfield region - the North Sea - and shows how the gradual expansion of European firms in oilfield exploration, drilling and equipment production partly resulted from the rising bargaining power of the UK and Norwegian governments vis-a-vis US multinationals.

There is, in effect, a substantial transition in the preceding chapters on multinationals to with the next section which focuses on organisational changes. In Chapter Eleven Györgyi Barta outlines some of the changes that have been made in the industrial geography of Hungary as a result of the decentralisation of management from the former central ministries to the enterprises. Her conclusion, that this "decentralisation" in fact extended external control from Budapest over the country's provincial industrial systems following branch plant development by multi-site enterprises rings a very familiar sound in the ears of students of industrial and regional change in capitalist systems, but is perhaps unexpected in socialist systems. Mark Bandman in Chapter Twelve continues his research into Soviet territorial production complexes, emphasising the need for flexibility and novelty in their management, a theme which ties up with points made in Chapter Two by Ivanicka.

Technological issues form the specific focus of the next three chapters and tie up with the remaining two, which examine business services, to round off the section. Appropriately, the first contribution on technology relates to a major source country, Japan. In Chapter Thirteen Kiyogi Murata and Atsuhiko Takeuchi outline the heavy regional concentration of machinery manufacturing, microelectronics industries and R & D, mainly in the Tokyo "technopolis", implying that tight and intricate local linkages, contact systems and "neighbourhood effects" contribute significantly to

PREFACE

Japanese innovativeness and competitiveness. Quite the opposite situation is demonstrated in Chapter Fourteen by Evangelia Dokopoulou. She shows how multinational corporate control over technology is used, often with the unintentional assistance of government policy, to stunt industrial progress in smaller and weaker European states like Greece. The point of her chapter is to emphasise that the concentration of the locus of control in the "North" is still a powerful force shaping the production systems of core regions in the developed nations despite recession: sales of secondhand and outmoded technology to a country like Greece are necessary for the MNEs to make profits and to retain control over competition. Yet, in some instances government purchasing policy can actually create competition from abroad which can discourage further modernisation by MNEs serving the host country market. In Chapter Fifteen, Guy Steed examines Ottawa's "Silicon Valley North" and casts doubt on the ability of centres of high technology industry in more peripheral or new regions, even in advanced states, to replicate California's Silicon Valley.

Eike Schamp uses the example of Lower Saxony in the Federal German Republic in Chapter Sixteen to clarify the importance of business services to manufacturers, stressing, quite rightly, that too little attention has been paid in the literature to patterns of demand behaviour for these services. Finally, David Wadley re-examines the urban "transition zone" phenomenon, using Brisbane in Queensland, Australia, as a case study, to propose policies to revitalise this critical kind of area. He argues that "if one believes the struggle against unemployment is worth pursuing, the transition zone warrants reappraisal as an entity which...could be dynamic and constitute an important urban labour shed." If time is to tell whether or not he will be right, more than local policy initiatives are going to be necessary.

F.E. Ian Hamilton.
Visiting Croucher Fellow,
Centre for Urban Studies & Urban Planning,
University of Hong Kong.

Chapter One

THE RISING IMPORTANCE OF SMALL AND MEDIUM-SIZED
FIRMS: TOWARDS A NEW INDUSTRIAL SYSTEM?

Genevievé Duché and Suzane Savey

The purpose of this paper is not to present a theoretical
analysis of the so-called crisis but to try to submit some
hypotheses about the articulation of the economic, social and
spatial shifts that can be observed for more than ten years
and to try to extract some possible consequences for the
future of the capitalist mode of production.

THE MAIN CHANGING FEATURES, OR A NEW ORGANISATION
OF PRODUCTION

Taking France as an example, it is important to find out
whether the inversion of tendencies which began in the early
1970s was specific to that country, and whether the structural modifications taking place were short-term or basic.

The Recent Changes in Production Space in France

Since the early 1970s the poorer regions in France, especially
in the South and West, have been positively affected by the
great changes under way, while the traditionally advanced
regions are more and more depressed (Savey, 1983). Between
1975 and 1980 all the southern and western regions experienced a larger increase in their gross regional product than
the old industrial regions. Languedoc-Roussillon was the
leader, with a 4.7 per cent growth, while Lorraine, the most
thoroughly industrialised region, had the lowest growth.
During the same period the change in industrial employment,
negative in the whole country (-4.2 per cent), was positive
in regions from Languedoc to Brittany and strongly negative
in Lorraine (-11 per cent). Between 1975 and 1980 the mi-
gration balance of population showed a very strong increase
in the South and West, which was new for these regions, and
a strong decline in the Paris region, the North and the East.
Ile de France lost 40,000 inhabitants every year during this
period.

1

This oversimplified concept seems to indicate that dynamism has changed spatially: it now belongs to the "poor" regions of France, at the expense of the "rich" ones. Another aspect of this paradoxical situation is that indications previously considered negative are accompanying the emergence of the new dynamism. Thus regions where gross regional product, new employment and population are increasing more quickly are those where:

(a) the role of small- and medium-scale industries is the most important in regional added-value;
(b) the role of small industrial units is the most important employment; Languedoc-Roussillon has the leadership from this point of view;
(c) the proportion of skilled workers is amongst the lowest in France;
(d) the average gross wage is the lowest, particularly in industry; and
(e) the rate of unemployment is very high; here again, Languedoc-Roussillon is the leader.

All these indicators seem to point to the emergence of a new model of spatial, economic and social organisation. The regions which are nowadays the most attractive for population and where the gross regional production grows fast are those where industry hardly existed in the past, where industrial units are small, where small firms are numerous, where wages and qualifications are the lowest, and where the rate of unemployment is at its highest.

Small- and Medium-Scale Firms and the New Dynamism
In considering this tendency towards spatial inversion in France, one of the main reasons for the new dynamism is the growing importance of small- and medium-scale firms in existing and new locations. Besides, some recent studies have emphasised the importance of small- and medium-scale firms as creators of new jobs, while big corporations lost a lot of workers in many developed countries. The French classification defines 3 classes of small- and medium-scale firms: very small firms have under 10 workers and do not need administrative staff representatives; small firms - 10 to 49 workers - are not legally required to have staff representative committees; and medium-scale firms, 50 to 499 workers.

According to research carried out by Birch (1981) between 1963 and 1976, 25 per cent of the gross increase in employment in the USA came from small and very small firms (Table 1.1). Moreover, this process has accelerated recently. The Japanese case also shows that small firms have begun creating employment since 1976, while employment has been decreasing in big corporations (Table 1.2). In the UK, the

IMPORTANCE OF SMALL AND MEDIUM-SIZED FIRMS

Table 1.1: Percentage Gains and Losses of Employment in Manufacturing by Enterprise Size, USA, 1969-76.

| Region | Size of Enterprise (employees) | | | | |
	1-20	21-50	51-100	101-500	500+
North East	100	−5.0	−11.3	−28.0	−55.6
North Central	83.1	16.9	−0.7	−28.2	−71.1
South	39.0	13.9	5.1	1.6	40.5
West	59.7	17.7	10.0	12.6	−100.0
Total	85.4	14.6	−5.2	−32.2	−62.5

Source: Ledebur et al., (1981) after Birch (1981).

Table 1.2: Evolution of Employment by Enterprise Size in Japanese Manufacturing 1971-77.

| Year | Size of Enterprise | | | | | |
	1-9	10-29	30-99	100-299	300-499	500+
1971	1245	1666	1991	1580	685	4458
1977	1420	1754	2939	1605	633	3979
Change	+175	+ 88	+248	+ 25	−52	−579

Source: Leclerc (1984).

Table 1.3: Industrial Employment Trends in the UK East Midlands by Enterprise Size 1968-75.

| | Size of Enterprise | | | | |
	1-20	21-50	51-100	101-500	501+
Rate of growth (per cent)	+27	+23	+15	−22	−59
New enterprises (created since 1968):					
number	1,588	52	10	–	–
employees	17,504	3,922	1,787		

Source: Gudgin (1984).

importance of small firms as new job creators has been pointed out by Gudgin, particularly between 1968 and 1975 in the East Midlands (Table 1.3). Also in the UK, the decline of industrial employment, in big corporations has led to depression in old industrial regions, while little towns and rural areas acted as receptacles for the new jobs. Since the early 1970s, as fewer firms have been relocating their productive capacity, new small- and medium-scale firms generated by the local environment have been the only glimmer of hope, as in France. In the latter, the annual average growth rate of enterprises with under 20 workers has been highest since 1975 (2.8 per cent). It is negative for firms having more than 100 workers.

This very small group of examples enables the following hypotheses to be put forward. The creative energy of employment, belonging to the big corporations until the mid 1970s, now belongs to the small, even very small, firms. Moreover, the former peripheries, first marginalised, then colonised by the subcontracting process, are now able to find in their own environment the resources for a new and modest development which is very likely to be permanent.

A New Organisation of Production
The inversion of previous tendencies suggests that the segmentation of production which bisects the world of enterprise, would give first place to small firms, and an even more important role than Taylor and Thrift (1983) gave them. Actually, the evolution of big corporations into global corporations was already decided in the monopolistic stage of the capitalist mode of production, while the tendency towards a scattering of enterprises and production units seems to be one of the main features of the beginning of a new stage, as well as the new dynamism of old peripheries in developed countries. We do not consider these tendencies as a return to the past, but as the symptoms of a new organisation, a new attempt by capitalism to subjugate the workforce through the organisation of new social relationships and the circumvention of workers' defensive structures. In this new stage, the internal dynamism of small firms, their internal social relationships, seem to be the new model, while the rural peripheries of developed countries appear to offer the best socio-economic environment for their location and for the development of new social relationships. The individual strategies are overcoming the collective strategies.

Figure 1.1 tries to collect together the main features of production structure, of social relationships inside the firms, of social struggles and of the relative importance of space in each stage of the evolution of the capitalist mode of production: the beginning of industry, competitive capitalism, monopolist capitalism, and what we call the monopoly-competitive stage. In this latter present stage, small- and

Figure 1.1: Implications of the Evolution of the Capitalist Production Mode for Production Structure, Social Relationships and Space.

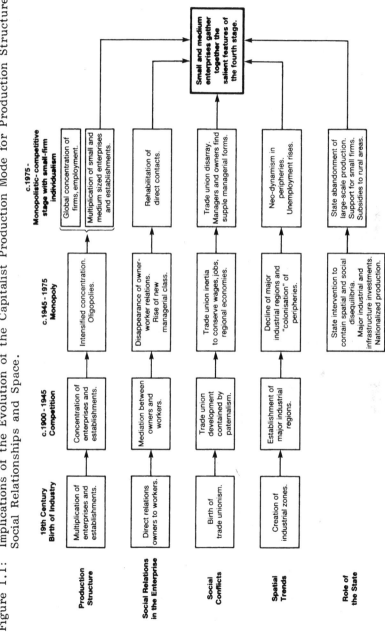

medium-scale firms are multiplying, along with small productive units. Direct contact between owners - or more
exactly executives - and direct productive forces is back in
favour. People able to generate the identification of the
workforce with owners or firms are highly favoured. Human
contacts are highly praised, replacing the rationality of the
big organisations' bureaucracy and technocracy in the general
discourse. Trade unions, which stagnated in the monopolistic-
capitalist stage, are now becoming disorganised, with the
workers no longer supporting them and the employers trying
to obtain a more flexible social legislation from the state. New
productive regions are developing in the old peripheries. And
the State fosters these new tendencies through new incentive
measures in small firms, and favours or special grants for the
peripheries.

Finally, this new stage is characterised by the development of small- and medium-scale firms in non-industrialised
environments, in areas lacking working traditions, and where
there is great demographic pressure and a high rate of
unemployment.

THE ROLE OF SMALL- AND MEDIUM-SCALE FIRMS IN
RESHAPING THE CAPITALIST MODE OF PRODUCTION

Why is the small firm, so criticised in the past, now the major
element in the new organisation of production?

Three main reasons explain the role of small- and medium-
scale firms in reshaping the capitalist mode of production.
First is their ability to accept some tasks or segments of the
productive process which have been externalised by big
corporations. Second is their structural vocation to develop
and to impose a new way of managing the workforce. Third is
their ability to contribute to the stability of a minimum social
concencus linked with the creation of jobs and the stabil-
isation of the unemployment rate.

These features may contribute to the emergence of a new
mode of accumulation. The main strategy of Fordism was an
adaptation of the market to the needs of production. In the
new situation, the productive machinery must now adapt to
the demands of market economy. Firms able to reduce their
fixed capital, to obtain a more flexible organisation of the
working process than the Fordist one, are the only ones
which can end the crisis. Let us now consider these three
reasons in depth.

Productive Potential of Small and Medium-Scale Firms, Shifts of Markets and Technology.

The emergence of electronics in the working process and the
necessity for firms to adapt to the market have two effects: a

decrease in the optimal size of productive units; and the possibility for small firms to penetrate markets which were until now the domain of mass-production giants. Small firms already coexist with big corporations in some dynamic fields, such as electronics.

Facing increasing complexity and reshuffling in market organisation, the best way for large multiproducing corporations to preserve their competitiveness is to create synergy through "channel" or "division" strategy. Small- and medium-scale firms cannot adopt this type of strategy, because their financial resources are too small. But, as they are flexible and mobile, they can choose new locations in more profitable segments of the production process. This is the consequence of their ability to innovate, which can balance the negative effects of their size. If they have access to scientific, technological and commercial information, small- and medium-scale firms have great ability to develop innovations and new technology. Their way of managing the workforce can mobilise resources and ideas very quickly.

Large industrial corporations try to take advantage of the technological innovation of smaller firms by developing some new ways of external cooperation. As the profitability of innovation investments needs the dispatching of these investments into several segments and agents of production and also technological transfers, it is a must for small- and medium-scale firms to enter a "channel" and have a cooperation strategy. But, in relation to technological progress and increases in productivity, especially for new manufactured goods, the importance of the necessary financial investment is decreasing, which makes it more accessible to the small firm.

Besides, the increase of service demand from enterprises or households will encourage the development of small firms, already very numerous in these types of activities. Moreover, there is a fairly successful behaviour of traditional sectors (clothes, shoes and so on) in small firms during the crisis period.

These better results achieved by firms having light equipment, weak productivity and low-skilled workers, especially women, have a cost: the degradation of working conditions and the decrease of wages. But they also show the ability of small firms located near the final market, to adapt quickly to the evolution of consumer demand. Finally, the modernisation of small firms is still under way, and we have not yet seen all its possible outcomes.

According to a paper written by Delattre and Eymard Duvernay (1984), the financial weight of the automation process in large enterprises leads these to externalise new segments of their production process. So the sub-contracting process might develop in favour of small firms. Until now, a great number of economists believed the management methods of big corporations were better, from economic and social points of view, than those of small firms. But changes in productive machinery and enterprise organisation entail the necessity of intensifying work itself. Therefore, the main role of the small firm is to contribute to a breaking up of the old "social" relationships.

Small Firms Break Up Trade-Union Organisation

Since the end of the 1970s one can observe a new aspect of the crisis: the search for a more flexible and adaptable workforce as instability of employment and wages increases. At this stage, the small firm can be considered as a model with more flexible working relationships and a weakening of the salaried class. Several factors explain this weakening: unemployment, which involves increasing numbers of skilled-workers and which increasingly constrains the most stable part of the proletariat; more frequent bankruptcies; and the development of political and ideological factors such as the proliferation of agencies specialised in working relationships, which give advice on how to fight trade-unions. In France, small firms with under 10 workers are not required to have workers' representatives.

Moreover, the development of services has already destabilised the trade-unions. It is very difficult to promote workers' organisations in these sectors. Spatial redeployment is another element of this change. For instance, in the USA, firms are encouraged to locate in one of the 20 states where collective agreements are not required. In France, between 1976 and 1984, 800,000 workers relinquished membership of the Confederation Generale du Travail and the Confederation Francaise Démocratique du Travail.

There is even a collapse of trade-unionism. For example, in December 1983, Star Industries workers demonstrated against the return of their union representatives, who had been dismissed because they had resisted a wage reduction.

Three factors, individual strategy, technological change, and management strategy, have a similar effect: they give rise to a more direct relationship between worker and management, and minimize the role of the unions. In this context, the small firm already presents a flexible social system. It: decreases the cost of manpower; develops direct relationships between productive forces and management; increases personal involvement of the workers in the firms and productivity; reduces absenteeism and claims.

A large part of the working population is ready to make many concessions. In early 1984, 69 per cent of unemployed people in France were willing to accept temporary work, 65 per cent agreed to work over 8 hours a day, 51 per cent accepted low wages. One unemployed person out of three was ready to move to find a job.

Finally, the small firm now seems to be the most representative structure of the new socio-economic relationship model. This model takes place inside the rupture of the social contract between capital and labour which was the major feature of the period of full employment. This rupture could condemn the global system and stop the recovery of accumulation. There is no likelihood of a return to full employment in the medium term, even with development of more flexible growth. Here again, small firms could play a special part in maintaining a social concensus leading to a new social compromise.

Employment in Small Firms

It is often said that future development relies on the growth of sectors of advanced technology, having a high capacity of innovation. These sectors now create employment, though not on a very large scale (see a forecast published in the American Bureau of Labour Statistics). In fact, the production of advanced technology sectors will increase quicker than that of other sectors, but the new jobs will not be very numerous because of the fast growth in productivity. In the meantime, the declining sectors and the traditional segments of the productive process in the large corporations will shed jobs massively.

These technological changes become operative through capital accumulation only over a long process (several decades). Thus, only the small firms, whose ability to create jobs has been stressed in this paper, will restrain the growth of unemployment. Besides, their way of taking on, their way of social management, are the first steps in a new social division of labour. The social compromise can only rely on a new division of labour, which means the reduction of working-time for everybody to reduce the number of unemployed.

Unemployed people are already willing to accept a reduction of working-time. Some people having jobs also prefer more leisure time to higher wages, but are not prepared to accept a reduction of their wages.

This type of evolution can go with the development of an underground or "black" economy which would worsen the working-life conditions of part of the population and make more difficult the financing of the social aids which have so far forestalled a social rupture. Finally there is the probability of a reactivation of competition, both between large corporations and between small firms which will create a new process of business concentration based on electronics monopoly. The concentration of capital and knowledge inside large corporations will depend on competitiveness between weaker and dependent firms. This movement will worsen the exploitation of the workforce and must be balanced by new social regulations at national and international level. But it is not yet time for all the present developed countries will win the technological battle.

CONCLUSION: TOWARDS A NEW INDUSTRIAL SYSTEM

This analysis leads us to formulate a double hypothesis. On the socio-economic level, the reshaping of productive machinery is possible, partly thanks to the tendency for small firms to develop autonomously. Currently, the small firms' revival seems to be related to their great ability to promote a new model of accumulation connected with their flexibility to adapt to the market, their ability to organise a new type of management which destroys the old social relationships, their ability to create new types of employment in the form of temporary and less skilled jobs which can absorb part of the unemployment created by big firms.

On the spatial level, the peripheries of developed countries, which until now had been receptacles for the decentralisation of big corporations, seem to find inside their own environment the capacity to create autonomous small firms. This ability seems to be linked with their lack of an industrial past and of working traditions and with the increase of demographic pressure and unemployment. (For further discussion of this point see Hamilton, 1986).

Thus, the proliferation of small firms in the peripheries seems to be the most important tendency of the new organisation of the capitalist mode of production, one of the ways to promote its own survival.

If these hypotheses are confirmed, their possible consequences on economy, society and space may be very dangerous.

First, it is obvious that the organisation of production is split into two parts: big corporations have abandoned to small firms the tasks they no longer wanted. Big firms rely on small ones to create the jobs which are necessary to the survival of the industrial system. But the small firms are not able to create as many jobs as are necessary. The increase of unemployment seems to entail an unavoidable new division of labour, between people having jobs and people having none. Yet, some palliatives are developing: part-time or "underground" jobs, development of informal sectors, increase of delinquency and crime. But until when will these palliatives be sufficient to forestall a revolt?

Besides, secondly, the new types of jobs introduce another division between workers: part of them, the highly-skilled, concentrate financial and technological information and decision power; the other part, the low-skilled or unskilled, are confined to tasks of mere execution but are more deeply motivated and more willing to identify with manager or firm, which means that they become more alienated. For the latter, the main problems are the weakness of wages, the decrease of purchasing power, the difficulty to keep their previous consumption level, while the former belong increasingly to the "jet-set". But how long will identification with the firm be sufficient compensation for the decrease of purchasing power? How long will the decline of social protection linked with the decline of unions permit the development of individual strategies at the expense of collective strategies?

On the spatial level, thirdly, the technological shifts and new organisation of production may generate a new model of polarisation. Some global corporations, reduced to their functions of management, innovation and decision, might concentrate in a few urban centres of very high level and rule over the major part of space through a network dispatching information and collecting products. The remaining space would become a global periphery where new factors of spatial differentiation could appear.

Finally, the most dangerous consequence of this evolution concerns the political sphere. If the present tendencies continue, a rupture of the social concensus may happen in developed countries. To avoid disaster, a change in social values would be necessary, with a will to share labour and wealth. Unfortunately, there is no symptom of such an evolution. The alternative might be the advent of strong political systems, perhaps of the fascist type, where the majority of the new jobs created would be in the police, the army, and the ideological State machinery. In fact, a more subtle evolution is likely, towards a three-stage society based upon a double division: first, exclusion from the working community vs. integration in it; then, inside the working community, access to decision power vs. mere execution of tasks. The excluded people might find a substitute for social advancement in a strategy to penetrate the working community, and a subsitute for social success in the obtention of more autonomy. Then the State power would have to invent a new system of regulation, oscillating between force and punctual concessions. But anyway, it would rely on a powerful logistic apparatus - even a disguised one - to resist the attempt at changes promoted by the workers themselves.

REFERENCES

American Bureau of Labour Statistics (1983) Business Week, 28 March

Birch D. (1981) The Job Generation Process and Corporate Evolution: A Micro-based Analysis. (Cambridge, Mass: Program on Neighbourhood and Regional Change, 1979-1981)

Delattre, M. & Eymard-Duvernay, F. (1984) 'Les Progrès des

P.M.E. dans la crise, signes d'un relachement du tissu industriel', Critique de l'Economie Politique, Jan-June, Paris, pp. 26-27

Gudgin, G. (1984) 'P.M.E. et créations d'emplois . Le cas exemplaire du Royaume-Uni, in: "Les P.M.E. créent-elles de emplois?, Economica. Paris

Hamilton, F.E.I., (ed.), (1986) Industrialisation in Developing and Peripheral Regions (Croom Helm, London)

Ledebur, C. et al., (1981). The Role of Small Business Enterprises in Economic Development. A Study Prepared for the Use of the Joint Economic Committee Washington, D. C., (Congress of the United States) May

Leclerc, E. (1984) Modernisation des P.M.I. japonaises et mutations des structures productives, in: Les P.M.I. créent-elles des emplois?, Economica Paris

Savey, S. (1983). 'Organisation of Production and the new Spatial division of labour in France, in: F.E.I. Hamilton and G.J.R. Linge, (eds.), Spatial Analysis, Industry and the Industrial Environment, Vol. 2 International Industrial Systems (Wiley, Chichester, 1983), pp. 103-120

Chapter Two

THE NEED FOR A NEW EVOLUTIONARY THEORY
OF TIME AND SPACE: CONTEMPORARY
CZECHOSLOVAK INDUSTRIAL CHANGE

Koloman Ivanicka

The real world exhibits eternal circulation of matter, energy
and information in which creation and constructivism meet
with entropy, destruction and chaos. Their substance, mutual
relation and inner motive power are not the mere dilemma of
our existence; they are practical questions, influencing
people's daily lives, to which society tries to find practical
answers. For example, how much, and how, do we pay for
the organisation and order we create? Is creation only an
episode in the entropic process or is it an eternal process, as
intrinsic to matter itself is as entropy? Creation is the substance of evolution, every stage of it being also a turning
point in creative development (Atkins, 1981). Man, the highest stage of creativity (Kuczynski, 1979), has gained control
over the genetics of living organisms and, through genetic
manipulations, can model organic matter as in the past people
mechanically modelled clay, wood, metal or plastic. Thus the
contemporary stage is typified by high technologies whose
effects on the further evolution and on social structures and
organisation may be unexpected and surprising (Ames, 1982).
    Shaping ideas occupies a new place in the scientific-
technological revolution, making it necessary to approach with
a new urgency the elaboration of Marx's "third reality" of the
unification of the world of ideas with the objectively existing
world in human knowledge (Marxs in: Marxs and Engels,
1966, p.626). To understand the world they live in, people
must comprehend the integration of Man and Environment.
Contemporary studies offer the building blocks for a new
evolutionary theory but their findings are fragmented - itself
a product of divisions in the organisation of science, research
and knowledge.
    Man is a dialectic unity of material, psyche and social
relations with the surrounding world. Being dynamic, people
are bound to their near and far environment by the systematic circulation of matter, energy and information through a
series of cycles and networks involving: physical phenomena
(e.g. oxygen, water, heat), food, electro-magnetism, biology

13

and demography, reproduction, energy production, production relations, inter-human relations, culture, education and exchange of knowledge. As society is continuously and intricately connected with environment by these cycles through multi-causal feedbacks, devastation or pollution can have an undesirable impact on people and damage - even disorganise - their somatic, psychic or social structures. A reappraisal of Man-Environment relations is the logical consequence of this knowledge: many advanced economies have shifted policy from the fight against Nature or its uncritical exploitation to one of the protection of environment, people having concluded that high levels of social organisation must not create chaos in Nature - a departure from past high entropic approaches and technologies and a transition to a programme for low entropic approaches and technologies, inevitably causing changes in inter-human relations. Thus multi-causal forces unleash both composition, organisation, new elements and disorganisation, chaos, chimeras, entropy in the environment (Rifkin, 1981) and, by feedback, creation itself can be modified, transformed or shifted on to another development trajectory. Counteracting and amplifying multi-causal links provides a framework for understanding the behaviour of the dialectic-synergetic system of Man (Ivanicka, 1980 pp. 29-31).

The concentration and accumulation of energy, driving and cycles, are key problems. Ecosystems and geosystems can concentrate and accumulate solar energy, transmitting it as high quality energy to the social system. Yet the succession of expanded reproduction, innovation, creation and evolution requires an optimal dynamic effect which can only be achieved if the forces of organisation and creation are stronger than those of entropy and destruction. Optimal efficiency in this sense bridges the boundaries between trends towards entropy and those to successive evolution. Low efficiency forms involving creation of less vital forms with a high input of energy, matter, information and low yields have no hope for survival. This universal principle is also valid when defining basic economic laws and is the precondition for economic growth (Ivanicka, 1985).

Classical methodological approaches were unsuccessful because complex reality was artificially and mechanically divided and then, after the loss of knowledge of multi-causal relations, was again connected non-synergically and non-dialectically in a mechanical way. Creation and evolution are very dynamic and systematically accelerated, so theories explaining Man's activity and the organisation of his time and space quickly become obsolete because they explain the history of the organisation rather than the present. Contemporary methodology, aiming at an evolutionary approach, emphasises changing structures and behaviour. It shows, for instance, that each industrial plant was once new and developing but, in the course of time, became mature, was adapted successfully or unsuccessfully to demands of the changing socio-economic environment, was transformed, or slipped into a chronic or terminal condition.

Industry - the main structure-forming force in the industrial revolution, changing the character of our planet, inciting population concentration in towns, making urbanisation dependent, intensifying agriculture, and creating modern communications networks - is now giving way in importance to information, just as in the 19th century industry susperseded agriculture as the key force in the space economy. Structural shifts are relative. As the scientific-technological revolution (or information stage) advances, absolute industrial production continues to grow. "Pre-production" stages are undergoing change, too, and within industry, older sectors, once the driving force, are declining in importance. Nowadays four new clusters of industrial systems are becoming prominent - electronics, biotechnology, systems for learning about cosmic space, and aquaculture - and are causing principal structural transformations both of industry as a whole and of the whole socio-economic and spatial systems (Rosciszewski, 1982).

The information stage sets in train employment shifts (Peters and Watermann, 1981, p.37; Nasbitt, 1982, p.1 - 38; Toffler, 1981, p.9), jobs being created in information-collection, processing and applications. Changes result in the requirements for the location of work and residence. Scientific-technological development using automation, computerisation and robotisation offers the option of increased labour productivity hand in hand with reduced working hours equivalent to a 3 or 4 day working week. Another trend is that transaction costs for innovation, communication and decision-making often exceed the savings from economies of large-scale production and concentration. Generalisations from the USA, where such structural shifts are at present both very rapid and advanced, show that, as a consequence of transaction costs, innovation per US\$1 investment is 4 times more effective in small organisational units than in middle-sized plants and 24-times more than in the large-scale plants (US National Academy of Sciences, 1983). This is the fundamental explanation of the reorganisation of large units into smaller, more flexible operational units, and of the statistical explosion of new and small industrial plants. Decentralisation of investments and the changes in the capital accumulation process are also fascinating aspects of this new evolutionary trend.

Evidence from the USSR shows that expensive innovation requires deeper and more complex organisational, economic, social and management operations than in the past, even if the R & D costs do not exceed the return to capital in roubles. Interesting organisational and management improvements can be observed in the creation of new micro- and macro-structures in nearly all developed countries. Introduction of economic stimuli and deconcentration into smaller production units can be observed, for example, in Hungary, even though it is the political aspects of this process that are most often discussed. To strengthen management in Czechoslovakia, a Ministry of Electronics was created because it was stated - though quite behind the times - that electronics is of key importance to all new industrial development, that a new integrated industrial system is being formed on the dynamics of which also engineering, metallurgy and the entire economic and social systems of the country depend. Present development has reduced the time between scientific discovery and application in new processes or products, making production structures so dynamic as to be almost fluid. Thus a new location theory demands an evolutionary approach embodying the complexity and integrity of processes in time and space.

Industrial, economic and social processes are learning structures. If industrial organisation structures are rigid, the removal of stereotypes to adapt the system to the expected evolution of production cannot occur and feedbacks lead to stagnation, later bankruptcy and destruction of entire industrial systems. Non-traditional processes and mechanisms are brought to the fore by industrial systems analysis in spatial sciences, as the system of values, general culture, continuous structural adaptation, the elasticity of feedbacks with the consumer, systematic raising of quality and reliability of operation hand in hand with decreased energy and materials requirements and higher levels of design and ergonomy of products. These processes make great demands on creativity, innovation, high levels of information and communication for all management, pre-production and production working teams.

External pressure of synergetic relations in the environment on the production system forces it to dynamise itself, nowadays by innovation. Thus the production system, ceteris paribus, continuously creates various innovation centres, research institutes, specialised training and applied institutions. So the original industrial production organisation is being altered into information-production and processing, with impacts also on management. If, once management was committed first to production, today introduction of innovations in production and tightening links between science and production have brought research into prominence in management, though production also has feedback effects through research on management. The demands of these linkages are very high both because science has its own technological information context and because linkages operate in a complex milieu of consumers tastes, domestic and foreign markets, product obsolescence, evolution of world science, prices (of materials, energy, information and research), licensing policy, financial barriers, and currency systems, political systems and embargoes. The variability of their relations cannot be understood in linear terms but demands analysis and synthesis in multi-dimensional space, the linkages therein creating a new type of socio-economic and management structure.

An evolutionary approach and the growth in real world complexity require a new definition of "environment", replacing the anonymous global one by a structuralised environment in which individual substructures are of systems character and can actively effect change and evolution in the industrial system (Hamilton, 1978). Thus the system "Man - society - nature - their reality" leads to the knowledge that environment becomes a component part of the dialectic-synergetic machinery (Haken, 1978; Prigogine, 1980) in which synergy makes demands on: the maximum harmony between Man and environment; the functional operation of objects, phenomena and processes; minimising energy, material and information losses; and maximising energy, material and information impacts.

NEW DIRECTIONS IN THE CZECHOSLOVAK PRODUCTION SYSTEM

A key problem of contemporary Czechoslovakia is the need for structural changes in industry. Demands for continuous growth in living standards urge decision-makers to re-evaluate orthodox approaches to expanded reproduction. Undoubtedly, that reproduction means both a continuous process of renewal of the expected outputs of the system and the renewal of conditions, instruments and mechanisms which make the outputs possible. If expanded reproduction successfully overcomes the tendency for the production system to head towards obsolescence and maximum entropy, then there has been a general increase of creativity, evolution and improved organisation. Through bifurcation there arise dissipative structures, new subsystems which are usually characterised by rapid growth, causing decline or extinction of some old production structures. Novelty and success inevitably create demand for extended reproduction. If new investments do not satisfy the customer, reproduction is not progressive and does not secure evolution, i.e. successful, gradual reproduction is simultaneously innovation, growth and evolution.

Besides natural wealth, manpower and capital, new sources of information and scientific-technological development play an important role in making the transition to low-entropic production processes with low energy and materials consumption and maximum efficiency of machinery yielding higher labour productivity. The generation costs of the ecologic

17

sphere, resulting from use of large quantities of resources, call for transition to new high technologies. Perception that industrial waste is evidence of entropy in energy and matter, and that from thermodynamic laws it is impossible to eliminate it without higher energy costs, is why great importance is attached to the restructuring of Czechoslovak industry.

Electronics and Robotics
Yet a dilemma exists over information collection, processing and application. Large investments are made in the modernisation of information infrastructure while in some institutions, firms and plants there is managerial resistance to pressures to increase employment in information-processing and to its conceptual re-evaluation. In practice, information and innovation have not yet assumed their key economic value (Ferianc, 1984). So far a fully satisfying mechanism of mutual communication between the official formal management structure of science and the broad basis of scientific-research workers has not been found. Several management mechanisms were introduced to increase dynamism in Czechoslovak industry: the plan, central channelling of investments, international division of labour and mutual scientific-technical cooperation within CMEA and a mass campaign in the media. Large budgets are granted to scientific-production associations and new institutions. Great patience is shown in the search for new organisational-managerial forms better adapted to the needs of industrial plants in the scientific-technological revolution. Innovation and restructuring of Czechoslovak industry involve rapid electronics development: in 1981 and 1982 Czechoslovak industry expanded output by 3.2 per cent, engineering by 6.5 per cent, while branches administered by the Federal Ministry of the Electrical Industry grew by 15.5 per cent, electronics itself by 24.4 per cent and microelectronic parts by 61 per cent (Zpravodaj Rožnov, 1983). Electronics is the only sector in which product prices have been reduced despite the general inflation of prices of energy, raw materials and intermediate products. The Czechoslovak electrical industry is orientated to satisfy the demands of general engineering, consumer electronics and controls of atomic power plants, and can strengthened in a selected range of these products, though this will only form a fragment of world production given the competition from major monopoly producers abroad.

Interest is concentrated on robotisation. The state programme in the 7th Five-Year Plan (1980-4) expected to produce 3,358 industrial robots and manipulators valued at 1,167 million Kčs (Czechoslovak crowns). From 1981 to 1983 production reached 2,044, 744 more than planned (Archiv VUKOV, Prešov 1984). At present there are 12 central producers of robots and manipulators, supported by several sub-contractors. VUKOV in Presov has gained the key position along with the Association of Engineer-Design and Production organisations which has 18 branches in the country. Reliability tests are carried but in 1,500 working places. Most investment in robotisation will be made between 1984 and 1988. There is extensive robotics cooperation with the USSR where the plan by 1986 is to introduce 40,000 robots into general engineering to release 70,000 workers for other sectors of the economy and to install 30,000 manipulators to save a further 45,000 workers.

Energy, Resource and Research Frontiers
The Czechoslovak Socialist Republic invests large sums in atomic power stations. By 1986, 20 per cent of the country's electric power will be produced in such stations, 50 per cent by 1990, and 60 per cent in 2000. Czechoslovak engineering produces reactors for atomic power plants which are also exported, mainly to other socialist countries. The Slovak Socialist Republic is a major producer and exporter of sanitary and purification installations and investments there are developing 2.5 times faster than in all Czechoslovak industry. As it is a knowledge-intensive sector its pre-production stages are also developing quickly, seeking new linkages with R & D and medical practice; structurally linked are changes in the pharmaceutical industry and production of medicines. Between 1979 and 1986, Czecholovakia is altering the production of medicines to meet World Health Organisation (WHO) standards, requiring extensive modernisation of plant, laboratories, research and application bases. The possibilities for small countries like Czechoslovakia to participate in space programmes are quite limited, so that it is not possible to create new territorial complexes and industrial systems as in the USA or the USSR. Yet Czechoslovakia has joined the CMEA INTERCOSMOS programme with its five permanent research units on cosmic physics, cosmic meteorology, cosmic communication, cosmic biology and medicine, and teledetection. INTERCOSMOS has launched 41 satellites, rockets and probes. At present about 200 work centres in Czechoslovakia are engaged in the cosmic programme and 27 in Earth Research. Several physical, meteorological, medical, biological measurement and optical devices have been developed, some of which, after adaptation, can be successfully used for civilian purposes, like special X-ray and thermo-regulative equipment. The presence of Czechoslovak astronauts in space has permitted experiments with production and industrial applications and to maintain contact with new international innovation impulses.

Not being a maritime state, Czecholovakia has great interest in the search for and use of new raw materials and energy resources for its processing industry. In 1972 an

agreement was signed for coordinated research in the exploitation of raw materials from continental shelves and ocean
beds. Its CMEA international coordination centre, called
INTERMORGEO, is located in Riga in the Baltic USSR. Some
promising sea-deposits have been found. Czechoslovakia also
participates in research into the titano-manganese sands in
the bay of Burgas (Bulgaria) and raw materials on the
shelves of the Caribbean Sea (in co-operation with Cuba).
The Institute of Mineral Raw Materials in Kutna Hora is the
coordinator of this programme in Czechoslovakia. Here
methods, prototype equipment and instruments are developed.

Since the 1970s energy price rises, interest has grown
in harnessing solar energy and power from small water and
wind mills. Elektrosvit Nové Zámky, Kroměříž and Vlachovice
produce solar batteries, MEZ Mohelnice wind power stations
and Kovopodnik Brno makes small water power stations. Several state farms and agricultural cooperatives employ biogas
produced in experimental, home-made devices. Mountainous
Slovakia prior to concentrated large-scale socialistic industrialisation had 2,400 small watermills with only 2000 MW
installed capacity - virtually equal to that planned for the
new atomic power plant in Mochovce which costs very must
investment (about 74 milliard Kcs) and offers high environmental risks. Many of these small watermills are out of use
but there are attempts to renovate them or to construct new
ones. Much attention is also being paid to harnessing thermal
waters in South Slovakia to complement traditional energy
sources. Use of small dispersed energy sources and formation
of small production units should be stimulated by Act No.
52/1982 which empowers National Committees in towns and
villages to install, control or close small economic activities.
The act gave local authorities the powers of the surveyor's
office and tries to correct the imperfections of centralised
economic management which did not always react to, and
meet, the demands of inhabitants for certain ranges of goods,
repairs and services (Kusenda, 1984).

The programme for the application of bio-technologies is
relatively extensive, Czechoslovakia being orientated towards
increased use of the genetic-ecologic potential of plants and
animals, production of medications, applications of bio-
technologies in mining operations and in waste water purification, and production of non-traditional biomass. There are
possibilities for non-traditional production of proteins in
cooperation with Hungary: production of proteins from grass
and leaves of various plants was recently introduced in the
Hungarian village of Tamasi in Tolna district. The Micro-
biological Institute in Trebon developed a successful method
for the production of algae.

Division of labour within the CMEA is important in
shaping Czechoslovak industry. Today problems of energy,
progressive technologies, robotization, electronics, complex

production equipment, licences and patents are prominent fields of international collaboration. Consumer goods and foodstuffs are important in CMEA trade. Now Czechoslovakia is taking on the role, within the European socialist macro-region, of a CMEA contact zone with Western Europe, actively participating in international socialist, European and world division of labour in that infrastructure, production and services in its border regions are being shaped in collaboration with those in regions of neighbouring countries. Development of new transit infrastructure between the CMEA and Western Europe (roads, improved railways, pipelines, power grids) is a stimulus to the creation of new economic activities in new locations.

CONCLUSION

Modern development is bringing about a series of new structural changes to every territory. Flows of new ideas and information are being accelerated. Thus the creation of an evolutionary and dynamic theory of time and space, which would replace existing location theories, is a very urgent task. The essential factor of contemporary evolution is the relation between consciousness and practice: evolution of the world we live in is closely bound with the evolution of thinking and values. Of crucial importance for the evolution of social practice is the system of generation and diffusion of innovation which requires new structures and the removal of outmoded ones. Differences in the rates of such changes between nations and regions will result in differences in socio-economic structures, posing further problems of development.

REFERENCES

Ames, E. Mary (1982) Outcome Uncertain. Science and the Political Process Avon Books, Washington
Archiv Vukov Prešov (1984) (Prešov)
Atkins, P.W. (1981) The Creation W.H. Freeman & Co., San Francisco
Ferianc, J. (1984) 'Otvarenie Perspektiv Intenzifikacie', Novo Slove, pp. 1-5
Haken, H. (1978) Synergetico. An Introduction Springer-Verlag, Berlin
Hamilton, F.E.I. (1978) 'The Changing Milieu of Spatial Industrial Research', in Contemporary Industrialisation, Longman, London, pp. 1-19
Ivanička, K. (1980) Prognoza Ekonomiko Geografickych Systemov Alfa, Bratislava

Ivanička, K. (1983) Zaklady Teorie a Metodologie Socioekonomický Geografie, SPN, Bratislava

Ivanička, K. (1985) 'Zakon Evolucie Priestorocasu Alebo Treti Zakon Energie?' Geograficky Casopis, 1

Kuczynski, J. (1979) Homo Creator. Wstep do Dialektiti Czlowieka Ksiazda i Wiedza, Warsaw

Kusenda, P. (1984) K Novej Pravnej Uprave Postavenia a Posobnosti Narodnych Vyborov SPN, Bratislava

Marχs, K. (1966) 'Rekopisy Ekonomiczno-Filozoficzne z 1844 r' in K. Marχs and F. Engels (eds.), Dziela Vol. 1, PWN, Warsaw

Nasbitt, J. (1982) Megatrends. Ten New Directions Transforming Our Lives, Warner Books, New York

Peters, J.T. and Waterman, R.H. (1981) In Search of Excellence, Harper and Row, New York

Prigogine, J. (1979) 'Čas, Struktura a Československy Casopis', Dyzika Sekce, 29,(2) pp. 97-208

Rosciszewski, M. (1982) Nowe Procesy w Suwatkowej Ekonomice a Ich Wplyw Na Wspolerawna Organizacje Przestrzenne PAN Warsaw

Rifkin, J. (1981) Entropy: A New World View, Bantam Books, New York

Toffler, A. (1981) The Third Wave, Bantam Books, New York

Zpravodaj VHJ Tesla (1983) Elektronicke Současty-Koncernu Rožnov Rožnov: VHJ Tesla

Chapter Three

PEOPLE-PRODUCTION-INTERNATIONAL DIVISION OF
LABOUR

Kajsa Ellegård & Claes Alvstam

Since 1975 world trade has shown significant changes. Until
then, the highest rates of growth took place in the industrialised world, whereupon there have been tendencies of
stagnation. Yet after 1975 there are remarkable increases of
the export values of manufactured goods from several developing world, indicating that the costs of production factors
have altered in favour of the newly industrialised countries.
    During the 1950s and 1960s industrial work at the in-
dividual level was organised in shorter and less skilled tasks
than before. Most industrial production today takes place in
plants originating from these decades.
    Thus big changes have occurred in conditions of indus-
trial production both at the global and the individual levels.
This chapter aims at connecting these two levels, usually
treated separately, to study effects of changes of the international division of labour on the organisation of work within
single production units. It is also possible to study the
reverse effect, i.e. how changes in the organisation of work
at the individual level affect commodity flows and industrial
location patterns at the global level, though that approach is
not taken here.
    The very complicated network of commodity flows that
exists at the present time within and between nation states is
examined in terms of how the production system is divided
into single, geographically dispersed units, belonging either
to the same group of companies or to independent enterprises
with close links between each other.
    A driving force behind recent changes may be increased
protectionism and new patterns of international trade policy.
Modern barriers to trade tend to be non-tariff ones, particularly domestic legislation and economic policy, favouring
home production and hampering imports. The location of
manufacturing may depend to a lesser degree on the geographical location of low-cost labour. Potential market growth
is more important. The huge increase in the volume of trans-
ported bulk commodities has now stagnated, and there are

reasons to believe that the growth of seaborne, intercontinental trade in raw materials will grow at a more modest rate in future. For instance, other materials are superseding steel, and re-cycling technology develops rapidly. The following step is a diminished dependence on massive labour inputs through increased automation. By the same token, wages will be less important as a location factor, while know-how grows in significance.

Our hypothesis is that fragmentation and geographical diffusion of the production system is an essential factor determining the work-tasks of individuals, both in their economic and their everyday life. A model is presented to analyse changes in single work-tasks, using the case study of how work-tasks have recently become more fragmented in a Swedish industry. Other questions arise. Is working life undergoing similar fragmentation elsewhere in the world. Do changes in production techniques and work organisation still occur with a time-lag between more and less industrialised parts of the world or are such time-lags disappearing, owing to the more rapid diffusion of technological innovations? The chapter is exploratory, given the neglect of this field so far by geographers.

TOWARDS A MODEL: STUDIES OF FRAGMENTATION

The concept of fragmentation denotes a division of a whole into pieces which are only remainders of the original totality. Fragmentation of manufacturing operates at least, at two different levels: (1) international trade, where flows have become more fragmented through a tremendous increase in the number of separate shipments between countries before the final product stage is reached, so that growth of trade in semi-manufactures is the most significant change in the world trade system after 1950; (2) individuals, for whom, over a long period there has been a process of fragmentation of work-tasks, each single task contributing a smaller part of the final product, through the consecutive phases of craftsmanship, professional work, to the currently dominating assembly-line production. (This process, however, is not unambiguous! Active trade unions initiate a parallel tendency to diminish the fragmentation of work-tasks in industrialised countries by calling for meaningful work, a call which succeeds where companies consider these demands compatible with their quality and productivity targets.)

The essential link between the two levels is the firm enterprise, the organisational unit. The same tendencies occur within manufacturing firms to split their production and business activities, with increased international intra-firm shipment of parts compared to trade between independent actors. Major Swedish manufacturing companies export about

50 per cent of their production to subsidiaries abroad. Intra-firm trade is considered to be 20-25 percent of total world trade. American and Swedish studies indicate that after a rapid increase of intra-firm trade during the 1960s, no significant relative growth is to be found during the 1970s. This apparent paradox may be the result of new forms of intra-firm trade. The direct majority control of a subsidiary - which is the most common criterion of intra-firm trade - has probably decreased, and more complicated, indirect linkages between firms have developed. Thus, there is, at present, a need for new definitions of intra-firm trade.

The connection between global and individual levels is the firm that acts at both levels at the same time. Figure 3.1, the model, describes these linkages which within a given production system, starts with commodity suppliers and continues with the separate companies. There is a production hierarchy, so that the model starts from the position of the production system in the total economy and ends up with the single work-task, representing the individual level (shown in Figure 3.2).

Figure 3.1: The production perspective on gainful employment, a production system. The product flow runs over time from the left to right. The shading is used to represent the ownership connections within the production system. The starting point is one company, the production of which is the centre of the production system.
Source: Ellegård (1983, p.50).

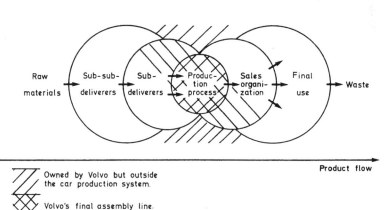

Figure 3.2: The production perspective on gainful employment, a production hierarchy. The number of employees in
the total economy constitutes the societal level. After a
continuous disaggregation, the total manufacturing production
is broken down to the individual level. The number of
individuals concerned at each level relates to Sweden and
Volvo in 1980.
Source: Ellegård (1983, p.52) .
1) Statistical Yearbook of Sweden 1980
2) Annual Report by AB Volvo 1980
3) Figure given by Volvo
4) Figures given by the body-shop at Volvo, Torslanda plant

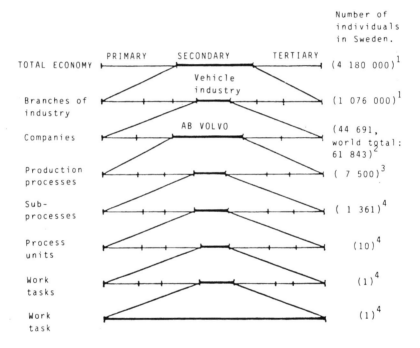

The Production System and International Trade

The central purpose behind the concept of a production
system is to embrace the entire product flow, from raw
materials through complete products and final consumption to
refuse. The aim is to use this entity to answer questions
like: How many units of production are involved in the entire
product flow? Where are raw-materials and semi-manufactures
bought and brought from? Which units of production are
connected within the same company group? How many subcon-

tractors are integrated in the company controlling the final production? Which countries are involved in the different stages of subcontract work? How big is the total volume and value of the trade that flows between the units in the production system before the final use?

The production system approach may contribute to the understanding of some of the peculiarities in international trade statistics, such as the rapid increase in some trade without corresponding increases in the final consumption. As international trade statistics use the gross-value principle, an increased number of passages over international borders by raw-materials and semi-manufactures results in a multiplied total value, as shown in Figure 3.3.

Figure 3.3: An example of the gross value measure in the trade statistics. Despite the same final value of the product (420), the value shown in the statistics increases more than three-fold, when the production system is internationalised and raw materials and semi-manufactures cross the national boundaries. It should be observed that the exaggeration effects may in reality be still greater, compared with this simple case.

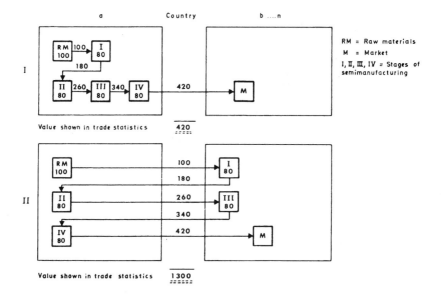

THE VOLVO CASE

A thorough investigation of the Volvo case (Ellegard, 1983) indicates that, until about 1978, Volvo increasingly integrated units in the production system for cars within its own structure. It also integrated activities outside the car production system. Volvo started making cars in 1926. As early as 1930 it acquired a supplier in the production system. In 1941 Volvo for the first time bought a plant whose activities lay outside the car production system. In the 1950s and 1960s output of cars increased markedly, several suppliers were purchased and the firm opened new production units internally. Assembly of Volvo cars was also started outside Sweden in the 1960s, and activities abroad increased in the 1970s.

In the late 1970s, certain car production activities were separated from the company: a kind of "disintegration" took place. This was partly internal, as when the parent company was divided by fission and different product units were given the status of "commission companies" which run their operations under their own business name, but entirely on behalf of the parent company. Volvo Car Corporation and Volvo Components Corporation were the two subsidiaries that assumed the parent company's previous role within the production system for cars. The "disintegration" was also partly external, in that part of the car production system, previously owned by Volvo, was sold to independent companies. Thus 15 percent of shares in Volvo Car Corporation were sold to Renault; majority holdings in one plant for car components production were also sold. Figure 3.4 (a-c) illustrate the location of Volvo-owned enterprises in 1949, 1970 and 1980 respectively. In 1949, Volvo owned one assembly plant and one engine factory. Furthermore, plants for manufacturing gearboxes and grinding-machines were included in the company group as subsidiaries. The only Volvo-owned enterprise within the production system located abroad were sales companies (Figure 3.4a).

By 1970, Volvo's direct ownership in the production system had increased considerably at the subcontractor level, by absorbing six sub-contractors and owning one as a subsidiary, though only within Sweden. However, 3 subsidiary plants had been built abroad for the final production stage, while sales organisation outside Sweden had been expanded to involve 15 subsidiary companies (Figure 3.4 b).

By 1980, through the subsidiaries Volvo Car Corporation and Volvo Components Corporation, Volvo owned 10 production units in the production system before the final assembly (still only in Sweden), 2 plants in Sweden and 5 abroad, and 24 foreign sales subsidiaries (Figure 3.4 c). This shows the continued heavy concentration in the home country of Volvo's owned sub-contractors while foreign-based sales

Figure 3.4a: Volvo subsidiaries and plants in the parent company in the production system for manufacturing Volvo cars in 1949, and subsidiaries outside the production system. <u>Source</u>: Ellegård (1983, p.71).

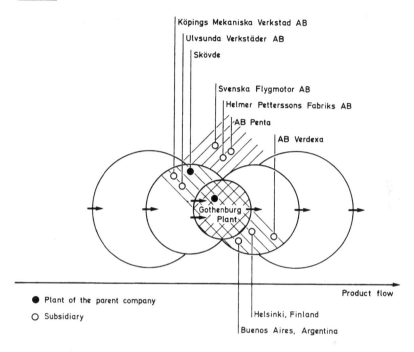

organisations embrace many directly-owned companies and sell about 80 percent of car output production outside Sweden.

Several final assembly plants located abroad were motivated by legal and political actions in the host countries, especially EEC tariffs and Local Content Rules as in Latin America and Canada, which prescribe a certain minimum of final value added must originate in the host country. This explains why trade between Sweden and host countries mainly comprises special components manufactured in Sweden. Where foreign assembly is motivated by tariff reasons, a higher degree of trade may occur to utilise scale economies among Swedish sub-contractors.

To investigate the extent to which production plants in Sweden receive components from non-owned sub-contractors, a pilot study was made of different sub-contractors to car bodies manufacturing at Torslanda in 1980. It showed that

Figure 3.4b: Volvo subsidiaries and plants in the parent
company in the production system for manufacturing Volvo
cars in 1970, and subsidiaries outside the production system.
Source: Ellegård (1983, p.74)
(A map showing Volvo plants in Sweden is given in
Fredriksson & Lindmark, 1979, p.176).

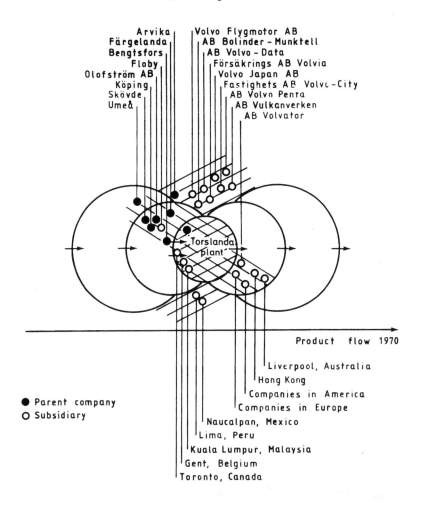

Figure 3.4c: Volvo subsidiaries and plants in the parent company in the production system for manufacturing Volvo cars in 1980, and subsidiaries outside the production system.
Source: Ellegård (1983, p.80)

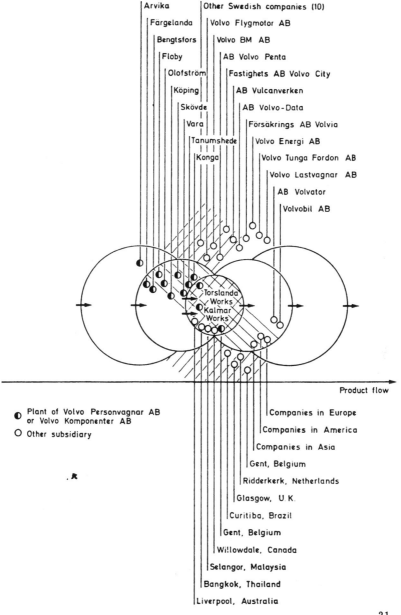

only 7 of the 31 direct sub-contractors were foreign, yet all suppliers of sheet to the press-shops were located abroad in Western Europe. (Since 1980, however, manufacture of fine sheet has started at the Swedish steel-mill at Domnarvet, and received orders from Volvo.) There are several different levels of indirect sub-contractors from the iron ore, bauxite and alloy-metals.

Volvo illustrates how the final assembly has been fragmented and located to different countries, and how local content rules fragment the sub-contractor levels too. Yet fragmentation has also internal causes like scale economies and productivity. When a production unit has reached full capacity, the decision has to be made whether to expand the original plant, to look for an external supplier or to construct one's own new plant to take advantage of latest production techniques. One example is the purchases by Volvo of German engines, and the engine production in France in cooperation with Peugeot and Renault, rather than to expand its own engine output in Sweden.

The globalisation of production is also clear in how components made in Sweden are carried all over the world for assembly. In 1983, more than 20 percent of the total Swedish export value of motor vehicles consisted of components and parts. Production techniques and know-how are exported at an even higher degree. There are several examples of how economically written-off equipment can be further used during its total technical life-time in less developed countries, implying that the technical time-lag between rich and poor countries may be maintained by transnational companies within the system of intra-firm trade.

Thus the production hierarchy must be examined to see how these macro changes affect the individual worker in the car production system.

PRODUCTION HIERARCHY

The model of a production hierarchy, shown in Figure 3.2, illustrates a successive disaggregation into a particular segment of the production of the entire society. Each step, however, omits valuable information, which makes comparison between different levels more difficult, a problem partly soluble by making several parallel disaggregations. Part of a production process may have radically changed after introduction of a new technique and may cause a split up of production to geographically separated locations within the plant, calling for more floor-space. Even small changes in techniques affect the content of single work-tasks, thereby radically changing conditions for the individual.

At societal level, effects of changes in the production units are illustrated by a link-up between the production

Figure 3.5: The production perspective on gainful employment, showing production hierarchy and production system. A
production process in a plant which is studied in the production hierarchy can always be studied from the viewpoint of a

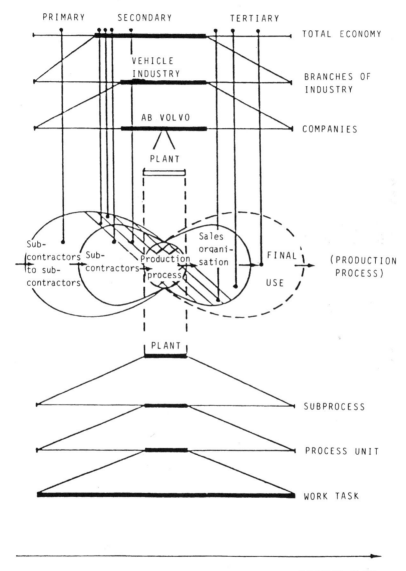

Fig. 3.5: (continued) production system as well. The figure shows how the linkages to the societal level in other branches of industry can be made. These linkages are symbolised by lines connecting one point in the production system with another point on the level of the total economy.
Source: Ellegård (1983, p.57).

Figure 3.6a: The bodies had originally a wooden framework, which was covered by iron sheet. The roof was covered by pergamoid, as the technique to press whole pieces of sheet of that size had not yet been invented.

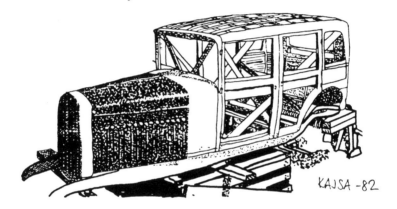

Figure 3.6b: Wooden framework with iron sheet cover in assembly-line production in about 1930. The covering with sheet corresponds to the assembly of the metal body in modern production.
Source: Ellegård (1983, p.89)

system and the production hierarchy. The unit in the centre of the production system is thereby brought into focus at that particular level in the hierarchy (Figure 3.5) making it possible to study how changes in that unit also effect on the preceding sub-contractors.

In the 1920s and 1930s, much wood was used in manufacturing Volvo car bodies, a raw material that has largely disappeared in modern production. Thus primary sector forestry has ceased to supply, and saw-mills and joiners in the secondary sector disappeared as sub-contractors. On the other hand, consumption of metals and plastics has increased, affecting the production of ores, crude oil and refinery products. Later stages of car production thus affect employment and production volumes in other manufacturing sectors. Changes in the raw materials used will also alter the composition of countries involved as suppliers in the production systems.

Thus, the lowest level of the production hierarchy is the single work-task, and concerns the design of the work done by the individual worker, as illustrated in the model of production systems and hierarchies. The single work-task is shaped by several factors, such as production technique, the share of volume produced in relation to total capacity, plant layout and principles governing work organisation.

FRAGMENTATION AT TWO LEVELS

Global Level: World Trade and the International Division of Labour.

Increased distances of sea-borne transport of materials and parts are related to the tendency for the national production systems to be weakened by increased international economic interdependence.

The very rapid growth of shipped quantities in world trade was accelerated by the huge increase in demand for material inputs in the industrial countries. In 1955, Japan imported 5.5 million tonnes of iron ores, compared with 130 million tonnes twenty years later. Continuously increased efficiency of transport implied decreased freight costs in market prices of finished products. Globalisation of world commodity trade let to quicker integration of the Third World in an internationally based division of labour and specialisation of production.

A parallel feature was the further fragmentation of production processes in the industrialised countries. For political, technical and economic reasons this fragmentation process has had great effects on the spatial division of production. Further the number of establishments involved in the production system for each product has increased considerably, partly through location of production units abroad, and the expanding tendency to buy semi-manufactures from foreign sub-contractors in the 1960s. Creation of the European Coal and Steel Community and the European Economic Community speeded up this development. By the late 1960s tariffs between the EEC and EFTA countries were abolished for industrial products. The share of internal trade in the total of the EEC countries rose from 33 per cent in 1955 to 55 per cent in the beginning of the 1970s, mostly due to trade in industrial commodities. The share of machinery and equipment in total trade increased during the same period from 15 to 30 per cent.

Since the mid-1970s, however, trade between the industrial countries has not increased relatively to world trade. Most rapid growth has occurred elsewhere, through a certain relocation of industrial production to Third World countries, the emergence of the newly industrialised countries, and increased purchases of industrial goods by less developed countries. Relocation of industrial production has taken place in two different ways. First, the relocation of early stages of the production system, e.g. pig iron, crude steel, refined copper and aluminium. The share of developing countries in international steel production rose from 1 per cent in 1950 to 8 per cent in 1980, and is expected to grow to at least 15 per cent in the 1990s. But only a few developing countries have been involved so far. Second, relocation of later manufacturing stages, as in the garment, light consumers' goods and electronics industries. During recent years this tendency spread to other sectors like motor vehicle assembly and its sub-contractor stages. Figure 3.7 summarises changes in the international division of labour, during the post-war period and their consequences for trade in raw-materials and industrial goods between the industrialised countries and the Third World.

However, car production, at least in small countries like Sweden, has not developed according to the pattern described in Figure 3.7. Fragmentation took place at a very early stage, as most components had to be bought from outside, including from abroad. Later, it became possible to build up national systems of sub-contractors, whereupon international dependence in fact declined. Not until recently, when some of the final assembly was located abroad, did dependence on foreign suppliers begin to grow again. Still the main part of the final assembly takes place in the home country based on deliveries from foreign as well as domestic suppliers, while the final assembly abroad uses deliveries from both Sweden and the new host country. Certain sub-contractors concentrate on supplying either the original or the new assembly plant. (see Figure 3.8).

Figure 3.7: A simplified model illustrating the changing pattern of the international division of labour and its consequences for trade flows of raw materials in the North, and Third World countries in the South.

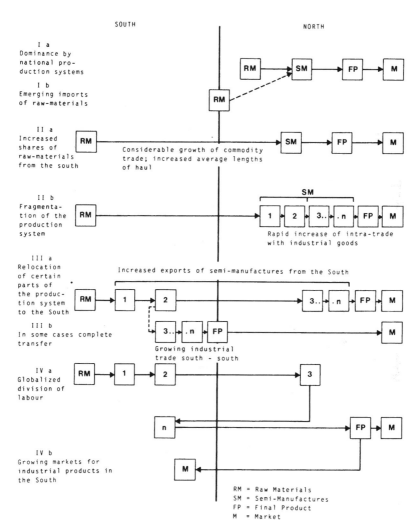

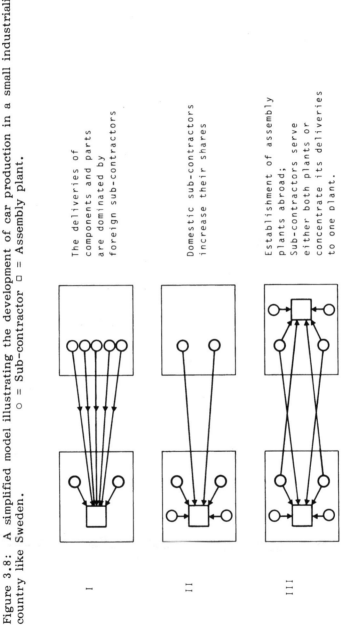

Figure 3.8: A simplified model illustrating the development of car production in a small industrialised country like Sweden.   ○ = Sub-contractor □ = Assembly plant.

The deliveries of components and parts are dominated by foreign sub-contractors

Domestic sub-contractors increase their shares

Establishment of assembly plants abroad; Sub-contractors serve either both plants or concentrate its deliveries to one plant.

38

Individual Level: Work-Tasks in the Single Plant.
The design of individual work-tasks depends to a high degree
on the production technique used. Manual processing demands
other kinds of knowledge about the process, materials used,
equipment and offers more alternatives concerning work
organisation than mass production or automation does.
Fragmentation started with the transition from manual to
automatic processing.

In Volvo car production, these two stages are illustrated
by work-tasks from the sub-process of body assembly in 1958
and 1980 respectively, a process in which the side-parts,
floor, roof and window-frames of the car are put together. In
1958, the technique used was manual. The main equipment
consisted of tools for point-welding, aggregates for gas-
welding, and fixtures to keep the parts together during the
welding. By 1980 most of these tasks had become automated:
all welding was done by 27 robots and one automatic welding
machine. During the 1950s growing demand called for volume
increases, while in 1980 the production capacity exceeded
demand. Work-tasks were designed through traditional time-
and-motion studies in 1958, and through the so-called MTM
method in 1980.

On both occasions the work-tasks investigated were in
functionally comparable units in the body assembly. They took
place at a processing station where 5 persons worked in 1958,
3 in 1980. The work-tasks were made in "cycles" lasting for
6½ minutes in 1958 and 1½ minute 1980. In 1958 most of the
time needed for the work-tasks was taken by the welding,
while loading dominated in 1980.

The fragmentation of work-tasks between 1958 and 1980
is illustrated in Figure 3.9a-c. First, the pattern of movements of individual workers is studied. No big changes took
place. Worker no. 2 (1980) made moves which were directed
towards the welding-machine, while worker no. 3 (1958) went
to the main jig repeatedly. The difference is due to the fact
that in 1958 the loading of components took place only at the
main jig, while in 1980 loadings were made at side-parts of
the station as well. Thus, more loadings were made in 1980
than in 1958.

When the individual spatial movement pattern during one
work-task is supplemented by the cycle-time of the work-
task, important differences between the two years emerge.
The work-task in 1958 lasted for about 6½ minutes, where 1
minute was devoted to loading. In 1980, the same task lasted
for 1½ minute, almost completely used for loading. This difference was an effect of the automation, as the manual
welding lasted for 5½ minutes per work-task in 1958.

We thus find, that similar work-tasks have become
fragmented between 1950 and 1980, as they are now divided
between workers and welding machines.

Figure 3.9a: The movements of an individual worker during loading at the station of the main jig in 1958 (upper part; worker no. 3) and the automatic welding-machine in 1980 (lower part; worker no. 2).
Source: Ellegård (1983, p. 121).

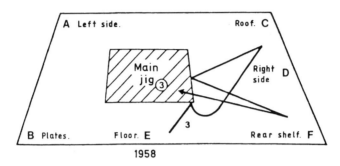

1958

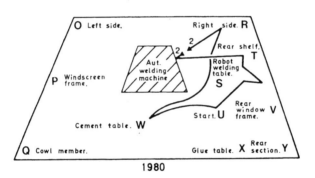

1980

If we finally make a joint study of the five work-tasks in 1958 and the three tasks of 1980, a new aspect of the frag-mentation emerges. In 1958 two workers made several loading together, i.e. they jointly carried and loaded big components to the main jig, whereafter they made the welding around the body in the neighbourhood of each other. In 1980, no joint loading-work was made. Two workers could work with the same component, but only in sequences, never together (cf. worker no. 1 and worker no. 3 in Figure 9c).

Figure 3.9b: A time-geographic presentation of two aspects of work-tasks made by an individual worker in 1958 (worker no. 3). Legend: See figure 9a.
Source: Ellegård (1983, p. 124).

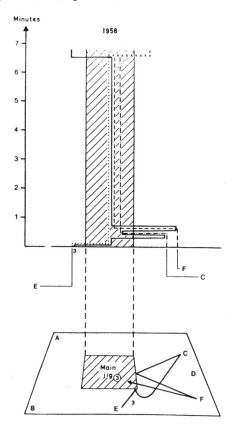

The effects of fragmentation are that workers have become more isolated from each other in their work-tasks. If the working-life of the individual is developing towards increased isolation, in a similar way in different production units within the production system, it is essential to find out whether these changes have similar effects on everyday-life in different cultural contexts. For example, will cultures with no traditions of Western-style work morals show more or less toleration of fragmentation and isolation?

Figure 3.9c: A time-geographic presentation of two aspects of work-tasks made by an individual worker in 1980 (worker no. 2). Legend: See figure 9a.
Source: Ellegård (1983, p. 124).

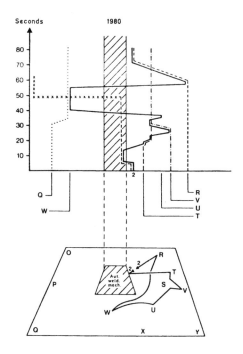

INDUSTRIAL GEOGRAPHY INSIDE FACTORY GATES

By means of models of production systems and production hierarchies, international trade flows and single work-tasks can be connected and analysed simultaneously. The aim has been to use the models as analytical tools, paying attention to events at different levels in the development of a region, a nation or a continent. The main reason for developing such a tool is the difficulty of explaining contradictory changes within as well as between different enterprises and sectors of industry. Another advantage is that the model permits the crossing of national state boundaries, a common problem in studies of industrial systems. Several studies of industrial geography stop at the factory gates. By detailed investi-

Figure 3.9d: A time-geographic presentation of two aspects
of work-tasks showing the spatial movement patterns of all
individual workers in 1958 (five workers). Legend: See
figure 9a.
Source: Ellegård (1983, p.125)

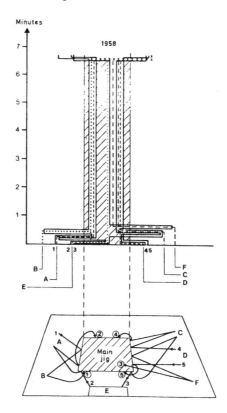

gations of the design of single work-tasks, it is possible to
provide better explanations of changes in the international
division of labour. This chapter focuses on fragmentation, but
is itself a fragment. Further research, aiming at a comprehensive empirical investigation of Swedish car production, will
test the hypotheses made here in detail to expand the model
connecting the international and individual levels.

Figure 3.9e: A time-geographic presentation of two aspects
of work-tasks showing the spatial movement patterns of all
individual workers in 1980 (three workers). Legend: See
figure 9a.
Source: Ellegård (1983, p. 125).

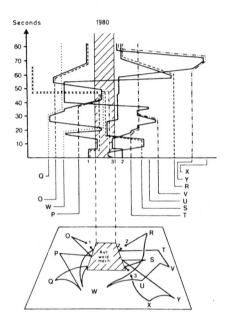

REFERENCES

Alvstam, C.G. (1982) 'International Trade in a Changing
     Environment - a Demand for a New Theory'. Paper
     presented at the IGU symposium on "Division of Labour,
     Specialisation and Technical Development" in Linköping,
     Sweden, 7-11 June
Ellegård, K. (1983) 'Människa - Produktion. Tidsbilder av ett
     produktions-system, Meddelanden fran Göteborgs Univer-
     sitets Geografiska Institutioner, serie B, no. 72
Fredriksson, C.G. & Lindmark, L.G. 'From Firms to Systems
     of Firms: A Study of Inter-regional Dependence in a
     Dynamic Society', in F.E.I. Hamilton & G.J.R. Linge,
     (eds.), Spatial Analysis, Industry and the Industrial
     Environment, Vol. 1: Industrial Systems (Wiley,
     Chichester)

Chapter Four

LOCATIONAL ISSUES IN WORLD ALUMINIUM: PAST,
PRESENT AND FUTURE

Bálint Balkay

The petroleum price explosions of 1973/4 and 1979/80, the
deep world economic recession and the economic misery of
most of the Third World - and that in the wake of the so
optimistic Declaration of a New International Economic Order -
have shed a sharp light on, among many other things, world
supplies of and world trade in minerals and mineral-based
commodities. Views concerning these issues have turned
several somersaults since the prosperous days of the 1960s.
The star performer of the minerals arena has been petroleum,
of course, but many lessons can be learnt also from aluminium, a metal that can be seen as paradigmatic in several
ways of the less glamorous minerals and mineral-based commodities. Aluminium is a fair benchmark among other things
because its price in real terms has stayed practically constant
- apart from the inevitable fluctuations - since about 1970.

DEVELOPMENT PATTERNS

Before 1945
Bauxite mining began in the late 19th century on the karst-
type bauxite deposits of France and of what were then the
'developing countries of Europe' (Yugoslavia, Hungary,
Greece and Turkey). There being no other significant outlet
to bauxite than the making of aluminium metal, the refining of
bauxite into alumina and the smelting of alumina into aluminium went hand in hand with the establishment and operation of the bauxite mines. These processes, however, were
concentrated in 'developed Europe', mainly in France,
Germany and Switzerland. Mining in the US and the con-
comitant processing began slightly later.

    In 1920, the European and North American aluminium
industries, small not only by today's standards but also in
relation to, say, steel, still processed practically no overseas
bauxite (Table 4.1). The European industry kept relying on

Table 4.1: Trends in Output in the Main Bauxite-Producing Regions, 1920 to 1982 1000 metric tons.

Country, region	1920	1930	1940	1950	1960	1975	1980	1982
Europe outside present-day CMEA	333	870	1389	1259	4349	9000	8564	8750
USA	530	336	446	1356	2000	1800	1560	700
South American continent	32	386	1250	3709	5694	8300	12100	8800
Present-day CMEA	–	33	871	1319	4763	10500*	10700*	10300*
Asia inc.islands	–	–	422	598	1824	3100	3950	3600
Africa	–	–	–	134	1607	9900	14400	10950
Caribbean islands	–	–	–	–	6500	13800	13000	9400
Australia	–	–	–	–	34	20000	27200	2300

*Including equivalents of the non-bauxitic aluminium ores processed in the USSR.

Remarks (1) The table shows 'the actors in the order of their appearance'.
(2) To emphasise the main trend, production figures of less than 10,000 tons p.a. by country have been omitted.

46

the bauxites of the Southern European countries, where prospecting and development were largely based on the visual identification of the striking red surface outcrops of the deposits. ALCOA, the Aluminium Company of America, sole US producer at the time, still processed indifferent-grade domestic bauxites. The first step in the globalisation of the aluminium industry was connected with the development of important hydro electric power sites on the southeast Canadian rivers: there being no bauxite in Canada, ALCOA (from which ALCAN, the Aluminium Company of Canada, was subsequently split by anti-trust action) had started developing bauxites in Surinam and (then British) Guyana. Even at the time, however, the prospectors of ALCOA and then ALCAN were engaged in an extensive and occasionally successful, largely pre-emptive search for bauxites in tropical regions, especially in West Africa, the Caribbean and South Africa. Colonial geological services, the French one in particular, also went looking for bauxite, and so did a number of independent prospectors, but industry took little enough interest in their findings at the time.

True, World War II entailed an intenser working of the South American deposits, yet the US relied mostly on the accelerated extraction of domestic bauxites, even though the supplies from South American were not menaced by any enemy. In the peak war year, 1943, production in the US exceeded six million tons; it had dropped back to one million tons by 1945, and has not topped two million tons p.a. since. During the war, Britain developed the Ghanaian deposits of Awaso. The Japanese war machine used Indonesian, Malaysian and to some extent Chinese bauxites; the Germans relied largely on Hungarian, to a lesser extent Yugoslav, bauxites. Prospecting proceeded at a forced pace: Jamaican bauxite was discovered in 1942, and so was a major deposit – Iszkaszentgyörgy – in Hungary, both too late to be developed to any significant extent before the end of hostilities.

Having no access to raw materials from abroad during war years, the aluminium industry of the USSR was forced into involuntary autarky. During the Cold War period, this autarky, which by then had risen to the rank of a policy, was extended to what is today the CMEA group of countries. The Hungarian bauxite resource was prospected and developed apace; new deposits were discovered in the USSR, too. Yet the combined sources were inadequate to meet the CMEA group's growing demand for aluminium. This is why the Soviet industry built plants to process non-bauxitic ores, attaining eminence in this field: in fact, at present, the USSR is the only country to process non-bauxitic ores on any major scale (2.5 million tons p.a. of nepheline at 25 to 30 per cent alumina content and 0.6 million tons of alunite at 16 to 18 per cent alumina content, in addition to 4.6 million tons of bauxite. (Mining Annual Review, London, 1983, p. 452.) Even so, the USSR relies at present on bauxite and alumina imported from outside the CMEA to feed 30 per cent of its aluminium industry.

From World War II to the Petroleum Price Explosion of 1973

Thanks to technological development based largely on the breakthroughs of the war years, a quantum jump took place in the post-war period in the globalisation of mining at large and of bauxite mining in particular, backed up by a process that is best described as gigantisation. Giant earthmoving, loading and hauling machinery made it possible to establish open-cast mines of five to ten million tons p.a. output and more; the development of ore, ore/oil (O/O) and ore/bulk/oil (OBO) carriers of up to 300,000 DWT size and of the appropriate port loading and unloading facilities - these factors made minerals extracted open-cast practically anywhere in the world but within reasonable distance from tidewater competitive with the output of the small open-cast mines of the main consumer regions, let alone the underground ones. In the case of bauxite, the rule of thumb for 'reasonable distance from tidewater' is that the mine should not be farther inland than x hundred kilometres if its output is x million typ. Of course, different rules apply to other minerals according to unit (dollars per ton) value. Conversely, even bauxite won underground can well be competitive in a sizeable consumer region remote from tidewater or from major ports: this is the case of Hungary. The result was the great swarming-out of the developed market-economy countries by aluminium companies for their raw material supplies into the tropical regions. The North American industry in particular geared itself to quasi-exclusive bauxite supplies from overseas. For both freight cost and strategic security of supply reasons, the US industry developed a clear-cut preference for Caribbean (overwhelmingly Jamaican) bauxites, whereas ALCAN ranged farther afield. At home, both preferred to locate processing plants on the seaboard (or, in the Canadian case, along waterways accessible to big seagoing freighters), and in places built private ports for themselves. The same 'extroverted' raw material procurement pattern was soon adopted by the two other US aluminium majors, Reynolds and Kaiser, and by the two European ones, Péchiney of France and Alusuisse of Switzerland; smaller producers such as BACO of the UK and VAW of the Federal Republic of Germany followed suit. The Japanese industry, which has no domestic ore base at all, displayed a preference above all, for Australian bauxites and contributed to their development by signing letters of intent guaranteeing sizeable volumes of purchase.

LOCATIONAL ISSUES

The aluminium industry links together three major siting-sensitive factors of production, bauxite, electric power and market outlets. Other inputs into the system, such as capital, capital goods, labour (and more specifically, skills), consumables and new technology are comparatively neutral spatially. However, when the pros and cons of the three major factors balance about evenly, some of these secondary factors may well be critical.

The bauxite mine must be located on a bauxite deposit of high enough grade, large enough tonnage and fair enough accessibility. Such deposits, being rather abundant all over the tropical world, the aluminium industry is not constrained by any shortage, relative or absolute, of bauxite; yet bauxite geography does have a big impact on siting patterns. Table 4.1 reveals that, today, the bulk of world bauxite output is being produced in the developing world and Australia, while the two biggest markets, North America and Western Europe, are sizeable net importers. The CMEA is also a net importer, albeit a minor one. The bauxite producers of the developing world and Australia have managed to set up between them the second most viable mineral producers' organisation after OPEC, in the shape of IBA, the International Bauxite Association. Australia belongs to the group of countries termed the resources periphery of the developed market-economy world which includes Canada, South Africa and, for some purposes, Norway, New Zealand and Iceland. With regard to natural resources, these countries behave similarly in many ways to the developing countries rich in natural resources.

For the aluminium smelter, it is not an absolute necessity to be sited next to a large power station producing cheap electricity, but the case for such siting is a very strong one and rests upon:

(1)   the cost of power made up 10 per cent of the price of primary aluminium before 1973 and 20 per cent of it today;

(2)   the long-distance transport of electricity is unviable albeit not unfeasible, and, even at shorter distances, it is cheaper as a rule to move the smelter inputs to the power station than power to the points of reception of the smelter inputs; and

(3)   the same holds, mutatis mutandis, also for moving primary aluminium to the semi-fabricating plant or to the market.

This is why siting smelters next door to power stations, with the power delivered at a relatively low voltage to the smelter direct by arm-thick low-loss bus bar, is by far the most favoured siting pattern. The second best one is to have the smelter at a distance of a few kilometres from the power station if, for one reason or another, siting next door is not viable. This is the most common location pattern of big export orientated smelters, whereas comparatively high-cost smelters sited in big markets in the US and Western Europe are often supplied from a reliable national grid.

For primary aluminium to be competitive, the electricity available to the smelter must be cheap as well as abundant. Until about 1970, the rule of thumb used to be that power for aluminium smelting should not cost more than about three to six mills (tenths of a US cent) per kWh. Even then, this condition was satisfied above all by hydroelectric power. This was the advantage that led to the establishment of the big Canadian smelters (ALCAN, one of the biggest aluminium corporations of the world, actually built and to this day owns most of the power generating facilities that feed its Canadian smelters), the Norwegian industry, a few facilities in developing countries, such as Edéa on the Sanaga River in Cameroun and Tema near the Akosombo Dam on the Volta River in Ghana, or in Iceland, which has no bauxite and a very modest metal market. (Contrary to Iceland, both Cameroun and Ghana have perfectly workable (and actually worked) bauxite deposits; yet both are supplied with alumina from abroad.)

As regards their environmental impact, smelters used to be great polluters: a typical uncleaned-up smelter emits 15 to 20 kg of fluorine compounds, 7 to 10 kg of carbon dioxide, 50 to 100 kg of carbon monoxide and 20 kg of dust per ton of metal produced. Also, some types of smelter emit noxious and carcinogenic tar fumes. Old smelters can and have been cleaned up, but if the necessity to do so comes in step with an electricity price rise, it is more reasonable to close the old smelter down and build a new one (most probably in another country or region where power is cheaper), using a technology that is clean, from the start.

In contrast to the bauxite mine and the smelter, the alumina refinery – in which bauxite, the ore of aluminium is refined to the smelter input alumina (anhydrous aluminium oxide, Al_2O_3) is comparatively indifferent to location. It is best situated somewhere near the transport route that joins the bauxite mine to the smelter, but that is no hard-and fast rule, since alumina plants, being generally much bigger than smelters, typically supply more than one smelter. In actual fact, the refinery is typically sited either close to the mine or close to the smelter, although the arguments for either of these types of location are not very strong. Indeed, there are telling exceptions such as the refinery in the US Virgin

Islands, which is comparatively remote from both mines and smelters, but has proximity to tidewater and is inside US territory for customs purposes. The reason for this indifference is that the costs of transporting bauxite from the mine to the refinery about equal the costs of transporting alumina from the refinery to the smelter.

The environmental impact of an alumina plant is due almost entirely to the waste it produces, called red mud. One to 1.5, seldom two tons of red mud are produced per ton of alumina. Red mud has a moisture content largely of caustic soda. The early thoughtless practice of dumping the red mud in the nearest body of water has been abolished nearly everywhere. Red mud is typically stored today in ponds confined by high earth dams. These storage areas are major and permanent environmental eyesores. Only recently, under pressure from rising environmental awareness, have attempts at using red mud gained momentum. Experiments to turn them into tiles and other building materials have been successful, and so have others to add them to the tar of tarmac roads. The problem is that these outlets are not of the same order of magnitude as the 'production' of red mud, let alone the old dumps. This is why, today, alumina plant sites where red mud ponds trigger less of a resistance, if any, are preferred and are found in many instances in the developing world or in the resources periphery of the developed market-economy world. This sort of a siting motive, however, is a fairly recent one, and, despite the above-expounded comparative siting neutrality of alumina plants in the pre-environmentalist days, such plants were, at least up to about 1970, and with the major exception of Jamaica, overwhelmingly sited also in the developed market-economy world. Why?

The asymmetry is in the nature of the economies in which the bauxite mines and the smelters, respectively, are sited. Up to about 1955, locating a major export-oriented smelter in the developing world was unthinkable, not so much because ownership was at risk (wholesale nationalisation of the aluminium industry's assets in the developing countries came much later), but because of the lack of infrastructure and of certain backup skills and facilities. Even in 1982, 84 per cent of world primary aluminium output and some 70 per cent of world alumina output came from the industrially developed countries, as against only 43 per cent of world bauxite output. Yet developing countries' smelter capacity is, at about two million tons p.a. (with the Asian centrally planned economies disregarded), about equal to those countries' modest aluminium consumption. But this balance covers up some fairly circuitous trading patterns. A great deal of the metal produced in the developing countries' smelters is processed into semi-finished goods in the developed market economies, and a great deal of the aluminium consumed in the developing countries comes from the developed ones, a substantial percentage of it in some wrought, that is, higher value-added, form. There is thus a considerable scope for expanded South-South cooperation in aluminium trade.

In the case of both the smelters and the alumina plants, then, the secondary siting factors, referred to above, turned out to be predominant. In a developing country, investment into plant is more expensive per unit of capacity; more infrastructural investment is required in almost every case, and such investment may double the owning cost of the facility; skills are harder to come by, and there are limits to the sophistication of the equipment that can be installed, not primarily because it is so much more complicated to run, but because of the shortage or absence of the aforementioned backup skills and services (in repairs and maintenance). Of course, in addition, the corporations of the developed market-economy countries at the time laid great store on having their plant away from possible nationalisation (outright or creeping), political upheavals, and overvalued or capriciously fluctuating currencies. As a result:

(1) alumina plants too were overwhelmingly sited in the industrially developed world, with the greatest single expansion in Australia: and

(2) bauxite-owning developing-country governments stipulated, as one of their prime demands vis-à-vis the world aluminium industry, that alumina production be gradually shifted into their own countries.

The criteria of siting the semifabricating facilities relative to the aluminium smelter on the one hand and the market (which, to all intents and purposes, tends to coincide with the market for the aluminium or aluminium-containing finished goods) are more clear-cut but also more complex. The best solution is to have both the smelter and its source of cheap power in or near the market. The advantages of being in mid-market may outweigh the drawbacks of expensive power (cf. the 'Ludwigshafen story' below). Yet smelters so sited tend to be extremely sensitive to power cost escalation. This, by and large, is the case with the Canadian and Norwegian smelters and used to apply more or less, before 1973, also to US smelters. On the other hand, if the smelter cannot be sited so favourably, then the arguments regarding the siting of the semi fabricating facilities become somewhat conflicting. The advantage of a comparatively large number of smaller, distributed semis-facilities (with outputs in the 5,000 to 20,000 tons p.a. range) right inside the market, supplied with metal from a comparatively remote smelter, is that such semifabricators are better at adapting to consumer preferences and market fluctuations. Also, to the extent that the semis-facilities are scrap-fed - and large volumes of scrap arise in the large markets - the semis facilities' dependence on freight costs from the smelter is reduced. The larger semis facilities sited close to the smelters tend to enjoy certain economies of scale, and they can be supplied with molten metal for their highly efficient cast-rolling facilities at a considerable saving in melting heat. On the other hand, aluminium semis are somewhat more costly to transport than ingots. Advantages vs. disadvantages line up differently for different products and different ownership patterns: at the one extreme, so-called direct finished goods which are produced at the smelter proper, such as certain castings (e.g. door handles), are best made at the smelter, and so are the products of cast-rolling like wire and cable, strip and, more recently, certain types of plate. At the other extreme, small-volume specialised products such as extruded goods of complicated purpose-oriented profiles are best made in the market. Semis facilities owned by the smelter owners tend to be bigger and closer to the smelter, whereas independent semifabricators tend to set up in the market. None of these 'rules' is hard-and-fast, however.

ECONOMIES OF SCALE AND BARRIERS TO ENTRY

Limited markets precluded any awareness of the economies of scale to be made in the aluminium industry roughly till the end of World War II. It was the subsequent process of gigantisation, with many breakthroughs in alumina plant and smelter design helping, that turned economies of scale into a prime consideration. In the 1950s, 100,000 tons p.a. alumina plants and 20,000 tons p.a. smelters used to be on the big side; today's largest alumina plant (Gladstone, Australia) produces 2.4 million tons of alumina a year, and the largest smelter (Bratsk in the USSR) produces close on 1 million tons of metal a year. Investment per unit of alumina refinery or alumina smelter capacity is, within limits, a logarithmically degressive function of facility size: it is about 1 million US dollars per thousand tons p.a. output for a 100,000 tons p.a. alumina facility and 0.46 million US dollars per thousand tons p.a. output for an alumina facility ten times bigger, both taken without the investment into the required infrastructure.

Economies of scale are less important in mining, but very considerable again in transportation; they are least important in semis manufacturing.

These conditions hold, ceteris paribus, for so-called greenfield sites where no other industry and, possibly, no infrastructure pre-exists. The expansion of existing facilities tends to be cheaper, in places considerably so, especially if, when laying down the original infrastructure, subsequent expansions have been envisaged. One important advantage of the expansion of an existing facility is that the skilled workforce of the original plant can be spread out to operate the expanded facility and to train on the job the additional labour hired. The operating costs per unit of output of the bigger plants are not dramatically lower (the consumption of most consumables, determined as it is by the laws of chemistry, is influenced by technological progress above all rather than by plant size), but there are certain, possibly important savings on labour, overheads and services.

All this adds up to fairly high barriers to new entrants into the industry, the principal problems facing them being (1) finding the capital for their new ventures, (2) finding market outlets for their products, and (3) finding a specialist partner who will run in their technology for them. This had resulted by about 1960 in an oligopolisation of the aluminium industry similar in many ways to that of the petroleum industry, with the role of the Seven Sisters being played by the Big Six, Alcoa, Kaiser and Reynolds of the US, Alcan of Canada, Péchiney of France and Alusuisse of Switzerland: in 1960, these six companies between them held 70 per cent of world non-socialist smelter capacity. Their share, however, had declined to 50 per cent by 1982. What happened?

A NEW EMERGING PATTERN

The central thesis, posited here is a double one:

(1) As time passes a country or region may develop certain well-nigh irresistible comparative advantages relating to a given industry. The redeployment of that industry into the country/ region in question, however, is by no means automatic. Opposed by vested interests, it is a slow process that, normally, is commensurate with the time it takes for the vested interests to write off their facilities rendered obsolete or otherwise non-viable by the new comparative-advantage pattern (and to do so without excessive loss of face).

(2) For nudging redeployment along, the country with the recent comparative advantages has essentially two means:

(a) factor starvation (that is, withholding supply of some of the factors of production required by the industry to function, with a view to shifting the use of the factors in question to new facilities in the country/region with the recent comparative advantages);

(b) underselling.

The emerging new siting pattern of the aluminium industry features both. Bauxite being abundant, and skilled labour and capital being as a rule available in sufficient volumes to such new facilities as can be shown to be viable, the factors of production relevant to the aluminium industry in which starvation situations may be considered are (a) energy, (b) technology and (c) market outlets. Of course, the energy price explosion was the single most important factor resulting in the emerging new siting pattern. Its principal impact, as far as the aluminium is concerned, was to greatly reduce the prior geographic mobility of energy, thereby upgrading the comparative advantages of smelter sites where low-cost (which is not necessarily the same thing as low-priced) energy is available. Most of these sites are in the developing countries.

Most smelter closures of 1981-1982, both permanent phase-outs and temporary 'mothballings', were attributed primarily to the rising cost of energy as supplied by third parties, while the old-established integrated producers who own most of the power generating facilities supplying their smelters, which in their turn use predominantly renewable (hydro) energy sources, have been able to weather the market downturn reasonably well. Those smelters, too, that are supplied with power under cheap long-term non-renegotiated contracts which have not yet run out, as in Greece (Dokopoulou, 1986) also have a considerable cost advantage over their competitors, albeit probably only a temporary one.

Consider for an example ALCAN's Ludwigshafen smelter in the Federal Republic of Germany, which, by its contract with the Pfalzwerke electricity utility company, was sold power at 4.5 Pfennige per kWh, which had been on the dear side when the contract was concluded in the 1960s, and was offset by the smelter's proximity to both tidewater and a sizeable market. When its contract ran out in September 1982, the utility offered to renew it at 7.5 Pfennige, which would have driven the smelter irretrievably into debt all the more so since most of its competitors in the country continued receiving power at 3.5 Pfennige, under contracts that had been concluded earlier and had longer to run. ('Der Stromschlag von Ludwigshafen', Der Stern, Hamburg, February 3, 1983, pp. 205-206). The point missed by Der Stern is that, the cost of one kWh to the utility being 6.5 Pfennige, the smelter was in fact kept in the black by the taxpayer. Hence, if the taxpayer is not prevailed upon one way or another to keep subsidising an aluminium industry on security-of-supply or other strategic considerations, then the only reasonable way for the Ludwigshafen smelter - and of its competitors in most of Western Europe - to go is to shut up shop and move near cheap power sites elsewhere in the world.

For another example, the Japanese aluminium smelters are supplied with electricity by oil-fired generating facilities. (Petroleum used to be, in the golden days pre-1973, the geographically mobile fuel par excellence.) The petroleum price explosions, the second one in particular, have put paid to this concept of smelter economics. As against a capacity of 1.6 million tons p.a., and an output that exceeded one million tons p.a. every year between 1972 and 1980, Japanese smelters produced only about 250,000 tons of metal in 1983, and entire smelters have been 'mothballed' or phased out for good.

The point to be stressed here that the impact of the new developments has been almost entirely on smelter siting.

Remarkably enough, there has been no serious attempt at technology starvation in the aluminium industry, probably because up-to-date technology is available from a variety of competing sources (from Japan, a number of engineering companies such as Bechtel, and also from the socialist countries, in addition to the Big Six who also compete in selling technology). Also, having the ultimate in technology does not matter a great deal except in the most developed countries which have access to it anyway. It has, on the other hand, turned out generally preferable to have, in smelters, semifabricating units and to a less extent also in alumina refining, a partner who can help in marketing or supply the know-how for plant run-in and ongoing modernisation. The most widespread arrangement these days is to offer the high-technology partner a minority shareholding. An example in point is Reynolds Metals' holding of just 4 per cent in the Valesul smelter of Brazil. One of the major changes int he world aluminium industry since 1970 has been that the big aluminium transnationals' preference for wholly- or at least majority-owned subsidiaries abroad has been replaced by their going in for minority shareholdings (which, incidentally, has reduced their exposure to risk, too). This result was achieved partly by the nationalisation of the older facilities (early on above all) and, latterly, by government and, in places, local private capital putting up the bulk of equity for the newly created ones.

Whereas the supply and demand of aluminium are about evenly balanced in the Third World, some of the big or relatively advanced developing countries have been importing large volumes of metal. These countries have a comparative market advantage in setting up import-substituting industries of their own, thereby reducing demand in the world market of aluminium. Moreover, precisely for the economy-of-scale reasons referred to above, these facilities are created, more often than not, with exports as well as import substitution in mind, which increases the pressure on the world market still further. Most smelter facilities set up on this pattern are backed up by domestic bauxite mines and alumina plants:

hence, as distinct from the impact of a changed world energy situation, these new facilities affect the world market of bauxite and alumina as well.

Underselling the metal produced by the older smelters is principally based these days on new low-cost sources of energy, among which natural gas in the OPEC countries and in some other developing countries is prominent. Hydro power sites in the developing countries could just as well be used (or developed) to smelt aluminium. This will certainly come about in the future. However, hydro power, if already available, tends - with a very few exceptions such as the Cabora Bassa facility in Mozambique - to be sold out, and new developments take a long time and are, more often than not, frightfully costly. The problem with these latter is to find for the power (or the water) other outlets in addition to aluminium smelting, with a view to solving/mitigating the tremendous cash flow problem caused by the obligation to repay the credits that have gone into the development of the site. Nevertheless, a new generation of big export-oriented hydropower-based smelters in the Third World will clearly be the next step in aluminium siting pattern evolution.

Natural gas produced as a co-product of petroleum in, say, an Arab Gulf country can, up to a point, be exported in liquefied form, in which case its price is only slightly lower than that of petroleum. The outlets for this form of exportation being, however, much more limited than the volume of gas available, the remaining gas can either be flared (a tremendous amount is being wasted in just that way) or used to supply/fuel some domestic industry such as aluminium smelting. The key point here is that, whereas the selling price of liquefied natural gas is quite high, the actual cost of production of the gas is almost nil. Hence, the price at which the gas is sold to, say, an aluminium smelter is, within the broad range so defined, largely a matter of bookkeeping conventions, and, at a pinch, it can be lowered readily to keep the metal produced competitive (that is, to underbid other smelters in less favourable energy supply situations).

It was these factors, acting singly or in combination, that have permitted a number of developing countries to actually increase their output of aluminium metal between 1980 and 1982, in a period when world non-socialist aluminium output as a whole shrank from 12.8 million tons to 10.7 million tons, (smelter output of the centrally planned economies as a group remained constant), and average smelter utilisation was just 76 per cent in 1982. This, in fact, is the forced redeployment of aluminium smelting for a case is made above. The process is certain to go on also in the future, shifting more and more of smelter capacity away from the developed world. Countries where import substitution was probably the major factor were Brazil, India, Argentina, Indonesia, Iran, China and North Korea. Countries where underselling from a position of energy cost advantage was probably the major factor were Bahrain, Dubai, Egypt, Cameroun; and countries with mixed motives included, as far as one is able to see, Guyana, Turkey and some countries of the "developed market economy minerals periphery", Australia, New Zealand, South Africa and Iceland. New capacity is actually being added on in Canada, Norway, South Africa, and a number of developing countries.

The ALBA smelter in Bahrain, the first to be built in the Arab world, went onstream in 1971. Its initial capacity, 57,500 tons p.a., has since been raised to 170,000 tons p.a. It is owned 78 per cent by the Bahraini and Saudi governments, and 17 per cent by Kaiser Aluminium. It receives power from a gas-turbine-driven power station and alumina under a long-term contract from Gove, Australia. The smelter is to be expanded to a final size of 250,000 tons p.a. The second smelter in the Arab world was the Egyptian one at Nag Hamadi. Built with technical assistance and part-financing from the USSR, it came onstream in 1975 with a capacity of 33,000 tons p.a. Its current capacity is 133,000 tons p.a. It receives power from the Aswan High Dam and alumina likewise from Gove, Australia. Expansion to 166,000 tons p.a. is underway (or possibly completed). The third was the Jebel Ali smelter in Dubai, owned 20 per cent by the Dubai government and 20 per cent by an entity called Aluminium Smelter Holdings. First onstream in 1979, it produced in 1981 142,000 tons p.a. metal for a nameplate capacity of 135,000 tpy. It has a gas-fuelled power station which also feeds a sea water desalination unit, and receives alumina from Alcoa of Australia. Plans call for an expansion to 180,000 tons p.a. For the Arab-Gulf as a whole, a smelter capacity of one million tons p.a. has been envisaged by GOIC, the Gulf Organisation for Industrial Consulting. Further smelters to be based on gas-fired power stations and on imported alumina have been envisaged by Algeria, Abu Dhabi, Libya. How have bauxite mining and alumina refining fared in the meantime? Under the combined impact of the backlash against the IBA cartel and the recession, the aluminium industry has moved away from producers in the developing world. The outright winner was Australia which, remarkably, is itself an IBA member. In 1984, Australia produced some 30 per cent of world bauxite output and 30 per cent of world alumina output, confirming the thesis that there is no evolution in siting patterns where there are no pressures. That said, a number of the newly established smelter companies in the developing world have envisaged backward integration into alumina making, which further reduces the bauxite producers' scope for getting alumina plants of their own under economically viable conditions.

THE FUTURE

All forecasters agree, and the writer tends to agree with them, that at about twice the growth rate of GNP in the OECD group (which is the market that matters for aluminium), demand for aluminium may be expected to show a wholesome growth. The problem is that given the very broad scope for both export-oriented and import-substituting aluminium industry development, supply is almost certain to outstrip demand practically at any time over the period considered. This spontaneous process is likely to be backed up by the big aluminium transnationals which, having largely retired into semis from the upstream phases of the industry, will presumably have an interest in fostering competition among the new entrants. This, incidentally, is the fate that the writer can see for any industry engaged in the prime processing of minerals, be it petroleum refining, petrochemicals, iron and steel, non-ferrous metals or even cement.

REFERENCE

Dokopoulou, E. (1986) 'Multinationals and Manufactured Exports from the Enlarged EEC Periphery: The Case of Greece', in F.E.I. Hamilton (ed.), Industrialisation in Developing and Peripheral Regions (Croom Helm, London) pp. 205-231

Chapter Five

SPATIAL AND STRUCTURAL CHANGES IN WEST EUROPEAN
PAPERMAKING

Peter Lewis

THE CHANGING CONTEXT

More than 500 paper mills and 1500 papermaking machines
have ceased production in Western Europe in the past ten
years: an average of one mill each week. Over 50,000 jobs
have been lost from the industry in the European Economic
Community (EEC), representing 20 per cent of the total employment in papermaking in 1973. The regional distribution of
this loss varies widely from about 5 per cent in Italy to over
30 per cent in the UK, with France, Belgium and Denmark
near the EEC average and the German Federal Republic with
the lower value of 14 per cent. Few new mills have been
opened; those mills that have provide an important guide to
risk assessment by investors in an industry that has shown a
poor return to capital during this period. The investment cost
of paper mills has more than doubled in the past decade
reflecting the expected factors of inflation, increased engineering costs of control systems, and higher labour costs
and rapidly rising costs of mandatory pollution controls. It is
an extremely capital intensive industry with a 3 to 5 year
lead time to start-up. These factors, added to a general
overcapacity in Europe as a whole, and the well-known cyclical nature of pulp supply and demand, inhibit cavalier
investment in new capacity. There has been much greater
pressure and willingness to refurbish existing machines and
add control systems, though this, too, is expensive.

Paper consumption continues to increase in all the main
grades of paper (a glossary of terms is given at the end of
the chapter) and the total output of European mills has risen
correspondingly. However, the overall increases in consumption and production disguise some substantial changes in the
structure and spatial character of the industry as it adjusts
to the progressive integration of the European economy for
pulp and paper. The removal of trade barriers at the beginning of 1984 to Scandinavia and other EFTA nations for pulp
and paper, and the scheduled extension of the EEC to include

Spain and Portugal, will effectively complete this integration. Yet the process of adjustment is by no means complete: many more paper mills are likely to close and a large number of papermaking machines will go out of production in the next 15 years, with a corresponding reduction in jobs and a major redistribution in paper production in total and by grade.

Stress and readjustment are not new features of the European papermaking industry, which has been characterised by relatively short periods of change in response to an innovation followed by longer periods of adjustment to the new conditions. Till the last 20 years these innovations have been technological, first with the change from manual to machine production, secondly, with the change from cotton rags to wood pulp. Both major changes led to a reduction in the number of mills and an increase in the capacity at a site; together these led to regional concentrations of paper production. The adjustments in scale and location, transforming one pattern into a distinguishably different one, occurred over many decades, with a slow initial response which accelerates and then diminishes rapidly. These are characteristics of a logistic function evident in all the principal changes in the European paper industry in the past century.

These major technological changes, and various minor technical modifications, preceded and stimulated changes in market area. Mechanisation changed the papermaking industry throughout Europe from an essentially local, market town-oriented industry to a regionally, and later a nationally, organised industry in which competition for all grades of paper production was possible: capacity increases and more efficient transport networks made competition effective over progressively greater areas. This type of change was reinforced by the introduction of wood pulp which resulted in expanded capacity at a site and in concentrated spatial cost advantages, leading to further expansions in market. Yet the market for paper remained essentially national.

The principal feature of the past 25 years in Europe has been the political initiation of the enlargement of the market rather than through technical innovation. The question of interest concerns the nature and speed of adjustment that the nationally-organised paper production structures in Europe will make to this supranational competitive market area in which production and supply costs vary very greatly. It is the largest coherent market in the world with over 330m people and an average GDP per person of more than US $8500 in 1980.

Certain common elements are evident in the way that the papermaking industry has responded to the technological changes. First, some sectors have grown while others have declined. In particular the technology initially favoured the bulk, lower-quality grades, but continued technical modification extended the impact to medium and higher quality grades of paper. Secondly, the range of mill products fell. Thirdly, a number of mills have survived by specialisation and by finding a market niche not readily filled by mills adopting the innovation. These market niches have been squeezed progressively by technical improvements to the original innovation. Fourthly, company amalgamation to secure markets has often been followed by the closure of those mills which were considered marginal in the context of the company's production profile. Till recently, this has occurred within a national context, but international infiltration is evident and could well increase.

All these features seem likely to dominate the next fifteen years of change in response to the enlarged European market for pulp and paper. Some gross indication of international changes can be inferred and monitored from trade figures.

TRADE IN PAPER PRODUCTS

As the scale of self-sufficiency has increased from the local to national to international levels, so the range of a typical papermill's products has become more restricted. It is axiomatic that specialisation leads to exchange. Interregional exchanges are not available but international exchanges are and reflect at a coarse level some aspects of the paper industry's structural and spatial development.

Western Europe is essentially self-sufficient in paper products over all grades and has remained so during the past twenty five years. (Table 5.1). Paper consumption, matched by production, increased from about 29 million tonnes in 1963 to 42 million tonnes in 1981. There is trade between Europe and North America, with Canada supplying newsprint and the USA supplying fluting medium, but its volume had fallen to about 13 per cent of total trade in 1981.

There are three zones of paper trade in Western Europe. The EEC is a paper importing zone; Scandinavia an exporting zone; the remaining countries are approximately balanced in production and consumption. Austria has tended to become a more important exporter, especially to West Germany, and, over the next fifteen years, Portugal is likely to be able to exploit its pulp production potential and make an increasingly important contribution to the European pulp and paper trading pattern.

Within the EEC, trade has increased since its enlargement from the original six members (Table 5.2). The Scandinavian and North American contributions have each fallen by about 3 per cent, but the former still dominates total paper trade. Over the same period Scandinavia's share of pulp has fallen from 60 to 40 per cent, while North

Table 5.1: Production and Apparent Consumption of Paper in Million Tonnes.

	1963		1973			1981		
	Consumption	Production	Consumption	Production	Kg/cap	Consumption	Production	Kg/cap.
EEC	24	18	30	23	120	33	24	127
Scandinavia	2.5	8	3	11	184	4	14	200
Rest of Europe	2.5	2.5	4	5	65	5	6	80
Total	29	28.5	37	39		42	44	

Table 5.2: Volume of Trade in Million Tonnes.

	EEC				Source of Imports (%)			
	Consumption	Production	Exports	Imports	EEC	Scandinavia	Austria	N. America
1973	30	23	4	11	25	53	3	16
1981	33	24	5	14	31	50	4	13

Table 5.3: Paper Production and Consumption in Million Tonnes for the EEC.

	Production	Imports	Exports	Apparent Consumption	Kg/cap.
1973					
France	4.785	1.535	0.591	5.729	112
Belgium	0.833	0.916	0.456	1.293	129
Netherlands	1.741	1.029	0.800	1.970	149
West Germany	6.355	3.149	1.094	8.410	137
Italy	4.100	0.513	0.280	4.333	80
UK	4.615	3.258	0.297	7.575	136
Eire	0.142	0.187	0.057	0.272	91
Denmark	0.239	0.559	0.042	0.756	152
1981					
France	5.151	2.130	1.061	6.220	116
Belgium	0.864	0.987	0.480	1.370	134
Netherlands	1.701	1.384	0.897	2.189	156
West Germany	7.498	3.771	1.709	9.560	156
Italy	4.935	0.858	0.498	5.295	93
UK	3.793	3.395	0.357	6.832	122
Eire	0.055	0.278	0.015	0.318	95
Denmark	0.253	0.728	0.149	0.832	162

America's pulp trade to Europe has increased from 28 to 38 per cent.

Table 5.3 shows that, within the EEC, there have been important changes in production and consumption since the Community was enlarged. Total output has increased in every country except the UK, Eire and the Netherlands. Both total production and consumption per person have increased in every country except the UK. Imports dominate exports, but all nations export some paper.

Tables of total mutual trade are too cumbersome to present for the 18 countries when they are split into various trading subsets, such as the EEC, the enlarged EEC, EFTA and the reduced EFTA, for three time periods, 1963, 1973 and 1981, in terms of both value and tonnage. The more important features are summarised. First, mutual trade has intensified, but changes in trade agreements have led to important changes in reciprocity. The original EEC nations show a much greater reciprocal trade structure in paper than the remaining nations in all three periods. Their trade has increased overall and the degree of reciprocity has intensified. Second, West Germany has become the principal supplier of paper by volume and value to all the other original EEC member states, which was not the case in 1963 or 1973. At the same time France has become Germany's most important supplier. Thirdly, the enlarged EEC was still in 1973 very much a union of two disparate trading groups, but, by 1981 the degree of mutual exchange was greater. The most notable result is that the UK provides the dominant export market for every other EEC nation and is itself a minor supplier to all other EEC nations except Eire. Indeed both statements are essentially true in the context of the whole of Europe.

Tables showing total trade by value or volume are difficult to interpret because each country typically has different quantities of exports. Furthermore the volume of trade from year to year is likely to fluctuate making overall comparison difficult. Part of this difficulty arises from the different marginal totals involved. For example in 1981 Benelux exported 204,000 tons of paper to France which represented 40 per cent of Benelux exports but only 21 per cent of France's imports. So long as the marginal totals are kept no information is lost and the situation can be described adequately either on an equal importer or on an equal exporter basis.

The two tables can be combined by standardising the marginal totals simultaneously by an iterative procedure until they reach unity within an acceptable tolerance (say 0.0001). Once all the marginal totals equal 1, one has captured the essential trade association of the original values and put it on a general basis with the following advantageous properties. Any increase or decrease in total trade that is distributed proportionately over the whole table does not disturb the association. Any increase or decrease in the total export or

65

import of any one or more exporting or importing countries that is distributed proportionately to all the importers or from all the exporters does not disturb the pattern. That is, if West Germany doubles its exports to all its trading partners the standardised values would persist. Any increases or decreases that do NOT affect a full row or column DO upset the association and provide a means of detecting changes, and, subject to some assumptions, significance of the changes.

In short such tables are unaffected by multiplicative row or column changes. If all the values are further standardised to sum to 1 overall then the values are very like probabilities and may be treated as transition probabilities of trade given the importing (or exporting) country. Such p_{ij} can be treated as a time series and testing for a Markov property is an obvious step for such an analysis of the complete range of values from 1963 to 1981.

In the case of just three points the proportions may be used differently. Over the three periods the p_{ij} for any pair of trading partners could increase, decrease or oscillate. Clearly there are six possible outcomes and if the p_{ij} are random a strict increase or decrease will occur in one third of the cases. For the original EEC nations in which Belgium and Luxembourg are combined for trade statistics the expected number of cells showing a strict increase or decrease is 7. This is the observed number too. For the original EFTA members the expected number is 19, the observed is 41. For the full table of West European nations, the expected number is 70, the observed is 103. Important structural changes seem to be occurring in international trade. These changes reflect shifts in the structure of production and consumption of paper.

STRUCTURAL CHANGES IN EUROPEAN PAPERMAKING

The main features of recent changes in consumption by grade of paper are shown in Table 5.4. Over the next 15 years, demand for paper is likely to increase, but is unlikely to be the same over the whole of Europe. A common feature of many estimates of expected future demand for paper has been the use of high correlation between GDP and paper consumption followed by the assumption that these correlations are independent of their spatial context. It is unwise to assume that European paper consumption characteristics will imitate those of North America in volume or grade as GDP increases. Indeed any such assumption is demonstrably incorrect. Although GDP in the whole of Europe (1980) was less than in the USA, paper consumption in those nations with comparable GDP values was very different from the consumption profile of the USA. Furthermore the way the pattern of consumption

Table 5.4: Projected Consumption by Grade of Paper in EEC for AD 2000.

| | CONSUMPTION | | | | PRODUCTION | |
	1973 Million Tonnes	1981 Million Tonnes	2000 Million Tonnes low	2000 Million Tonnes high	1973 %	1983 %
Newsprint	4.4	4.6	5.02	5.28	40	39
Packaging, Wrapping	10.3	10.1	11.66	12.59	66	68
Board	4.9	5.1	5.59	5.88	90	88
Tissue	1.0	1.6	1.93	2.13	92	88
Printing, Writing	8.7	10.1	11.80	12.80	92	88
Other	1.0	2.5	3.00	3.32		
Total	30.3	34.0	39.00	42.00		

67

changes over time also differs from region to region. This is an important proviso in projecting demand for Spain or Italy by comparison with the UK or West Germany.

In Table 5.4 projected demand by grade to AD 2000 is restricted to the EEC. The demand profile is consistent with that in these nations over the previous twenty years and this author estimates that demand for paper is likely to lie between 38 and 41 million tonnes by the end of the century for the EEC and between 48 and 53 million tonnes for the whole of Europe. These values are substantially less than some projections prepared for the industry and if much higher values begin to look realistic by 1990 then conclusions concerning the distribution of mills and machines at risk will need modifying. Nonetheless the projected demands give a 5 to 8 million tonne increase for the EEC and a 6 to 11 million tonne increase for Europe which is a substantial increase. Similarly the difference between the upper and lower estimates is 3 to 5 million tonnes and this too is a large volume of paper representing many mills and many jobs.

Changes in Machine Size and Mill Size

The principal structural responses in the European paper industry to an increased demand of 8 million tonnes from 1963 to 1973 and of 5 million tonnes from 1973 to 1981 were for machines to become larger and for mills to become larger with fewer machines needing less labour and having a higher degree of instrumentation control over quality. Machine size distribution for Europe has increased steadily from a median of 210 cm and a central half of machines between 160 and 250 cm in 1963. By 1973 the median was 220 cm and the central half of machines ranged from 170 to 280 cm. By 1983 the median was 230 cm and the central half ranged from 170 to 310 cm. The steady increase in variance, the progressive reduction in small machines and the increase in the number of large and very large machines are striking features of Figure 5.1. By 2000 AD, the distribution of machine sizes seems likely to be a median of 250 cm, a central half ranging from 180 to 360 cm, with less than 100 machines in Europe below 150 cm in width. The total number of machines is falling and could well be no more than 1500 by 2000 with the bulk of the lost 800 machines in the under 250 cm range.

All EEC nations show a steady increase in machine size, but only Italy has a substantial lower tail. France is likely to increase the proportion of machines between the median and upper hinge sizes. Spain and Portugal are likely to lose a large number of small machines as in each country the median machine size is near the lower hinge and their upper hinge is near the European median. Austria and Switzerland have made a systematic reduction in small machines over the period and their machine size profiles are very similar to the general

Figure 5.1: Changing papermaking machine widths, Western Europe, 1963–2000.

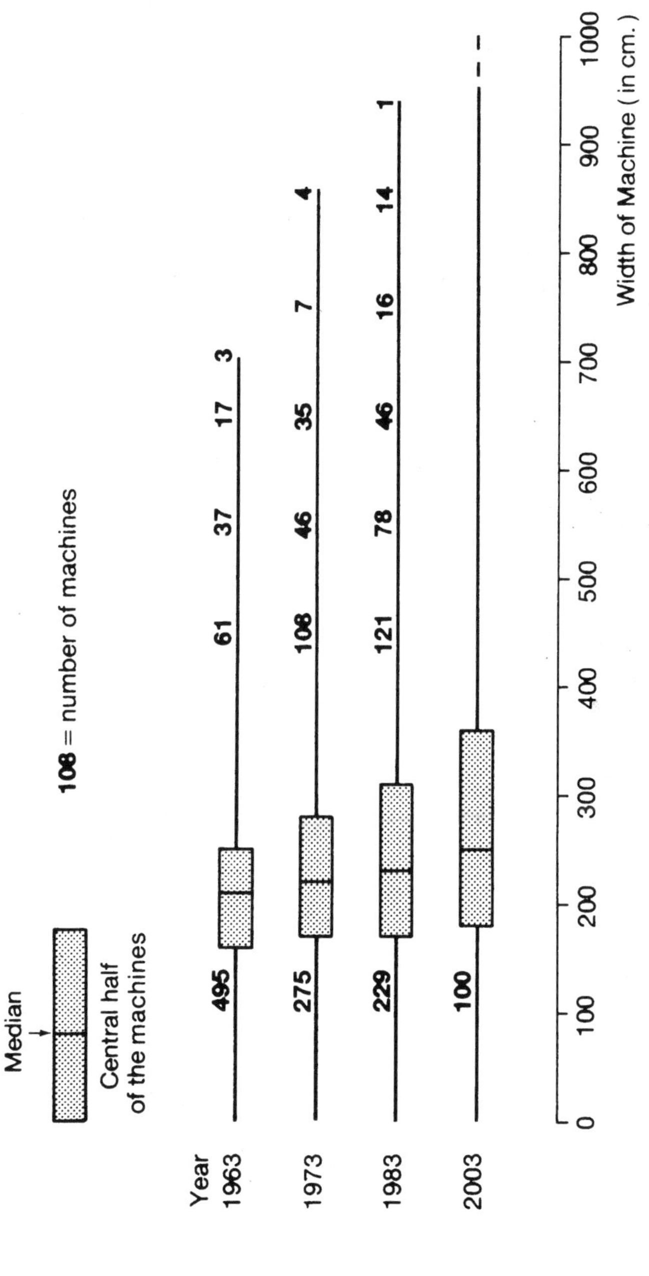

European pattern, trends which are expected to continue. Scandinavian firms continue to increase their machine sizes and there seems every reason to expect the number of smaller machines to be reduced as mill managers introduce new, more advanced equipment competing for grades of paper which till now have been considered unsuited to such large, fast machines.

The size distribution of mills by country for selected EEC nations is shown in Table 5.5 for 1973 and 1981. In all cases the number of mills has fallen and the productivity of mills has increased. The weak competitive position of the UK is emphasised by this measure and unless productivity is increased, further reductions in British mills and machines seem inevitable and yet unlikely to stem the increasing flow of imports.

Production and Competition by Grade

Paper is not a homogenous product and summary figures for changes in paper production and consumption disguise major differences in the main grades in terms of production possibilities and consumption patterns. The summary projections in Table 5.4 show that the EEC as a whole is expected to increase its consumption of all grades of paper but that this increase is not the same for all grades. Such differential growth has typified the previous 20 years and is likely to apply to the structural changes by grade in the next fifteen years.

Newsprint

The EEC produces less than half the newsprint it uses. The largest consumers are West Germany and the UK, each with 30 per cent of the EEC total, followed by France (14 per cent), the Netherlands (10 per cent) and Italy (7 per cent). Italy and the UK are the two extremes in self-sufficiency with 84 and 26 per cent respectively but quite different demand structures. France, West Germany, the Netherlands and Benelux are all very near the EEC average value of 40 per cent production. Within the EEC the general tendency has been for domestic newsprint production to fall. Suggestions that it is politically unwise to let it fall much below the present level do not seem to recognise that there is an equal vulnerability to the imported pulp needed to maintain that production. The UK has changed in 20 years from having a large national newsprint production, using imported pulp, to the present situation of importing newsprint directly, principally from Finland, and producing barely a quarter in domestic mills.

This shift reflects the cost advantages of those countries which can benefit from the economies of scale of integrated

Table 5.5: Papermill Characteristics for Selected EEC Countries.

Size Range Tonnes/Year	West Germany 1973	West Germany 1981	France 1973	France 1981	Italy 1973	Italy 1981	UK 1973	UK 1981	EEC 1973	EEC 1981
< 5000	84	49	73	42	398	150	30	27	601	271
< 10000	39	26	40	26	64	47	24	18	176	120
< 25000	60	49	61	51	63	61	44	35	254	215
< 50000	36	37	30	34	32	35	27	29	150	150
< 100000	21	23	13	16	19	21	14	8	79	83
< 100000	12	18	7	9	6	6	10	7	39	47
Number of Mills	252	202	224	167	582	320	149	124	1299	886
Output in Million Tonnes	6.355	7.498	4.785	5.151	4.100	4.935	4.615	3.793	22.810	24.884
Tonnes/year/ Employee	106	146	121	167	104	131	67	80	97	133

71

pulp and paper mills with large, fast, modern machines using a high proportion of local mechanical pulp. The contrast is evident in the machine sizes. In Scandinavia the median machine size used for newsprint produces 120,000 tonnes a year compared to 50,000 tonnes a year for the median machine in EEC. The upper hinge size is 180,000 tonnes a year in Scandinavia; 120,000 tonnes a year in the EEC. If major newspaper-using nations of the EEC wish to retain national production the cost advantage of installing 2 or 3 new large machines seems overwhelming and the smaller machines and mills will be vulnerable. In addition, the integrated Scandinavian mills seem likely to increase their share of the EEC market.

Packaging and Wrapping

Such papers are a major component of total paper consumption and about two-thirds are produced at mills within the EEC. The trend to an increasing use of waste paper is likely to continue and become more widespread under pressures of economy and conservation. Two distinct types of production are evident in Europe as a whole. Many small mills make limited quantities of paperboard and wrapping papers on small, slow machines for a local market. In contrast, a few, large mills make enormous tonnages on large, fast machines. Although linerboard and fluting medium can be imported by the EEC from the USA at competitive prices because of the cost advantages of the integrated East Coast pulp and paper mills, it seems more likely that most of the increased demand will be met by EEC producers on a few, new large machines, which will replace many smaller machines and mills. This pattern of replacement occurred successively in Sweden, UK and West Germany and is evident in France. Italian mills seem likely to follow this trend and the same vulnerability to such change seems inevitable in Spain and Portugal.

Board

Demand for board within the EEC resembles demand for newsprint but, in contrast, about 90 per cent of the board is produced in the EEC; over a third using re-cycled fibre. Very many, tiny mills run board grades on old, slow machines making diverse qualities for local customers. Recently, large machines have started to run these grades with consequent advantages of scale economies. If, as seems likely, the grades are increasingly made in bulk then large integrated mills will dominate and the structure of this sector of the paper industry would change substantially in the next fifteen years, with many small mills closing. There will be strong competition between EEC and Scandinavian producers and the cost advantage is with the integrated mills found in Austria, West

Germany, France and Iberia. The small board mill is unlikely to be important in Europe by the end of the century.

Tissue

The EEC is practically self-sufficient in tissue papers: indeed most nations are self-sufficient. It involves the lowest tonnage and by 2000 could be over 3.0 million tonnes; substantially more than the projected total. Typically tissue mills are near the market. The trend in the EEC is to move chemical pulp to the production site and mix it with mechanical pulp and waste paper. In France, Italy and West Germany the mechanical pulp is usually domestic and may be local. In the UK, West Germany and France, tissue mills are large and modern with two large, modern, fast machines. Such mills are likely to increase to meet the expected growth in demand and to replace the remaining small mills making hard toilet paper or using old, slow machines for tissue grades. Such a change will be most noticeable in Italy and Spain.

Printing and Writing Paper

This is a large and growing market as important in tonnage as packaging and wrapping grades, but more important in value and diversity. Its future is the most critical in the structure and distribution of the European paper industry in the next fifteen years, just as, in fact, it has given most structure to the industry since 1960.

A basic distinction is made between woodfree papers and wood-containing papers. The term 'woodfree' means the papers do not contain mechanical woodpulp although, of course, they do contain chemical woodpulp. Wood-containing papers do contain mechanical pulp.

The EEC imports more wood-containing than woodfree papers. Imports have increased from 25 per cent in 1973 to 35 per cent in 1981, with the UK showing the greatest dependency, Italy the greatest self-sufficiency. Demand for such papers seems likely to grow, putting increasing pressure on the many small machines making such papers especially in Italy, France, West Germany and, later, in Spain. The large, fast machines in the EEC are as efficient as the Scandinavian and North American producers. One may suspect company infiltration is more likely in market erosion of domestic producers than an increase in direct imports from Scandinavia or North America.

Woodfree printing and writing paper production is very considerable and is the most likely to grow. Typically the EEC nations are 90 per cent self-sufficient with about half the production on small machines able to make less than 20,000 tonnes a year. There are some large, highly efficient and competitive machines whose influence is widely felt in continental printing-grade markets.

73

CHANGES IN WEST EUROPEAN PAPERMAKING

The pattern of woodfree printing and writing paper production illustrates some important general features. Traditionally, such papers have been considered as speciality papers made for specific customers who specified grammage, sheet size, colour, brightness and porosity. Production runs were short, grade changes frequent, market demand met by many small, versatile machines and marketing depended on strong, established mill-customer links. The traditional furnish was the long fibre sulphite pulp and the qualities demanded by the customer were controlled by careful preparation of the stock. The pulp drained slowly at the wet end of the machine and these factors meant that the papermaking machine had to run comparatively slowly.

Since the 1960s technical improvements have made it possible to use the short fibre sulphate pulp and to retain good brightness, good control of pulp quality without long stock preparation and yet retain paper strength. Sulphate pulps drain faster and so permit increased machine running speeds. In the same period, improvements in the quality control of weight, density and two-sidedness have all led to faster machine operation and greater output. There has also been a quite remarkable standardisation of printing grades, the reduction in the range of papers offered meaning that each grade of paper can be produced as a longer run, with consequent reductions in unit cost. The increases in order size and in the length of unbroken run emphasise the discrepancy in profitability of mills: economies of scale are reduced with small runs and interrupted runs further reduce profitability.

As the range of papers is standardised and as quality control increases, so the advantage of large, fast, instrumented machines increases leading to a reduction in the number of small machines in small mills serving local, traditional markets. Such mills will be unable to compete in the long run with the bulk production of what have till recently been considered as speciality woodfree printing and writing papers. Hundreds of small mills are vulnerable to this change and there are comparatively few opportunities for survival by specialisation: there are fewer market niches than small mills. Strategies adopted by UK mills include concentration on non-standard weights of paper, increasing purity levels, providing supercalendered papers by passing the paper through heavy steel rollers to give a compact surface or by turning to new uses such as papers for medical purposes. These strategies are evident in European mills but there is no reason to suppose that a substantially higher survival rate will occur than in the UK.

The expected increase in demand for woodfree printing and writing papers will largely be met by bulk production mills. Such mills already provide a benchmark of cost and quality which acts as a constraint on contemporary production. Inevitably this constraint will induce a shift from many small mills to fewer large mills as new, fast machinery replaces other, slower machinery. It is less evident whether there will be a significant reduction in the existing high level of national self-sufficiency in such woodfree printing and writing papers within the EEC nations by an increase in direct imports from Scandinavian mills.

This uncertainty reflects the fact that market specification remains extremely important in such papers. In assessing the likely impact on such mills there are in fact three stages to production which must be considered: the supply of pulp; its conversion to increasingly standardised grades of paper, in reels; cutting the paper into sheets to meet particular customer demands in the EEC.

An integrated mill where the pulp and paper making operations coincide has a cost advantage over a non-integrated mill where the pulp is dried and then shipped to the paper mill for conversion. For those EEC countries which depend almost completely on imported pulp this discrepancy in costs gives an initial advantage to Scandinavian producers. However this cost advantage is reduced by the sheet cutting operation as prepared paper is more expensive to handle and needs a more extensive organisational and marketing structure which together reduce the initial advantage in production costs. The importance of merchanting has become evident in the UK over the past decade as various paper merchanting companies have reorganised their warehousing and distribution centres. The slightly smaller integrated bulk producers in the UK should be able to retain much of their market share.

Integrated mills exist in the EEC. Such mills should keep a slight cost advantage over Scandinavian competitors. Paper from integrated mills may be cut on site or sent in reels to a merchant and be cut into sheets on demand. The cost advantage lies with the latter strategy, whether the mills are Scandinavian or in the EEC; consequently marketing infiltration by Scandinavian producers in the EEC or by French, West German and UK producers elsewhere in the EEC seems likely to increase and to be important in determining the survival of national woodfree printing and writing mills.

TOWARDS CONCENTRATION AND BULK GRADE

The proposition is that the many traditional, small, un-integrated mills with small, old machines making paper for local markets are the most vulnerable. They will be increasingly unable to compete with the fewer, large, modern mills producing bulk grades. The range of papers coming into this category of bulk grade has increased steadily over the industry's history. Board and particularly woodfree printing and writing grades will be vulnerable to such pressure in the next fifteen years. The customary response that large numbers of small mills will survive by providing speciality papers unattractive to bulk producers is not borne out by the experience of the last twenty years. Such mills tend to survive for only a short time as the depredations of the UK industry and parts of the West German and French papermaking industries indicate. This is especially important for the small woodfree printing and writing mills which face new competition from three distinct locational cases with little clear advantage to one or the other but each is distinctly superior in quality and cost to the small, older, slower mill. Some small, specialist producers will survive, and have emerged already in each European country, but only a small proportion of them will do so by 2000.

GLOSSARY OF TERMS

Paper: a web of vegetable fibres usually deposited onto a moving wire screen from suspension in water. Much of the water drains away, the remainder is evaporated as the paper passes through heated metal rollers. To give extra finish the paper may be passed through steel rollers or calenders.

Paper
Machine: paper making was mechanised by the Fourdrinier machine which remains the basic design but it has been modified considerably since its introduction about 180 years ago. Yankee, Former and Cylinder machines are such modifications.

Wood Pulp: replaced cotton rags as the dominant raw material 100 years ago. Rag pulp is still used for some fine papers.

Mechanical Pulp is made by grinding the round timber or wood chips so that the fibres are separated. About 98 per cent of the wood's original material remains in the pulp. Used mainly in newsprint, board and cheaper tissue.

Chemical Pulps are made by cooking the wood chips under pressure in a solution designed to remove the lignin (up to 30 per cent of the timber). The yield of pulp is about 50 per cent of the original timber. The terms semi-chemical, sulphate and sulphite pulp refer to different chemical solutions. These pulps still contain some lignin and vary in colour from a pale to dark brown.

CHANGES IN WEST EUROPEAN PAPERMAKING

Bleached Pulp is mechanical or chemical pulp treated with chlorine, oxygen and an alkali to make the pulp white and increase brightness.

Waste Paper: increasingly important pulp source in W. Europe.

Paper:
papers made from chemical pulps are sometimes referred to as woodfree, meaning free from groundwood. Woodfree originally meant the pulp (or furnish) was rag or esparto grass.
Magazine Printing is a calendered paper with at least 50 per cent mechanical pulp and used in periodicals. It may be coated.

Newsprint normally has at least 75 per cent mechanical pulp; the rest is sulphite or bleached sulphate.

Packaging papers include:

Fluting or Corrugating Medium made from semi-chemical pulp or waste paper used as the corrugated layer of corrugated fibreboard.
Kraft liner is made from sulphate pulps and is the surface layer of corrugated fibreboard.
Test liner uses waste paper pulp with a surface layer of sulphate and is the surface layer of corrugated boards.

Wrapping grades include:

Sulphite papers which are principally chemical pulps but may have some mechanical pulp for cheap bulk. Is used for creped and sanitary paper.
Kraft paper is made from sulphate pulp and may be bleached. It is used for sacks, bags and wrapping.

Folding boxboard is a foldable paperboard of multiple layers whose surface is a bleached chemical pulp. It is increasingly coated, waxed or plastic faced for used in food packaging.

Coated paper is finished in a coating plant either at the paper production site or elsewhere. It gives a more uniform surface suited to particular end uses and especially able to take modern printing inks.

Fine paper encompasses a wide range of printing, writing and drawing papers, computer stationery, art and postcard qualities.

Speciality papers include a whole range of papers designed for industrial and commercial processing and include electrical, base papers, diazo, transfer, release, medical and filtration papers.

Hard fibreboard is made mainly from waste paper and consists of many separate sheets pressed together when wet and then dried and glazed. It is used for insulation, suitcases, door panels and shoes.

Chapter Six

SPATIAL PERSPECTIVES ON THE DYNAMICS OF
THE WORLD PAINT INDUSTRY

Peter Herdson

This chapter on the dynamics of industrial systems worldwide
takes a Multinational Enterprise (MNE) viewpoint and examines
the development of the MNE within the production system.
The underlying trend is growing interdependence both within
the developed industrial market economies and between them
and the less developed middle and low income economies.
Faster pace of change is seen in the introduction of new
technology and market innovation. With improved communications comes increased awareness of trends in world markets
and the MNE has greater capability to respond to these
trends. The development of the MNE is examined in relation
to its spatial dimensions and perspectives which change over
time and are a determining factor shaping company strategies.
    The paint industry worldwide demonstrates the dynamics
of the industrial system in 2 ways. First, paint is a major
raw material for a wide range of manufacturing industries and
for buildings and structures as a protective and decorative
coating. Thus, the industry reflects trends in the economy
and in the level of economic development. Second, the paint
industry itself displays increasing interdependence between
world regions, resulting from the changes in technology and
from growth in multinational companies. Paint products and
market segments range from low to high technology and from
local to international and world markets.

CONCEPTUAL FRAMEWORK

The conceptual framework is depicted in Figure 6.1.
    Multinational companies might be defined as having
manufacturing plants in two or more foreign countries providing a given proportion (say more than 10 per cent) of
total group turnover. The latter may be under financial,
managerial or technical control of the former (Ghertman &
Allen, 1984 : 2). The MNE is usually a market leader in its
home country in specific segments of the market. Key fea-

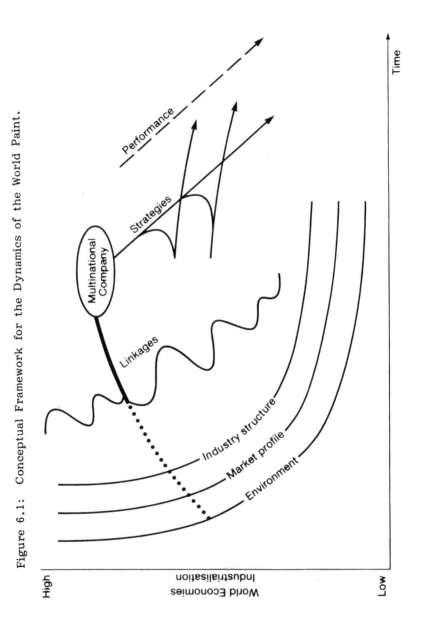

Figure 6.1: Conceptual Framework for the Dynamics of the World Paint.

tures of the MNE are ownership, size, product portfolio, and geographical locations including major (core) locations and management. Its characteristics are transnational mobility and control of its resources.

Several major paint companies, notably in the USA, license technology worldwide but with manufacturing operations confined to home markets. These are firms with an international perspective but a policy to remain nationally based. Such transfer of technology is a form of multinationalism which is becoming increasingly important.

Through strategies (short and long term planning) MNEs can reshape market structure and lead in market innovation: expansion is by exploiting technologies and growth markets. Key features are mergers and acquisitions, external relationships and alliances. Strategies are formulated within the context of the firm's awareness and perspective of the environment and market place.

This perspective derives from the firm's linkages and spatial dimension, its customers and suppliers, local plant, subsidiaries, associates, licensees: and its points of intersection with competitors. It is influenced by its locations in world markets at any point in time and a spatial learning process develops within these constraints (McDermott & Taylor, 1982 : 75).

Spatially the MNEs develop from a position within the industrialised economies in two directions: toward the newly industrialised middle income countries and within the major industrial market economies to strengthen their technology and for larger markets. Technology and innovation develop under the impetus of the market, the industry itself and government.

Environment and market profile are important because the MNE operates within the needs and constraints of the market and of environmental conditions, both socio-economic and political. Economic criteria include GDP and GDP per capita (level of market development) and growth in GDP.

Industry structure relates to customer and supplier concentration and the place of the MNE will depend on opportunities and barriers to entry into national markets.

The performance of the MNE can be measured in structural adjustment to changing market conditions including divestment and acquisition of business. It involves changes in product portfolio, geographic spread of activities, and management organisation: financial performance is highly relevant.

MNEs will move toward an equilibrium at any point in time, with concentration matched by increasing customer strength, widening geographical markets and competition, new entrants with technology and innovations. The kind of equilibrium, if any, reached in a given market depends on the

amount and type of information at the disposal of participants
(Jacquemin & De Jong, 1977 : 2).

In this context the MNE needs to establish, maintain and
strengthen linkages worldwide to maintain leadership. A key
aspect of this is the interaction of the MNEs within the context of their spatial disposition (McDermott & Taylor, 1982 :
204).

KEY FEATURES OF THE PAINT INDUSTRY

Paint can be defined as surface coatings which are chemical
formulations for protection and decoration of substrates being
composed of a film-forming binder consisting of resin, dispersion medium of solvents or water and pigment. Varnishes
are clear with no pigment. Powder paints are a mixture of
pigment and resins (100 per cent solids).

Overall demand for paint tends to follow broad economic
trends such as the level of consumer expenditure and industrial production because of its diverse spread of customers:

Building paints for new construction and maintenance
include professional and do-it-yourself (DIY) usage (the
latter mainly in higher income countries). This sector is
largely national in character with sales distribution and
advertising promotion vital to success. Large numbers of
customers are a feature but there is a growing concentration
in the retail sector with specialist DIY chains and superstores. Although building paints are comparatively low technology, product innovations are essential for firm survival.

Industrial paints (factory applied) cover a wide spectrum
of industry, such as metal-using, wood, plastics and generally use low technology. Many customers are served by many
local suppliers. But high technology sectors are significant,
including paint for motor vehicles, metal containers for food
and beverages, aircraft, ships and oil-rigs. These markets
have few suppliers and are dominated by multinational customers. R & D is essential for industrial paints and can give
high returns in the long-term.

Suppliers generally locate near markets with low capital
outlay and generally low technology. A large number of small
manufacturers of paint is characteristic of most national
markets because the paint industry is quickly set up when a
less developed country industrialises, with any requirement
for technology bought in under licence.

Costs of raw materials can vary between 35 and 75 per
cent of selling prices reflecting the range of product and
value-added. Low volume growth in developed markets and
competitive pricing are key issues for profitability. Manufacture is by batch process, with many products and colours
coming off the production line. Economies of scale in production are not as important as sufficient size of business to

finance R & D and publicity budgets. Products and tech-nology vary as a high proportion of building paints are water-based; industrial ones are solvent-based. The trend is to higher solids (less solvent) and to water-based paints in response to higher costs, competitive conditions and en-vironmental pressures including the cost of dealing with effluents. R & D expenditure in paint companies in developed economies can range from less than 1 per cent of sales for building paints to as much as 15 per cent of sales for high technology sector industrial paints.

Chemical Groups own many of the major paint companies as a downstream activity. Paints account for 5 per cent of chemical industry sales. Some oil companies, retailing firms and others have acquired paint firms in many cases as a cash generator. Long-term trends concern the paint industry's position vis-a-vis substitute materials to existing painted substrates and a wider definition of paint as a speciality chemical (higher added value products in the chemical in-dustry).

Statistics on products and markets published by Govern-ment agencies and Paintmakers Associations vary in coverage and reliability. Cheaper (tempera) type paints and small firms are often excluded from such statistics, while companies which are part of groups or privately owned may not disclose infor-mation. Nevertheless, company reports and materials in trade journals are important sources of information: for some countries virtually the only source. This chapter is based on available published information.

WORLD PAINT MARKET PROFILE

Market Size and Growth
The relative size and growth of world economies in GDP and paint usage are indicated in Figure 6.2. Paint usage corre-lates with GDP, a proportional breakdown of world markets being similar for GDP and paint.

Major markets for paint usage are North America and Western Europe, together accounting for approximately 70 per cent of world total. Japan accounts for a further 11 per cent, though this includes a much higher 25 per cent for the country's vehicle production. Of these key economies in market size and technology base, the fragmentation and structural complexity in Western Europe contrasts with North America (Jacquemin & De Jong, 1977 : 156). Within Europe the major national markets are the UK, West Germany, France and Italy: smaller markets are Benelux and Scandinavia; while growth markets include Spain. The continent thus has a diversity of national market characteristics.

The Centrally Planned Economies of Eastern Europe and the USSR (not shown in Figure 6.2) have relatively high

Figure 6.2: World Patterns of GDP and Paint Usage.

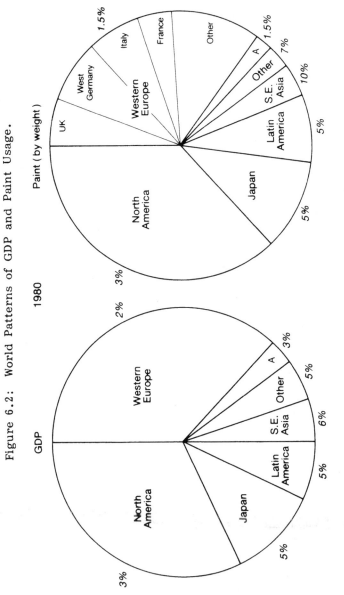

paint usage and would account for 24 per cent of total world market. China has a very low paint usage.

Growth rates are modest in the industrial market economies of North America and Europe: higher rates of growth are evident in the less developed middle and low income economies in line with GDP growth rates.

The paint usage breakdown in Figure 6.2 is based on weight (tonnes) due to the paucity of value data: and it relates to a world market of 14.5 million tonnes valued at approximately US $20 billion (1980) excluding the centrally planned economies of the USSR, Eastern Europe and China.

International Trade

International trade to developing economies accounts for a small (2-3 per cent) proportion of total paint production in industrial market economies. It tends to be short term and be replaced by local production with continuing demand for intermediate materials, through the licensing of technology.

Paint trade between industrial market economies accounts for up to 5 per cent of production and has been rising slightly due to increase in demand for high technology paints. Major exporters are Benelux (one third of production) whilst the UK, West Germany, France and Italy export around 10 per cent of production, West Germany having a growing trade with Eastern Europe in paints. Trade flows can develop due to the short-term effects of exchange rates which create significant price differentials.

PAINT MARKET DEVELOPMENT

Level of Industrialisation

Paint usage correlation with income per capita is shown graphically in Figure 6.3. High usage of paints is achieved in the industrial market economies of North America, Europe and Japan; up to 21 kilos per capita in the USA. This is due to the high incidence of maintenance painting of buildings and the level of manufacturing industry. These are considered mature markets with low growth but technology and innovations can regenerate growth.

Middle income countries such as those newly industrialised show a marked increase in paint usage at upwards of US $2000 (1980) per capita income which is also associated with development of economic infrastructure. These countries include Venezuela, Brazil, Mexico and Argentina in Latin America and Malaysia, Taiwan, South Korea and Singapore (the latter with high usage of marine paints) in Southeast Asia. Spain, however, would be included in this category. High-income oil exporters such as Saudi Arabia have high usage of building paints for infrastructure, but not in re-

Figure 6.3: Paint Usage and Income Per Capita 1980.

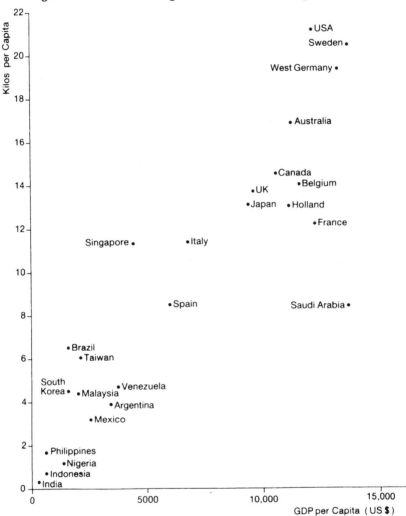

lation to income per capita. Low-income countries include potential of the large economies (high population) of the Indian sub-continent, Indonesia and China.

The variability in the figures for the industrial economies is illustrative of the differences in individual market development. Thus, Italy has a particularly high usage of paints in furniture and domestic appliance industries. Again, West Germany shows a particularly high usage per capita (based on weight of paint) because of high usage of thick emulsion wall-paints. But the UK has declined in relative position since 1980 due to its decline in manufacturing industry vis-a-vis continental EEC countries.

Economic Cycle

The past two decades cover the period of world economic growth up to the 1973 first oil crisis, recession and recovery to the 1979 second crisis followed by recession and anticipated slow recovery during the 1980s. These economic cycles have a significant effect on the developing interdependence between countries and the expansion of the multinationals. The period up to 1973 saw expansion of US multinationals into Western Europe: paint companies followed motor manufacturers GM and Ford, looking to the enlarged EEC market. At the same time, EEC multinationals were expanding. Following the 1973 oil crisis there was restructuring in the industry, including some withdrawal of US companies caused by shortages of cash in parent companies. The UK manufacturing industry declined relative to the EEC after the 1979 oil crisis and presented a different view of the prospects in the UK for EEC multinationals.

Furthermore, the timing of the economic cycle can be out of phase between countries and economic regions. The relative phasing of the economic cycle gave opportunities for entry to the US market in the early 1980s assisted by exchange rates in favour of Europe. A number of European paint companies made a US acquisition at this time including AKZO of the Netherlands and BASF of West Germany.

Two crucial points in multinational strategies arising from the above are: first, the need for a full perspective of the phase reached in the economic cycle in specific markets; and second, a strategy plan to enable action at the right time. Several major European MNEs were slow to respond, for example, to the 'open window' for US entry in the early 1980s.

The Role of Government

Government plays an increasing role in influencing market development for socio-economic and political reasons both through legislation and directly as a major customer for paints. In industrial market economies government environmental controls aim to reduce solvents in paints and encourage the switch to water-based and higher-solids paints. Such government pressure is particularly evident in the USA, Scandinavia and West Germany. At the same time, however, many governments are concerned to maintain a competitive market economy. Yet anti-trust policies are nationally based and are often in conflict with needs of the MNEs in international markets (Fishwick, 1982 : 8-10). This is especially evident within the EEC as companies have to relate to a wider 'home' market.

In developing economies governments may restrict imports and seek import substitution by duties and other controls to encourage the development of an indigenous paint industry. Nationalistic attitudes have in many instances brought constraints on foreign ownership and control in MNEs in Africa, Latin America and Asia, a force which can affect MNE commitment to a local associate company.

Technological changes

Technology concerns higher value added and more knowledge-intensive business relating to processes, products and markets. New technology is generated in developed economies under pressure from customer industries which demand better performance including lower costs. Within the paint industry, companies also seek higher added value and lower costs. Government environmental controls are a stimulus, too. The transfer of technology to less developed countries must be appropriate to local conditions of manufacture and customer needs.

Technology generated within one specific economy can be transferred to neighbouring economies, with implications for paint manufacturers not directly involved in the originator economy. For instance, new motor repainting technology came from the European continent into the UK which was a more conservatively-structured market.

Transfer of technology can be by foreign direct investment by MNEs or by licensing. This is occurring increasingly between industrial economies, a trend which can lead to rejuvenation in the industry life cycle. For example, new motor paint top coats technology was generated in the EEC and transferred to the USA while the reverse direction developed with cathodic primers technology.

INDUSTRY STRUCTURE

To understand market structure and development it is necessary to distinguish the various segments of the paint industry (Figure 6.4).

Overall, the industry is very fragmented with large numbers of small firms supplying local customers in both industrial and building sectors of the market. Some reduction in numbers of paint firms has taken place but 1700 paint firms continue to exist in Western Europe alone in the 1980s. However, a few companies do account for an increasingly significant share of the market in all countries. These are companies with national distribution and often formed by

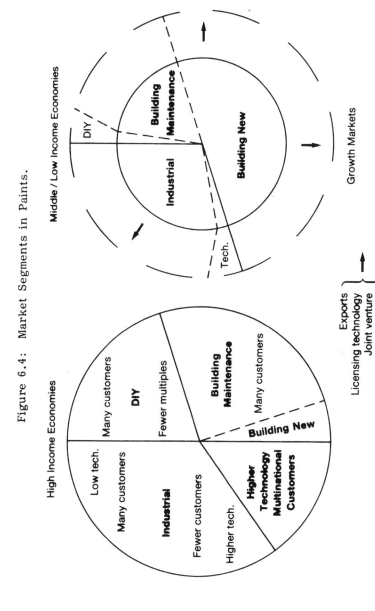

Figure 6.4: Market Segments in Paints.

mergers of a number of medium-sized companies, a process which happened in Western Europe in the 1960s and early 1970s. Concentration has been increasing in the EEC since its formation, both in the paint industry and its customer industries. But MNEs are entering national markets by foreign direct investment and so, at least in the short term, increasing local competition as, for example, motor manufacturers and their paint suppliers within the EEC.

The level of this concentration is indicated in Figure 6.5. Western Europe, where the top 5 companies account for 20 per cent of total paint sales, is more fragmented than the USA or Japan. Smaller national markets have the higher concentration (for example, one firm dominates in Norway).

Middle income economies in Latin America and Southeast Asia show relatively high concentration at upwards of 50 per cent of the market held by the top 5 companies; in a majority of cases these are owned by foreign MNEs. (A notable exception is Venezuela which has taken national ownership, though technical links are maintained.)

Concentration by market segment tends to be very high in higher technology markets in which multinational customers are a feature. Concentration in the vehicle industry worldwide by suppliers and customers is highlighted in Figure 6.6. Alignment of customers with suppliers is a key strategic issue.

Local retail do-it-yourself markets can have a high concentration and be difficult for MNEs to enter. Market leaders may dominate through tied distribution, as in Sweden and The Netherlands, or advertising budgets as in the UK.

Concentration in the market place tends to be toward an equilibrium or balance (never actually achieved) with suppliers and customers growing in size to match each other in bargaining strength. Examples are in retailing with the larger multiple DIY chains and superstores with own label paints and in higher technology with an ever widening geographical dimension of the market.

Opportunities for entry to national markets arise through growth prospects and motivation to exploit technology. Claiming a significant market share (10 per cent or more) generally requires local investment in manufacture in an established market by acquisition or merger. In paint this is true for national markets in the EEC, including high technology sectors such as paint for vehicles. Barriers to entry depend on the degree of existing concentration in the markets and national characteristics as, for instance, the great strength of market leaders in West Germany for vehicle repainting through their control of distribution.

Government can influence decisions through anti-trust legislation and on the other hand giving encouragement to develop locally to provide import substitution.

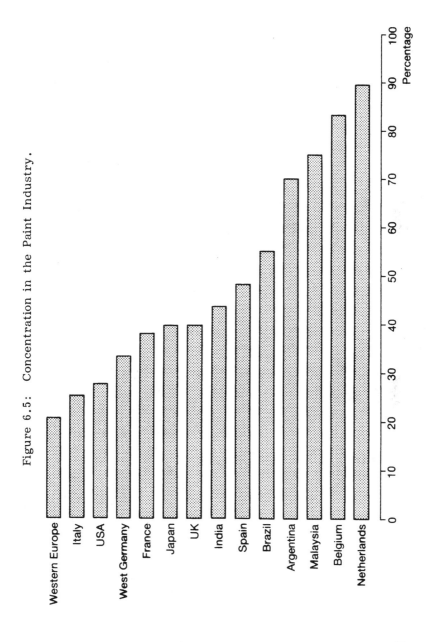

Figure 6.5: Concentration in the Paint Industry.

Figure 6.6: Paint Companies and the Automotive Industry.

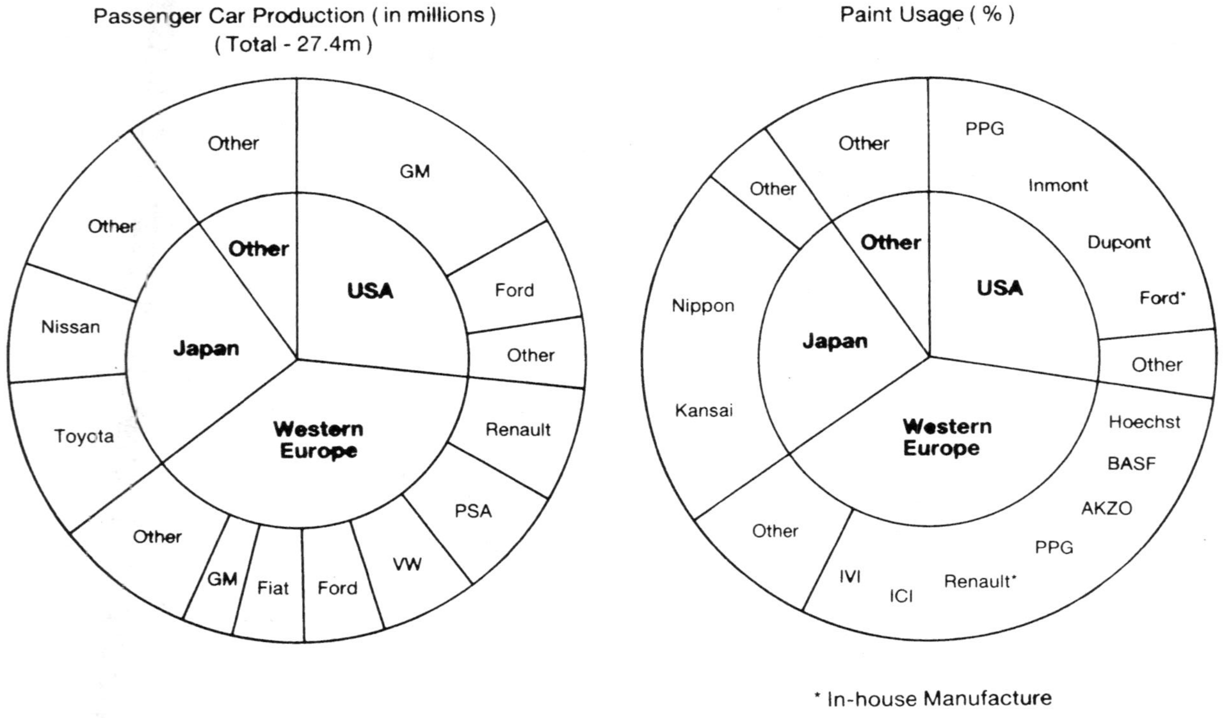

Passenger Car Production (in millions)
(Total - 27.4m)

Paint Usage (%)

* In-house Manufacture

MULTINATIONAL PAINT COMPANIES

Key Features

Core locations of the major MNEs are in the industrial market economies of the USA, Western Europe and Japan: of 12 major MNEs, 5 are in the USA, 5 in Western Europe and 2 in Japan. These companies are market leaders in their home markets supported by leadership in technology. Ownership of many is by Chemical Groups in which paint may feature as a small part of total turnover, with important implications for Paints' group strategy. Product Portfolio for a majority of the MNEs includes decorative paints (local markets) and usually increasing concentration on specific segments of industrial paints with, in many cases, a high proportion of turnover in higher technology fields such as motors paints. R & D is important and licensing of technology is extensive, including cross-licensing between MNEs. Organisation and management is restructured to deal with multiple core locations following acquisition and concentration on business segments oriented to international markets. Profitability of paint tends to correlate with specialisation in product fields, and profit is available to finance further R & D. Thus, a significant share in a large home market provides the base for significant R & D expenditure.

Presence in World Markets

Foreign direct investment by the MNEs is portrayed geographically in Figure 6.7. MNEs are strongly based in the USA with usually around 80 per cent or more of their turnover in the home market. Traditionally, these MNEs have had a dominant position in Canada through local subsidiaries and have gained dominant market positions through acquisitions in the newly industrialised Latin American countries in the growth period before 1973.

American MNEs have established a leading position in the European motor paints business based on acquisitions by 3 or 4 companies each in the 1960s. Overall US presence accounts for around 5-7 per cent of the West European total paint usage but nearer 25 per cent of motors paint usage. Several US paint companies divested of plant in Europe in the 1970s when group cash became short (e.g., Celanese, SCM). Recently, the US market position in Europe has been increased by acquisitions, notably of the major motor paints manufacturer in Italy. This involved PPG's acquisition of IVI, a subsidiary of Fiat. Since 1980 there have been a few modest acquisitions in the USA by European MNEs to form a base for expansion and access to technology.

Following formation of the EEC in 1958, many mergers of local firms increased concentration in the market, including forward integration by the German Chemical Groups BASF and

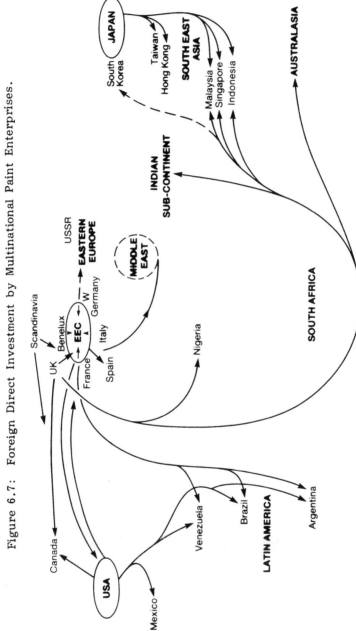

Figure 6.7: Foreign Direct Investment by Multinational Paint Enterprises.

Hoechst and by the Dutch firm AKZO. In a few cases, moves were made against bids by US companies, but acquisitions have been patchy with no one company having substantial presence in all major European countries in any one product sector (Tugendhat, 1971: 243).

UK majors like Imperial Chemicals Industries (ICI), International Paint (Courtaulds) and Berger (acquired by Hoechst) have substantial proportions of sales outside Europe in subsidiaries and associate companies in the British Commonwealth. Traditionally these MNEs have been orientated toward these widely dispersed and varied markets.

Japanese paint majors have followed customer industries into Southeast Asia with extensive local investments; but so far not to any significant extent further afield. No foreign MNEs are established in the Japanese market due to local conditions of marketing, though one or two joint ventures are now operating there. In the future Japanese paint companies may follow car manufacturers into the USA and Europe.

The Middle East has seen a significant increase in demand for paints met by imports and a number of MNEs - notably those firms already in the area with marine paints and anti-corrosion paints which have formed joint ventures with local companies. Turn-key projects for plant construction and paint technology include a paint plant located in Iraq which was supplied from Hungary using ICI (UK) paint technology as part of the package. This illustrates the 'East-West-South' phenomenon elaborated by Gutman and Arkwright (1981).

Exports of paints to Eastern Europe, notably from West Germany and Austria, have been followed by a number of linkages to provide technical know-how on paints and related engineering by MNEs. Thus a coil coating plant was set up in Yugoslavia with the technical guidance on design from a leading West European paint company.

Some paint companies have been establishing business in China either in the form of technical support through joint ventures or licensing of technology with a view to the country's long-term potential.

The Strategy of the Multinationals
Some key aspects can be considered in relation to Figure 6.8 which refers to core locations and date of acquisition for 3 major MNEs. These are AKZO (Netherlands) and ICI (UK) in which paints account for 10 per cent and 5 per cent of Chemical Groups turnover respectively: and Pittsburgh Plate Glass (PPG: USA) in which paints account for nearer 30 per cent of group sales.

The AKZO Chemical group acquired Sikkens early in 1969 as a market leader in the Dutch paint market, a small home base so that the company exported nearly 50 per cent of production to neighbouring countries. Major acquisitions were

DYNAMICS OF THE WORLD PAINT INDUSTRY

Figure 6.8: Multinational Enterprises in Paints: A Comparison of AKZO, ICI and PPG.

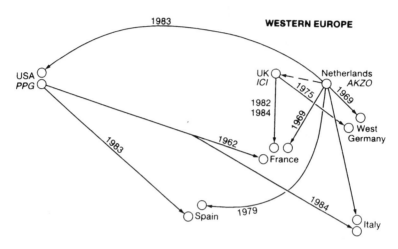

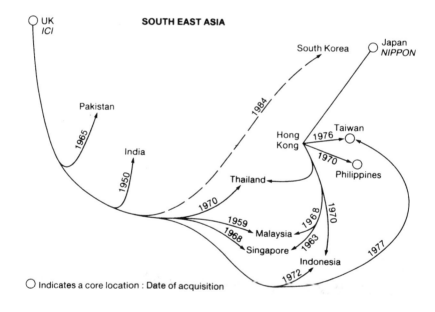

○ Indicates a core location : Date of acquisition

made also in 1969 in West Germany and France at a time when these markets were fragmented. During the 1970s AKZO spent money to build up its market position and the groups acquired a Spanish paint company. Some 70 per cent of its sales are in Western Europe.

The company has decorative and high technology industrial business (including motor paints) and R & D expenditure to support these segments. AKZO appears now to have a Pan-European business in terms of management and operation based on a number of core locations. Furthermore, the company recently acquired a modest base in the USA for technology and sales and set up a joint venture in Japan. The UK market is served by exports only.

PPG (USA) was an early entrant into Europe, following US customer industries such as motors, and in 1962 it acquired a leading paint company in France. Motor paints business expanded partly through exports within Europe to achieve a leading position in the market supported by world technology leadership in primers. Recently, a major acquisition was made in acquiring the Fiat paint subsidiary (IVI) as well as entry into Spain by smaller acquisitions.

PPG established a leading position in world motor paints based on its R & D resources for the key US market (75 per cent of turnover is in USA). It subsequently exploited this through local manufacture and licensing directed by management reorganised on a product-geographical basis. This has led to changes in policy from licensing towards local direct investment. Thus the proportion of turnover outside the USA has risen substantially, particularly in West Europe (which now accounts for 25 per cent of group turnover).

ICI acquired a medium-sized paint company in West Germany in the mid-1970s, but significant moves into Europe came only in the early 1980s with two acquisitions in France to achieve a leading position in Europe for can coatings and vehicle refinish paints and within France in retail paints. Traditionally, ICI was orientated to the British Commonwealth with several core locations worldwide, but not in USA or Japan. The group is strong in technology, including motor paints, but the UK has represented a declining market vis-a-vis Europe. One quarter of turnover is in the UK and more than 50 per cent in the Commonwealth. ICI has now established a substantial base on the continent of Europe with Business Area organisation on a Pan-European basis to achieve the benefits of synergy from acquisitions.

Southeast Asia (Figure 6.8) highlights a developing middle/low income region which includes motor assembly in which two MNEs have substantial positions through local associate and subsidiary companies. Entry to these markets was mostly achieved in the growth period pre-1973, but has continued with Taiwan, Philippines and South Korea in the latter through licensing technology.

DYNAMICS OF THE WORLD PAINT INDUSTRY

One problem highlighted in this area is the relationship of an MNE and its associate company in a country which adopts a policy of local control as this can restrict implementation of changes in method of operation.

Performance

In terms of MNE strategy, this chapter has stressed the following points. First, the key areas of the USA, continental Western Europe and Japan are markets and centres for technology in which MNEs are seeking to achieve significant presence. Second, access to growth markets in developing economies is important.

A feature is the evolving interface between MNEs to safeguard leadership in selected businesses and technologies. The tendency to concentrate on specific segments of the market is intended to gain leadership and concentrate R & D, production and management. Important here is the definition of business segments and emphasis on company strengths (Ohmae, 1982 : 154). A crucial aspect following acquisition is management on a geographical basis incorporating multiple core locations to maximise resources and opportunities. It is essential to seek to achieve the synergy expected from acquisition, in manufacture and marketing.

The pattern of strategic expansion for the MNEs can be related back to earlier core location(s) and the spatial perspective derived. For instance, AKZO paint subsidiaries were located in small home markets and orientated to wider European markets. AKZO were leaders in implementing Pan-European strategies. ICI was orientated to the British Commonwealth and had achieved leadership in world paints on that basis, but was slow in achieving penetration of EEC markets. PPG was located in major motor vehicle markets which became increasingly international and has thus been able to exploit its technology worldwide.

Financial performance reflects the relative success in achieving strategic objectives of a strong base in the key markets of the USA and continental EEC for high technology segments; but with more variability in the fragmented EEC.

FUTURE TRENDS

The major markets in industrial economies will continue to dominate in technology and techno-commercial innovation in response to customer demands, government environmental controls and the industry itself. New technology can rejuvenate industry product life cycles so that growth segments will be a continuing feature of the market even in the so-called 'mature' highly industrialised countries.

98

Further concentration within EEC will strengthen it as a base for technology although this may be slow, depending on performance of the economies and local political pressures. At the same time, its continued variety of markets provides stimulus to technological development. Increasing demand for techno-commercial support in the developing market economies and in the centrally planned economies present opportunities for the MNE. Technology transferred to the less developed countries must be appropriate to local needs.

The market is moving towards a wider geographical equilibrium in terms of balance between multinational companies as suppliers and customers in a competitive environment. Multinational paint companies will display a continuing trend toward greater interdependence for technology and innovation together with closer links with suppliers and customers. The interface between competing MNEs will demand particular attention: from licensing, through internal expansion by direct foreign investment to new forms of alliances to safeguard technology and competitive positions. Management needs to achieve a balance of resource allocations and control within a multinational context: hence, the increasing importance of strategic management.

Further geographical expansion of MNEs and growth in regional MNEs in developing economies can be expected. Local MNEs in the developing countries will evolve technology appropriate for local conditions whether these are climatic, social or economic.

Government will continue to exert pressures on industry to safeguard the environment and to maintain competitive industrial activity. In this respect it can be restrictive unless it applies perspective in defining products and geographical markets. National markets can in fact become more competitive with foreign direct investment of the MNEs. In the EEC, for example, social and political decisions have to come at the international level. In newly industrialised economies the need is to look to the advantages of MNE presence for techno-commercial innovation and not to impose too restrictive controls on management. The need is to encourage regional development for local companies so that they may contribute to regional, and hence, national economic health.

Of increasing significance, and a subject for research, is the interface between the MNEs in seeking leadership and balance of power in markets and technology. Spatial perspectives must be the basis for strategic planning in the MNE. Establishing and maintaining linkages (internal and external) in space is a crucial element in company structure. This trend has socio-economic and political implications: thus, the interface between multinational businesses is becoming too complex for governments to fully control on a purely national basis.

REFERENCES

Fishwick, F. (1982) Multinational Companies and Economic Concentration in Europe, Gower

Ghertman, M. and Allen, M. (1984) An Introduction to the Multinationals, MacMillan Press Ltd., London

Jacquemin, A. and De Jong, H.W. (1977) European Industrial Organisation, MacMillan Press Ltd., London

McDermott, P. and Taylor, M. (1982) Industrial Organisation and Location, Cambridge University Press, Cambridge

Ohmae, K. (1982) The Mind of the Strategist, McGraw Hill

Penrose, E.T. (1959) The Theory of the Growth of the Firm, Basil Blackwell, Oxford

Pickering, J.E. (1974) Industrial Structure and Market Conduct, Martin Robertson & Co

Porter, M.E. (1980) Competitive Strategy, MacMillan Press Ltd., London

Tugendhat, C. (1971) The Multinationals, Eyre and Spottiswoode Ltd., London

Chapter Seven

TWO MULTINATIONALS IN COMPETITION

Risto Laulajainen

There is an established school of thought holding that it is more worthwhile to base research into business corporations on a cross-sectional sample rather than on a detailed analysis of one or two companies. The main argument is that corporate individuality precludes results that are truly representative of anything except the example companies themselves. When the study objects are large, however, a counter-argument is raised: that large companies by virtue of their size and importance are a study object of their own, distinct from small firms, and that their small numbers make statistical generalisation impossible. Furthermore, traits which remain concealed in a cross-sectional study may come to light in a longitudinal one, and that a small number of research objects more easily allows the inclusion of a time perspective. This chapter uses the longitudinal approach and analyses both common traits and differences in the development of two large corporations: Atlas Copco AB of Sweden; and Ingersoll-Rand Corporation of the USA. It appears natural to investigate companies that are, in one way or other, comparable, for example, in that they belong to the same industry and hence, implicitly, compete with each other. Indeed, that corporate destinies in western societies are decided in the marketplace, where the fittest survive and prosper while the rest are acquired, laid down or go into liquidation. Thus competition is an integral part of our investigation and competitors, facing a roughly similar environment and having been successful to the extent of surviving, share important common traits. In other words, the demand for representativeness is fulfilled to a degree, although not in a statistical sense.

Cross-sectional studies customarily rely heavily on surveys, while longitudinal ones lean on written sources and in-depth interviews. This chapter, being based largely on material which either has been published or, given sufficient interest is publishable, does not permit a complete account of the more subtle aspects of company life, but it should compare with the structured questions of most surveys which

101

necessarily convey a straightforward idea of decisions and reasons. Large corporations, often with a long past, have made available a great deal of relevant material, grossly overlooked by the profession.

STRUCTURAL TRAITS AND TRENDS

This case study concerns two century-old mechanical engineering companies which, starting from widely separate geographical bases and having initially quite different technological prerequisites, have become increasingly involved in an intense competition worldwide during the past four decades and have gained a number of common traits in the process.

Origins
The origins of both the companies were in the primate cities of their respective countries, New York and Stockholm. Ingersoll-Rand (IR) resulted from the merger of Ingersoll-Sergeant Drill Company (1871) and Rand Drill Company (1871) in 1905 and Atlas Copco (AC) that of Nya Atlas AB (1873) and Diesels Motorer AB (1898) in 1917 (Gårdlund et al., 1973; Kother, 1971).

Ingersoll-Sergeant was founded to exploit an invention, a mechanical rock drill. The Rand company was created to boost sales of explosives by mechanical drilling and air compressors were added the following year to supply power for drills. Booming New York City offered a ready market. The Rand company received its financial backing from the existing business. The roots of Ingersoll-Sergeant were in a small repair shop, but access to risk capital was easy in the financial hub of the nation.

Things looked different in Stockholm. The first edition of AC, Atlas AB was founded by a group of financiers to supply the barely twenty-year-old State Railways with cars. The technology employed was modern but not revolutionary. Production capacity was oversized; demand had to be shared with a number of competitors. It was soon necessary to supplement rail cars with any saleable mechanical engineering product. Scale economies disappeared, and when daily managerial talent was also lacking, bankruptcy was inevitable. The dominating bankers reorganised the company as Nya Atlas AB and subscribed most of its capital in 1892. These men had interests in many other companies. One was Diesels Motorer AB, exploiting the brand-new patent of Rudolf Diesel in Sweden. The chairman was simultaneously president of Nya Atlas. When production capacity for diesels proved insufficient, orders were placed at Nya Atlas. When the two companies started internationalising (below), they sometimes joined forces and had a common representative or sales office abroad. As their ownerships also overlapped heavily, and partners were about equal in size, the merger in 1917 was a logical rationalisation measure.

The two American companies had come to the same conclusion in 1905. The idea came from a banker, the dominant shareholder in Ingersoll-Sergeant. The motive was to collect under the same roof the relative strengths of Ingersoll-Sergeant in rock drills and of Rand in air compressors. The former company was about three times larger than the latter one.

The year 1905 is, in a way, the beginning of this study. Consistent and continuous financial information on both AC and IR has been preserved since that year.

Profitability
Financial information on a business company crystallizes in its financial result, i.e. profit. Profit in proportion to the magnitude of company operations is profitability. According to traditional economic theory, the goal of business is maximum profitability. Yet measuring profit and profitability is subject to many vagaries, varying accounting practices between companies, time periods and countries. Comparisons are thus broad indications of trends, not valid point estimates.

The profitability measure used relates the total compensation paid to capital, including taxes and appropriations plus depreciation, to this very capital. Taxes are considered profit-sharing by the public sector. Appropriations are included because they have been extensively used for monitoring profit in Sweden since about 1960. They are tax-free if deposited in the central bank, often at zero interest, and used only by government consent during a cyclical downturn. Depreciation, both accelerated and decelerated, is also used for profit monitoring, although the practical possibilities in a mechanical engineering company are restricted as the appropriate capital stock is comparatively small.

IR has been more profitable than AC in almost each year (Figure 7.1). The difference cannot be explained away by different accounting practices. The depressions and world wars are visible in both the curves although to varying degrees. Trends, when discernible, are the irregular rise during the period 1920-1950/55 and the decline thereafter. The latter trend is more definite and it is steeper at IR than AC. If the years 1950-1955 are taken as a rough watershed, the first subperiod was less profitable than the second one.

Growth by Different Methods
Sustained profitability suggests that, given environmental constraints, the prerequisites for growth, the other possible business goal, have been good. Either profits have been ploughed back, permitting self-financing, or they have been

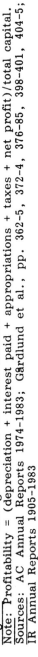

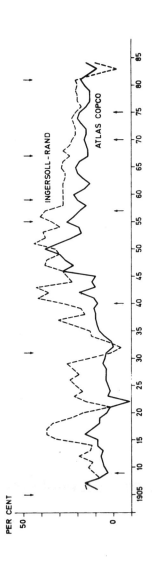

Figure 7.1: Profitability.
Legend: Arrow = Change of chief executive officer.
Note: Profitability = (depreciation + interest paid + appropriations + taxes + net profit)/total capital.
Sources: AC Annual Reports 1974–1983; Gårdlund et al., pp. 362–5, 372–4, 376–85, 398–401, 404–5;
IR Annual Reports 1905–1983

distributed as dividends, attracting new risk capital.

Corporate size is measured here by sales volume, constant 1982 prices. Despite the long time period with consequences for the accuracy of the price deflator, the broad features have been preserved. The corporate series are expressed in national currency. As the rate of exchange remained fairly stable for long periods of time (US$ 4 SEK 1907-1949 and USD$ 5 SEK 1950-1980; International Financial Statistics 1951-1983; Riksbankens årsbok 1934, 1942, 1950) it is possible to gain a rough visual comparison of the two series (Figure 7.2). In 1981-1983 the SEK figures should be discounted by up to 30 per cent to make them approximately comparable with the US$ figures.

IR has always been the larger company, as expected considering the sizes of the national economies. IR's relative size has, however, undergone substantial changes, being twice that of AC in 1983 (US$ = 8.4 SEK), about the same size in the early 1960s, perhaps 8 times larger in the late 1920s. Yet up to the early 1960s, (excluding the war years), IR had experienced more cyclical fluctuation than AC. As the product lines were broadly similar (below), the fluctuation seems to have been connected with the volatility of the American economy.

The companies made explicit decisions to grow on two occasions (see Figure 7.2). At AC the decision was made in the late 1940s. It was realised that long production series were instrumental for profitability (Figure 7.1) and were possible only by selecting a narrow market segment. This necessitated specialisation on the most promising product lines, disposal of the rest. The company had gained a president with a background in marketing and who, in this respect, deviated strongly from the technical tradition of the company. The technical staff had developed some outstanding products but was unable to see and exploit the marketing potential. Because of the restricted national market, the decision was tantamount to internationalisation (Gårdlund et al., ~1973, pp. 115-8, 135).

At IR the reasoning was completely different. Some time in the late 1950s, people had got tired of the repeated business cycles typical of a specialised capital goods producer (Figure 7.2). Diversification was seen as a means of achieving a more balanced future. As there was reluctance to prune away existing product lines, growth was the automatic result and was also favoured for its own sake. Domestic competitors strove for it and, if successful, were able to achieve scale economies in production, financing and research, thus threatening the existence of IR as an independent company. Part of the growth effort was directed abroad, the reasoning being that, in an internationalising world, the only way to preserve relative size was to face competitors on their home markets (Phatak, 1971, p.41).

Figure 7.2: Sales in Constant (1982) Prices.

Legend: The left-hand vertical scale applies to 1905-1950 and the right-hand scale to 1950-1983. The vertical bars on the curves indicate parent companies (left) and groups (right).

Notes: The curves are roughly comparable up to 1980 whereafter the AC curve should be discounted by up to 30% to achieve comparability. Price index, Sweden: 1905-1913, Industrial raw materials, metals (1881-1885 = 100); 1913-1920, Svensk Finanstidning (1913 = 100); 1920-1935, Raw materials for iron and metal industry (1913 = 100); 1935-1968, Machinery and transportation equipment (1935, 1949 = 100); 1968-1983, Mechanical engineering products, excl. vessels and boats (1968 = 100). U.S.A.: 1905-1939, Metals and metal products (1926 = 100); 1939-1964; Machinery and motive products (1947-1949, 1957-1959 = 100); 1964-1983, Machinery and equipment (1957-1959, 1967 = 100).

Sources: Price index, Sweden : 1905-1913, Kommersiella meddelanden, 1921; 1913-1962, Ekonomisk översikt, 1928, 1955, 1962, 1963-1983, Statistiska meddelanden. U.S.A. : 1905-1957, Historical Statistics, 1960; 1958-1980, Statistical Abstract; 1981-1983, Producer Prices. Other : AC Annual Reports 1974-1983; Gårdlund et al., 1973, pp. 364-5, 374, 380-5, 400-1, 405; IR Annual Reports 1905-1983; IR Sales Figures 1905-1041; Parkhill.

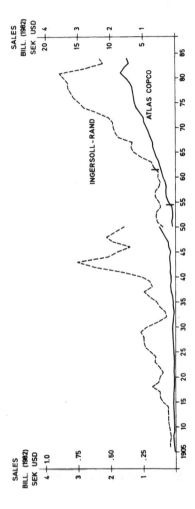

In general opinions hold that the growth decision was implemented in different ways in the two companies: AC relied more on internal growth, IR leaned heavily on acquisitions. Environmental possibilities combined with managerial goals to be instrumental. IR benefited from a large national economy and had a number of potential acquisition objects available. As one of the goals was diversification, the number of objects became still larger. At AC the situation was exactly the opposite, a small national economy and the desire to specialise: expansion by acquiring foreign companies was subject to the consent of the central bank and integrating the purchases could be painful (Gårdlund et al., 1973, pp. 142-3).

To sharpen the picture, acquisitions are put in relation to the acquiring company. When the price was paid in treasury shares, a usual method at IR, the logical reference point is the outstanding capital stock on the previous balance sheet. When the price was paid cash, it is compared with the acquirer's capital. When neither measure is available, the relative size of the labour force is a rough substitute. And finally, there are cases which can only be labelled as "medium" or "small". For sake of completeness, sales of subsidiaries and divisions are given in a corresponding way.

The stereotyped view of AC's internal growth and IR's acquisition policies becomes modified through this technique (Table 7.1). When known and approximated percentages since the late 1940s are totalled, AC comes close to 80 per cent and IR to 100 per cent. Naturally, the dollar amounts are larger at IR because of its larger size. This and the clustering of its transactions to the more recent past seem to have created the said perception.

Regarding individual acquisition objects, there has been a pronounced difference in philosophy, at least since the 1960s. IR has been interested in market leaders or number twos, AC contented itself with smaller companies with technical know-how or marketing channels.

Prominent among IR's acquisitions are the Torrington Co., number two among US ball bearings producers and ranking 8th to 10th on a global scale; Lee Norse Co., in 1964 larger than such a renowned producer as Joy Mfg. Co. (Financial World, 1983, p. 16), and Lawrence Mfg. Co., representing perhaps one third of the national capacity. Millers Falls Co. is an example of breaking the rule and being unsuccessful. It could not dethrone Black & Decker Mfg. Co. as the dominant supplier to the home handyman and had to be redesigned for the professional tool market (Business Week, 1974, p. 76).

Typical of AC's modest acquisitions is Habegger AG of Switzerland (1968), a designer of full facers without production capacity, manufacturing being done as contract work. It was not until some ten years later when the line was strengthened by Jarva, Inc., one of the three leading US

Table 7.1:   Important companies/divisions acquired/sold.

Company/division	Year	Relat. size %	Product line at acquisition/sale
Acquisitions			
Atlas Copco AB			
Ekenbergs Söner	1873	15	Mech. eng. products
Brynäs Varv	1883	50-60	Ships
Norrby Gjuteri (50%)	1913	med.	Castings
Björneborgs Bruk	1942	3	Castings
Injector	1947	17	Fuel pumps
AB Eccoverken	1948	med.	Small air compressors
AB Växlar och Signaler	1951	5	Points and signals
Hesselman Motor Corp.	1956	2	Pumps, electrical eqp.
A.R.P.I.C., Antwerp (Belgium)	1956	5	Air compressors
Svensk Diamantberg-borrning AB	1960	28	Prospecting eqp.
Monsun-Tison AB	1974	2	Hydraulic components
Jahrls Mekaniska Verkstad	1974	1	Drilling equipment
Belna A.B.	1975	2	Portable drills, loading eqp., hydraulic comp.
Jarva, Inc., Solon (Ohio)	1979	3	Full facers
Worthington Compressors, Inc., Holyoke (Massachusetts)	1980	3	Air compressors
Turbonetics, Inc., Latham (New York)	1980	5	Gas compressors
Standard Industrial Pneumatics Inc., Cleveland (Ohio)	1980	5	Small air compressors
Klein, Schanzlin & Becker, Saarbrücken (West Germany)	1981	med.	Gas compressors
Linde A.G., Köln (West Germany) Ingersoll-Rand Company	1984	4	Gas compressors
Imperial Pneumatic Tool Co.	1903	small	Hand tools
Charles H. Haesler	1903	small	Hand tools
Cameron Steam Pump Works	1909	med.	Pumps
Leyner Engineering Works Co.	1912	small	Patents, rock drills
General Electric Co., part	1934	med.	Blast furnace blowers
Aldrich Pump Co.	1961	1	Pumps

108

Table 7.1/continued

Company/division	Year	Relat. size %	Product line at acquisition/sale
Millers Falls Co.	1962	2	Hand tools
McCartney Mfg. Co.	1963	1	Process equipment
Pendleton Tool Industries, Inc.	1964	11	Hand tools
Lee Norse Co.	1964	5	Coal miners
Improved Machinery, Inc.	1964	8	Pulp & plastic machinery
Lawrence Mfg. Co.	1966	med.	Full facers
The Torrington Co.	1968	35	Bearings, needles, control mechanisms
Sigmund Pumps Ltd., Gateshead (UK)	1970	1	Pumps
Negri Bossi SpA, Milan (Italy)	1970	2	Plastic machinery
Wesco Industries Corp.	1972	1	Textile machinery
Schlage Lock Co.	1974	5	Closers, exit devices
California Pellet Mill Co.	1974	1	Pelletizing machinery
Terry Corp.	1974	2	Steam turbines
S & S Corp.	1976	4	Coal haulage mach.
Western Land Roller Co.	1977	1	Pumps
Knight Industries, Inc.	1980	1	Eqp. for oil and gas industry
Cabot Corp., machinery division	1980	12	Oil and gas rigs
Paymover	1982	small	Aircraft support vehicles
Eagle Picher Industries, Inc., part	1983	small	Underground mining products

Sales

Atlas Copco AB			
Ekenbergs Söner	1888	med.	Mech.eng. products
Brynäs Varv	1890	med.	Ships
Norrby Gjuteri (50 per cent)	1921	8	Castings
Diesel engine division	1948	39	Diesel engines
Björneborgs Bruk	1960	6	Castings
Ingersoll-Rand Company			
Condenser division	1977	1	Condensers
Vlchek Plastics Co.	1977	small	Plastic machinery

109

Table 7.1/continued

Company/division	Year	Relat. size %	Product line at acquisition/sale
Negri Bossi SpA, Milan, Italy	1979	small	Plastic machinery
The Torrington Co., part	1980	med.	Industrial needles

Notes: med = about 2-5 per cent, sma = about 1 per cent; both are guesstimates. Transactions involving product lines not currently or no longer manufactured at the company are underlined. Only acquisitions and sales involving product lines are considered. Product lines discontinued almost immediately after the acquisition are not included in Figure 7.3.
Sources: AC Annual Reports 1968-1983; Gårlund et al., 1973; IR Annual Reports 1958-1983; Lufttrycket, 1981-1984; Parkhill; Tryckluft, 1973-1982; Utveckling, 1982.

manufacturers, that the Swiss unit was gradually phased out. Broadly similar strategy can be contoured in the entry into gas compressors and the US compressor market between 1980 and 1984. The most outstanding example is, however, A.R.P.I.C., a fairly small plant in 1956 and today AC's largest production unit, reportedly the largest compressor plant in the Western World - although challenged by IR's plant at Painted Post, New York (below).

When IR's acquisitions are seen in the light of the outspoken desire to smooth out cyclical fluctuation by diversifying, the policy appears to have been successful (Figures 7.1 and 7.2). The 1981-1983 slump in sales cannot be taken as evidence to the contrary as it has also affected AC. It should preferably be studied in the context of several, broadly related companies. What is quite possible, instead, is that an acceptable result could have been achieved by a more selective acquisition policy and a broader geographic base as was the case with AC. This AC policy was put into practice only after World War II; initially AC was simply compelled to diversify 'anywhere' due to the unsuccessful initial choice of product line and over-sized capacity.

Diversification and Synergy
Selection of product lines, whether for internal development or acquisition, involves essentially three kinds of consideration: growth potential, counteracting cyclical fluctuation; and synergistic effects.

110

Growth potential is intimately connected with the environment. Developments in communication technology, synthetic substitutes of natural products and automation are examples of opportunities facing a capital-goods producer. Cyclical fluctuation can be counteracted by introducing product lines with minimal fluctuation, or ones which are off-phase with the current lines. The first alternative usually necessitates entering the consumer convenience goods market, an unattractive avenue because of the negative synergy in marketing. Instead, complementing current product lines with technologically related products or products selling to present or similar customers, as well as internalising suppliers and markets, is likely to result in positive synergy. In practice, this necessitates some diversification.

Differing origins and growth philosophies notwithstanding, there has been a substantial similarity in product lines between the two companies as to content and even timing since the beginning of the century (Figure 7.3). Common product lines have been rock drills, compressors, pneumatic tools, diesel engines, diesel-electric railroad equipment and full facers, all with substantial growth potential at this level of aggregation during the period. IR had the lead in most of them. AC was first only in diesel engines and diesel-electric railroad equipment, both economically less successful than anticipated at both companies and subsequently divested (sold or closed).

The problem with AC's diesel engine production was the ambition to reach technical perfection, and through it licencing goals which were beyond the muscle of the company (Gårdlund et al., 1973, pp. 144-9). Diesel-electric railroad cars were intended for rail lines with small traffic intensity and therefore lacked market potential. The demise of the diesel engines at IR has parallels with this. The original idea was to develop a power source for compressors. But the temptation to use the engine in locomotives soon emerged. Unfortunately, the technical requirements are not fully compatible and this apparently channelled energy into fruitless efforts. The locomotive business as such suffered from being a joint venture with partners who also manufactured competing electric and steam locomotives (Anonymous, Vol. 7, p. 3).

In view of the similar fates of the diesel business at both the companies, it is tempting to speculate whether full facers are going to last for any length of time. IR has already divested the product line while AC continues with it.

What is unusual is the simultaneous introduction of pneumatic tools at both the companies in 1901. At AC this presaged the future business idea for many decades. Ironically, the man introducing compressed air had acquainted himself with it at IR's main plant at Easton PA three years earlier (Gårdlund et al., 1973, pp. 55-6). It was no less ironic that, although production based on compressed air

Figure 7.3: Important product lines.
Sources: AC Annual Reports 1968-1983; Anonymous, vols. 4-7
Business Week, 1974, p.77; Gårlund et al., 1973; IR Annual
Reports 1958-1983; Parkhill.

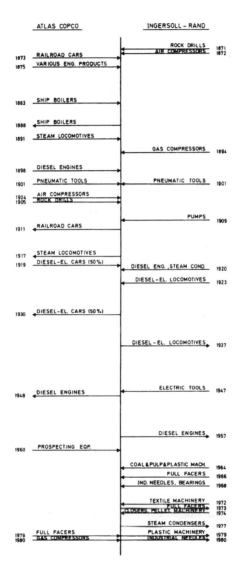

grew to reach the indisputable leading position within AC during his term of office as president 1909-1940, he never realised the inherent potential and favoured the far less profitable, although technically more intriguing, diesel production, the early love of the chairman and dominant shareholder.

The importance of pneumatic tools to AC was less in the tools themselves (they played a major role only in the late 1940s and 1950s) than in the introduction of compressed air to the company. Admittedly, the deliveries of the first air compressor and rock drill were certainly not considered milestones when they left the shops; they were simply two of many others which the company delivered when ordered. It was the market pull which warranted continued production and, in due course, allowed the discontinuation of railroad equipment.

The breakthrough did not materialise until the early 1950s. While the human role was important, it needed a technically outstanding product. The product was a light-weight method of drilling hard rock, developed in cooperation with Sandvik AB, a special steel producer, in hydroelectric power projects since the 1930s and supplemented by defence works during World War II. It was followed by other breakthroughs, viz. screw compressor in the 1950s, an oil free compressor in the 1960s. Thus AC was able, by virtue of products developed within the company, to preserve the growth phase until it could face competition, and often from IR, on more equal terms (Figure 7.2).

IR answered the 'Swedish Method' of drilling by developing heavy machinery in the mid 1950s in which weight was compensated by hydraulic manoeuvering and which prepared a considerable headache for AC's marketing people (Gårdlund et al., 1973, p. 166). The turbo compressor, the 'big brother' of the reciprocating (and screw) compressor, took IR to blast furnaces in 1912 and strengthened its presence in gas and oil production with pipelines as from 1949. AC entered this typically domestic US business only in 1980. A third significant step by IR was the screw compressor in the mid-1960s, the first in the USA. The marketing opportunity, however, was partly lost to a new company, Sullair Corp. (Business Week, 1974, p. 76). AC was not yet a factor on the US market, but one of its former executives was among the founders of Sullair!

The narrative so far covers all the important product lines of AC, arranged into three business segments: construction and mining technology, compressors and hand tools. Finding synergy within and between segments is easy.

Compressed air is still a common power source for rock drills, some underground loading equipment and hand tools, although it is giving way to hydraulics in rock drilling, diesel power in loading equipment and electricity in hand tools. The technological links are thus becoming weaker and the familiar combination, one technology - one customer, is losing relevance. Then the common denominator can be found in the size of the customers. For mining and construction technology and some compressors, the customers are mines, large-scale contractors and industrial plants, i.e., fairly large or large units. For tools and small compressors this may, but need not, be true. Automobile factories and shipyards, for example, fit the picture but repair shops and craftsmen do not, calling for a separate distribution network.

IR's situation in these product lines is naturally similar. But to IR's list must be added needle bearings, industrial needles, textile machinery, underground coalmining machinery, pulp and paper machinery, plastic moulding machinery, pelletising machinery, closers and exit devices.

Synergy between textile machinery, industrial needles and needle bearings is apparent. The needles were divested, however, in 1980. Underground coal cutters and coal hauling equipment are another obvious group with links to hard rock drilling. Pulp and paper machinery, plastic moulding machinery and pelletising machinery form a loose group but the moulding machinery was divested in 1979. The remaining two also have a certain overlap in customers. Closing and exit devices appear, superficially, to form an isolated group. The perception is modified when it is recalled that the primary market is in new construction, i.e., an industry segment using rock drills. At this level of disaggregation it appears strange to blame the company for lack of synergistic logic (Financial World, 1983, p. 15).

The scope of product lines has consequences for research and development, a virtual must in sophisticated mechanical engineering. Since the mid-1970s when information has been made available, the R & D budget of IR has been close to 4 per cent of sales against 3 per cent at AC (AC Annual Reports 1977-1983; IR Annual Reports 1972-1983). As IR has twice as many product lines as AC, the effort which it can devote to the central lines of AC must be less in dollar terms than its larger size and higher percentage alone would suggest. In other words, IR's larger size is no guarantee of overall technical leadership. Neither percentage includes technology acquisitions which, in relative terms, have been more extensive at AC.

SPATIAL OUTCOMES

At Home
Change in size has had numerous spatial repercussions. The original companies were located in what nowadays are the central city of New York and Stockholm. Only the more recent Diesels Motorer (1898) was located in the suburbs from the

114

Figure 7.4.   Plants in Western Europe.
Notes: One symbol may represent several plants if they are comparatively close to each other and particularly if they are small. Divestments are indicated only if all units at a locality are affected.
Sources: AC Annual Reports 1968-1983; Anonymous, vol. 8; Gårdlund et al., 1973; IR Annual Reports 1958-1983; IR Corporate Functional Listings; IR Directory, 1983; IR International, 1976; Lufttrycket, 1981-1984; Modin, 1949; Parkhill; Tryckluft, 1973-1982; Utveckling, 1982.

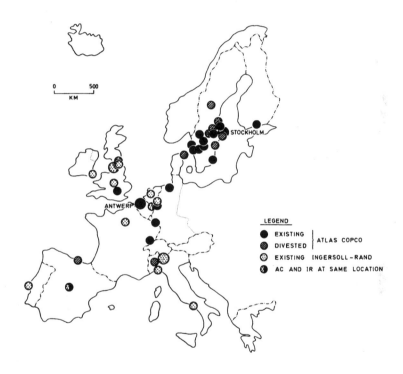

start. Expanding business made sites congested and city growth made the plots too valuable for manufacturing. IR and New York were larger than AC and Stockholm, and there the need to move out came earlier. Ingersoll moved some 100 km west to Easton (PA)/Phillipsburg (NJ) in 1893. Rand first moved 30 km north to North Tarrytown (NY) in 1886 and then a further 300 km north-west to Painted Post (NY) in 1899 (Figures 7.5 and 7.7). The Easton/Phillipsburg location is still the manufacturing hub of the merged company. Atlas moved its shops only in 1925, to the site already housing diesel facilities (Gårdlund et al., 1973, p. 95). That remained the firm's manufacturing centre until the 1970s, when the A.R.P.I.C. plant surpassed it in size.

When the manufacturing hubs had become established, both companies and IR in particular, remained comparatively immobile. IR established a plant at Athens, PA, close to Painted Post in 1907, acquired a New York-based pump manufacurer in 1909, moving it to Phillipsburg in 1912. That year it also bought a rock drill manufacturer in Littleton (Denver, CO) but divested the distant operation in 1930. The next step came only in 1961, in the large diversification effort.

AC's domestic moves outside Stockholm form three distinct temporal clusters. First came two acquisitions on the Baltic coast during the initial tumultuous decade, to be divested shortly afterwards (Table 7.1). The next cluster consisted of three acquisitions 1942-1951, covering the industrial heartland of Sweden. The last cluster, 1971-1983, was prompted by the shortage of production capacity, high labour costs in Stockholm and government decentralisation policy using the untaxed investment appropriations as a carrot (above). Ten new locations were involved, of which only two were for the purchase of technology (Figure 7.4). The last cluster comprised mostly small production units and appears to have been a temporary phenomenon to be followed by contraction. The waning sales have contributed (Figure 7.2), but equally important has been the revolution in the technology of production and materials handling. Today a given floorspace and labour force produce from three to seven times the volume they did in the early 1970s, a development which few could foresee.

The IR story repeats many of these traits, although they are flavoured by the larger spatial scale of the American continent and the policy of diversification by acquisition. Two subperiods are differentiated, 1961-1970 and 1971-1983. The first subperiod was dominated by acquisitions, while the company's own establishments have gained in relative weight since 1970.

The first subperiod sets itself apart from previous times by the wide dispersion of plants (Figure 7.5). The spread was facilitated by improved transport, although the immediate reason was the location of the acquisition objects, in turn

Figure 7.5: Ingersoll-Rand plants, new, in the U.S.A. 1961-1970.
Legend: E = Easton/Phillipsburg; P = Painted Post; A = Athens.
Notes: One symbol may represent several plants if they are comparatively close to each other and particularly if they are small. Some localities may be unidentified.
Sources: IR Annual Reports 1961-1970; Parkhill.

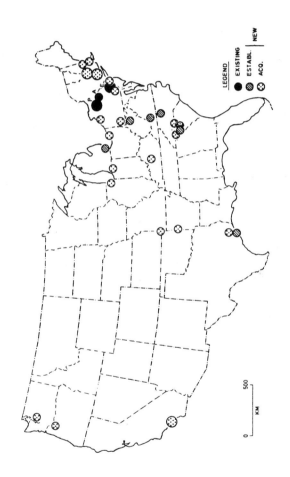

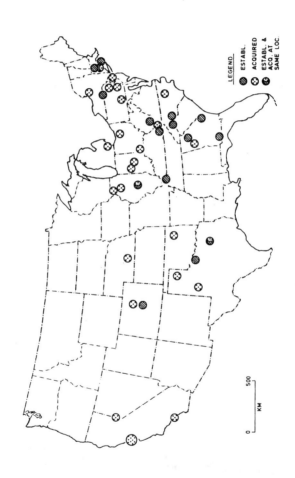

Figure 7.6: Ingersoll-Rand plants, new, in the U.S.A. 1971-1983.
Notes: See Figure 5.
Sources: IR Annual Reports 1971-1983; IR Corporate Functional Listings; IR Directory, 1982, IR Facts at a Glance; Parkhill; Thomas Register.

often connected by proximity to the market. Hand tools well suit the booming construction in California and the New England tradition of precision mechanics. Bearings further increase New England's relative weight. Coalmining machinery is found in the Appalachian coalfields, while further south industrial needles had followed the textile industry to the Appalachian Piedmont. The symbols on the Gulf Coast and in the prairies indicate manufacturers of process equipment and a packager of heavy machinery, both offsprings of the gas and oil industry. Seattle (WA) contains the manufacturer of full facers.

During 1971-1983 the acquired plants were mostly in the Manufacturing Belt, oil-producing states and California (Figure 7.6). Localisation in the oil states witnesses the endeavour to have part in gas and oil drilling, booming for most of the 1970s. California figures primarily because of closure and exit devices, an offspring of the continuing boom in construction. The Manufacturing Belt features, as previously, the numerous acquisition possibilities, although some plants are also connected with the Californian acquisitions.

One half of the plants established by IR were in the south-eastern states, covered most of the existing product lines and were set up to employ relatively abundant and low-cost labour in making mature products for the mass market, preferably under the tutelage of a parent plant in the Manufacturing Belt (Schmenner, 1982, pp. 98-100).

The subperiod, and its last years in particular, contains, as with AC, several divestments (Figure 7.7). They cluster in the Manufacturing Belt thus conforming to broad national trends. No particular product line is specifically affected.

Abroad

The spatial pattern of AC in the USA has parallels with that of IR. Plants are in the eastern Manufacturing Belt, i.e., closest to Europe (Figure 7.8). The original plant was there, as are the present US offices. AC's recent American activity seems to be the final step on its path to a truly global enterprise: the USA is the only large remaining market where AC's presence has so far been parenthetical (Figure 7.9). The first attempt was made in 1913, but the market proved impenetrable for the then weak company (Gårdlund et al., 1973, p. 66). The next attempt was made in 1950, but again the necessary effort was underestimated and operations dwindled (Gårdlund et al., 1973, p. 318). Perhaps only the third attempt, initiated in 1979 and also involving production capacity, will achieve the desired market penetration.

At aggregate level, internationalisation of a business firm is given in a time sequence in which direct export (without intermediates), representation by an agency, own sales office

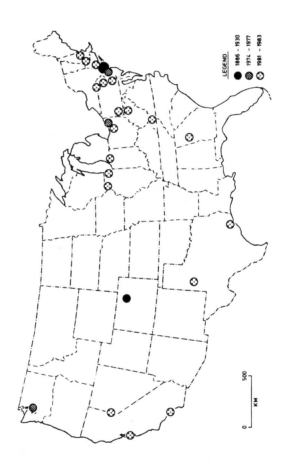

Figure 7.7: Ingersoll-Rand plants, divested, in the U.S.A.
Notes: See Figure 5.
Sources: IR Annual Reports 1976–1983; Anonymous, vols. 1 and 2; IR Facts at at Glance; Kother, 1971; Parkhill.

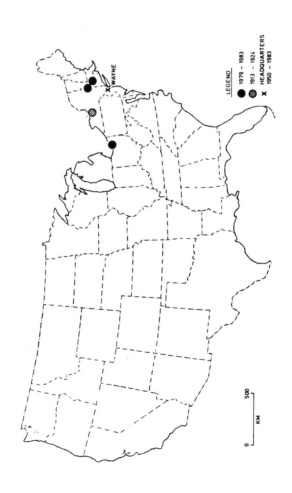

Figure 7.8: Atlas Copco in the U.S.A.
Notes: See Figure 4.
Sources: AC Annual Reports 1979-1983; Gårdlund et al., 1973, pp. 66, 85; Tryckluft, 1/1980, p.8; 2/1980, p. 4; Veckans Affärer, 1981, p. 21.

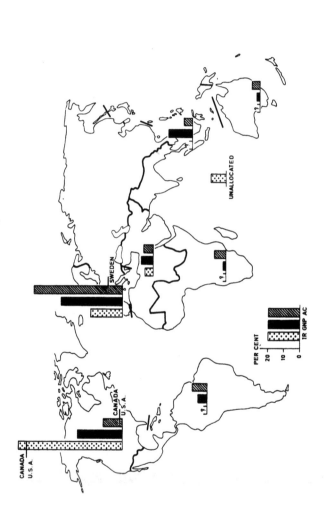

Figure 7.9: Relative sales and market potential in about 1980.
Notes: Socialist countries excluded. The bars for IR are approximations, as the statistical breakdown is incompatible with that of AC.
Sources: AC Annual Report 1980, p.3; IR Annual Report 1980, p. 19; Statistical Yearbook, 1983; Tryckluft, 4/1980, p.7.

Figure 7.10: Agencies and sales offices abroad 1871-1939.
Note: Data on IR's early activity in Latin America is
incomplete.
Sources: AC Annual Reports 1968-1983; Anonymous, vol. 8;
Gårdlund et al., 1973; IR Annual Reports 1958-1983; IR
International, 1976; Johansson and Wiedersheim-Paul, 1975,
Fig. 2; Modin, 1949, pp. 123-6; Tryckluft, 3/1980, pp. 7-8.

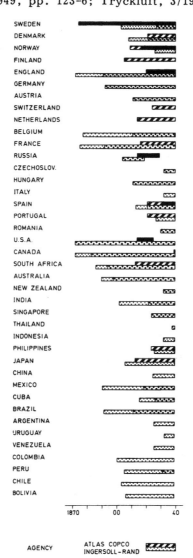

123

and manufacturing are the primary phases. The date of the first exports is generally unavailable and that of opening of an agency may be unreliable. Manufacturing is plagued by the wide range of operations. One theory (Johansson and Wiedersheim-Paul, 1975) suggests that the process begins in partner countries which are culturally close to the base and proceeds then to more distant countries. Although the theory ignores market potential and political factors and faces serious measurement problems, it is a working hypothesis. The application is strictly Swedish and reflects the pre-1914 conditions (Figure 7.10). From the American perspective, Canada and the British Isles, followed by the rest of the English-speaking world, thereafter France and Latin America, would appear more reasonable. The broad features of the theory are undoubtedly corroborated by the two companies (Figures 7.10 and 7.11).

The preeminence of IR should be emphasised, becoming international at least 15 years earlier than AC (Figure 7.10). For example, Sweden got an IR agency in 1902, or two years before AC had its first foreign representative in nearby Finland. Up to World War II, AC's foreign representation was confined to Europe and a couple of countries where business could be conducted in English. IR, instead, had developed worldwide operations. Internationalisation of manufacturing also started far earlier at IR, but has proceeded much further at AC (Figure 7.11): about 50 per cent of AC's manufacturing capacity has been abroad since the 1970s (Tryckluft, 1/1973, p. 8; AC Annual Report 1983, p. 48). A case in point is the A.R.P.I.C. plant (above). Only 15-20 per cent of IR's manufacturing takes place abroad (IR Annual Report 1983, p. 16). With 60-65 per cent of the sales being domestic and the major competitors being US companies there has been insufficient incentive to get really involved abroad.

Times may be changing, however. Foreign companies are entering the US market with competitive technology. Previously, Europeans compensated for the 15-20 per cent transport cost and customs duties (Tryckluft, 2/1980, p. 4) by lower wages and were constantly threatened by an antidumping charge. Now that the wage advantage is largely gone (Figure 7.12), they have started acquiring or establishing plants in the USA. To compensate for lost sales, US companies must go abroad on a larger scale than hitherto. The high rate of the US dollar in the 1980s further prompted the move. The drop of IR's foreign sales from 37 per cent to 31 per cent in 1980-83 is a serious enough indication (IR Annual Report 1980, p. 19; 1983, p. 16).

The problem of where to go is strongly conditioned by market potential and location of existing plants. Managements monitor the choice as, other things being equal, scale economies can be reaped by expanding plants (cf., however, Schmenner, 1982, p. 8). Market potential is mostly in Western

Figure 7.11: Manufacturing abroad.
Note: Minority ownership excluded
Sources: See Figure 4.

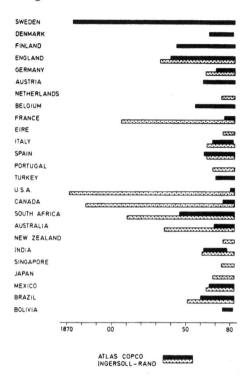

Europe, although the growth in percentage terms may be elsewhere. Most of IR's plants are there too, specifically in the UK and Italy (Figure 7.4). The pattern contrasts sharply (reflecting cultural closeness?) with AC, which has most foreign capacity in Belgium and West Germany. Cost levels and their development in these countries and in Sweden then become topical for mutual competitiveness in Europe.

Raw materials and components currently account for almost 60 per cent of production costs, wages and salaries for 30-40 per cent (AC Annual Report 1982, p. 49; IR Annual Report 1982, p. 35). Costs of raw materials and components also include, to a large extent, wages and salaries. At least raw materials, such as steel, are purchased mostly locally. Salaries per capita tend to be higher than wages per capita, and the ratio varies between countries, but the gap has been closing everywhere. Wages should, therefore, be broadly representative of production costs at large. From this angle,

125

Figure 7.12: Wages in mechanical engineering industry
1957-1982
Notes: Adult men and women, fringes included. ISIC 38.
Source: Wages and Total Labour Costs, 1966, 1972, 1975, 1984

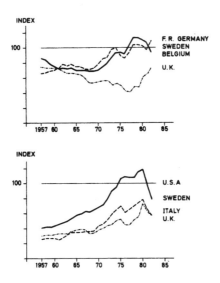

AC steadily lost competitive power in Europe between 1957 and 1976, the Swedish, Belgian and West German wages rising more rapidly than wages in the UK and Italy; only in 1980 did the trend seem to turn again (Figure 7.12). IR, too, must have suffered from the split of capacity between many plants, a by product of the generous acquisition policy. Thus, it appears that IR will strengthen its capacity in the UK and/or Italy, consolidate production in the largest plants, the numerous product lines permitting, and divest the rest (Business Week, 1984, p. 54).

Globally in the long term, the odds continue to be in IR's favour simply because the ratio of domestic sales to domestic capacity is higher, rendering protection when domestic costs develop unfavourably in comparison with foreign ones. If Western Europe is considered AC's 'home' market with 50-55 per cent of global sales (8-9 per cent in Sweden) and perhaps 80-90 per cent of production capacity, the ratio is about 0.6. At IR, with 60-65 per cent sales and 80-85 per cent capacity in the USA, the ratio is about 0.75.

The location of manufacturing has a bearing on the location of research and development. Applied R & D is located at or close to the appropriate major plants. AC has R

& D for mining equipment in Stockholm and air compressors in Antwerp, Belgium. That for gas compressors is still split between the USA and West Germany. IR has all its important units at home, in Phillipsburg (NJ) and Painted Post (NY) (Figure 7.5) for materials testing; in Easton (PA); San Francisco (CA) and Connecticut for rock drills, security locks and bearings, respectively (IR Annual Report 1975, pp. 15-17). More fundamental research is located where it can benefit from ready access to ideas and appropriate labour. But this may be equally possible abroad and at home, depending on circumstances and corporate philosophy. IR established a unit in Princeton (NJ) in 1965, while AC chose Lausanne, Switzerland in 1974, assumedly more attractive to the international labour market than far-off, northern and high-tax Sweden.

SIMILAR AND DISSIMILAR

A plea has been made that fruitful research can be conducted into large corporations, little amenable to formal statistical testing, using case studies. Generalisations can be attempted by taking related companies and following their destinies over a long period. Due to their size and compatibility of product lines, the companies are likely to be competitors. To survive they must then conform loosely to the same industrial standard, which subjects them to equalising pressure. The companies need not be identical, as the business goal, such as certain profitability or growth rate, can be achieved by a number of strategies. It is unlikely that the unity or the diversity will be properly elucidated in a cross-sectional study intended to be representative of the industry at large.

The ideas were tested on two, century-old mechanical engineering companies, one Swedish, the other American.

Similarities were in company origins at the source of market potential and financial resources; the timing of the pronounced growth phase, beginning in the late 1950s and early 1960s; roughly comparable profitabilities from that time onwards; an approximately 50 per cent overlap in product lines (by definition: 'related'); and a broad compatibility with the theory of cultural closeness when internationalising. Dissimilarities were in early business ideas; the declared, although not necessarily realised, growth philosophies; acquisition as opposed to internal growth; and the competitive consequences of the choice of the country for major manufacturing operations.

REFERENCES

Anonymous, Ingersoll-Rand Company 1871-1964, Vols. 1-8, unpublished, Washington, NJ

Atlas Copco AB (Publisher), Annual Reports 1968-1983, Stockholm

Ekonomisk Oversikt (1928; 1955; 1962), Kommerskollegium, Stockholm

Gårdlund, T. et al. (1973) Atlas Copco 1873-1973, Atlas Copco, Stockholm

Ingersoll-Rand Company (Publisher) Annual Reports 1905-1983, New York, NY/Woodcliff Lake, NJ

Ingersoll-Rand Company (Publisher) Corporate Functional Listings, Spring 1983, Woodcliff Lake, NJ

Ingersoll-Rand Company (Publisher) (December 1983) Directory, International, 1984, Woodcliff Lake, NJ

Ingersoll-Rand Company (Publisher) (December 1982) Directory, United States and Canada, 1983, Woodcliff Lake, NJ

Ingersoll-Rand Company (Publisher) Facts at a Glance 1981-1984, Woodcliff Lake, NJ

Ingersoll-Rand Company (Publisher) (1976) Ingersoll-Rand International, Woodcliff Lake, NJ

Ingersoll-Rand Company (Unpublished) Sales Figures 1906-1941, New York, NY

International Financial Statistics 1951-1983, International Monetary Fund, Washington, DC

Johansson, J. and Wiedersheim-Paul, F. (1975) 'The Internationalisation of the Firm - Four Swedish Cases', The Journal of Management Studies, 12, 305-22

Koether, G. (1971) The Building of Men, Machines, and a Company, Ingersoll-Rand Company, Woodcliff Lake, NJ

Kommersiella Meddelanden (1921) nr. 18, Kommerskollegium, Stockholm

Lufttrycket (1981-1984), Atlas Copco AB, Stockholm

Modin, K. (1949) Atlas Diesel 1873/1898/1948, Atlas Diesel AB, Stockholm

Parkhill, S.M. (Unpublished) Ingersoll-Rand Company 1871-1983 in Capsule, Washington, NJ

Phatak, A.V. (1971) Evolution of World Enterprises, American Management Association Inc., New York, NY

Riksbankens Arsbok 1934 (1935) 'Oversikt av Riksbankens avista försäljningskurser under åren 1901-1934', Tabell 39, Sveriges Riksbank, Stockholm

Riksbankens Arsbok 1942, 1950 (1943, 1951) 'Vaxelkurser i Stockholm aren 1933-1950', Tabell 53, 41, Sveriges Riksbank, Stockholm

Schmenner, R.W. (1982) Making Business Location Decisions, Prentice-Hall, Englewood Cliffs, NJ

Statistical Abstract of the United States 1960, 1963, 1965, 1969, 1973, 1981, US Bureau of the Census, Washington, DC

TWO MULTINATIONALS IN COMPETITION

Statistiska Meddelanden 1963-1984, Statistiska Centralbyran, Stockholm

Thomas Register of American Manufacturing 1976, Vol. 7, Thomas Publishing Company, New York, NY

Tryckluft (1973-1982), Atlas Copco AB, Stockholm

United Nations (1983) Statistical Yearbook 1981, New York, NY

US Bureau of the Census (1960) Historical Statistics of the United States: Colonial Times to 1957, Washington, DC

US Department of Labor (1983) Producer Prices and Price Indices 1982, 1983, Wasington, DC

Utveckling (1982) Atlas Copco AB, Stockholm

Wages and Total Labour Costs for Workers, International Survey 1957-1982 (1966, 1972, 1975, 1984) Swedish Employers' Confederation, Stockholm

Veckans Affärer, (23 juli 1981) 'Atlas Copcos Strategi på Jättemarknad: Förvärv av Företag ger bas för Tillväxt', nr. 26, pp. 19, 21

Chapter Eight

TELECOMMUNICATIONS AND THE GLOBAL FIRM

Henri Bakis

The world seems to have shrunk relatively: time and space
are no longer what they were even 3 decades ago. As Read
(1977 : 195) has stated, 'global interdependence - of which
telecommunications is the very nerve system - is widely
acknowledged as a salient trait of the new world order'.
Rapid technological change, the diffusion of new products and
services, are stimulating analysis of the direct and indirect
effects of the present and future impacts of innovation in
telecommunications on the spatial organisation of international
industry. Research into local and regional impacts of telecommunications has been undertaken for some time, especially
with reference to metropolitan decentralisation of non-
manufacturing functions. Yet the international framework into
which local and sub-national linkages and effects are tied has
attracted limited attention. Analysis of the internal telecommunications of a multinational company - such as International
Business Machines (IBM) chosen here as a case study - can
provide valuable insights into information flows between units
of a firm as well as into the hierarchy of regional sub-
national, regional sub-continental and world patterns of
spatial interaction comprising, and dependent upon, those
information flows.

COMMUNICATIONS NEEDS AND THEIR SATISFACTION

The use of telecommunications and data processing within IBM
is worthy of attention for 3 reasons. First, this company
operates in more than 100 countries and specialises internationally its manufacturing and non-manufacturing units
(Bakis, 1977). Second, while IBM looms large in the data
processing industry, it has increased its interests in telecommunications. Third, by profiting from the internal pricing
of its own data processing equipment and by perfecting the
computerisation of its own internal operations, on the global
scale IBM has achieved a significant market lead. It has

bestowed upon its subsidiaries, like IBM-France, technologies which in no way differ from those of the company at global level and, hence, point to the essentials of the corporate future which, in IBM's case, is already partly 'present' as most of its current telecommunications will be commonplace among the larger multinational companies by the mid-1980s and perhaps among most by the end of the century.

Born in 1911 as one of the first holding companies, under the name Computer Tabulating and Recording Company (CTR), the firm grouped together and controlled 13 companies scattered among 20 different locations in the US, Canada, UK and Germany. A branch was opened in 1914 in France. Thus, by contrast with traditional companies which expanded outwards from a 'historical' centre, CTR at the outset was 'globally splashed' in Onyemelukwe's terms (1974) and had to overcome the problems of spatially separated subsidiaries. Yet the relative independence of the various units constituting the holding company enabled CTR to make do with existing communications media: mail, telephone, telegraph and personal visits. The situation hardly changed when the company became IBM in 1924. Branches were initially charged with marketing equipment and subsequently with assembling components received from the USA. Centred in their respective markets, the subsidiaries needed to communicate with the head office about the supply of equipment and spare parts and for liaison between branch and head office management.

Conditions altered dramatically from the mid-1960s with the launching of the 360 range of computers and the advent of teleprocessing. Both combined to revolutionise the international management of manufacturing, R & D and marketing. IBM decided to launch a range of computers of increasing capability with standardised software. This initiative - a marketing masterpiece - enabled customers to complete their systems in step with the growth of their requirements without having to rewrite programmes. Third generation machines, the IBM 360 range, technically overtook all existing equipment by inserting integrated circuits.

It was a bold decision costing US $55,000 million in 4 years and company organisation had to be adapted to ensure that the gamble paid off. Thousands of employees were taken on in 5 new factories opened during the 1964-67 period in the USA and overseas while many others were significantly extended. Production units began operating according to a more advanced international division of labour to gain advantages from manufacturing computers in specialised factories of foreign IBM subsidiaries. The mid-1960s saw the emergence of teleprocessing as a tried and tested means of transmitting data from computer or terminal to computer. IBM began using it in the US for on-line applications and for the transmission of files. The European network began to spread in 1969. It is questionable whether the investment in the 360 range would

131

have paid off without widespread joint use of data processing and telecommunications equipment far in advance of the current state of the market.

Until the mid-1960s most contacts in the company continued to be made by face-to-face meetings, telephone, telex and mail. But technological progress then facilitated the promotion of a series of telecommunications products directly relevant to business. Thus, 'telecopy' enables a written document to be transmitted via a telephone link (this is analogous to remote photocopying although there is strictly no technological similarity). 'Teleconference' allows discourse between geographically separated groups in specially equipped video or audio studios: this goes beyond the simple replacement of face-to-face meetings because it permits additional discussions that distance would otherwise render impossible. And the radio-telephone enables a travelling representative to remain in contact with his office, while other devices can locate a person within a building and answering machines fulfil the role of letter boxes for absent people.

CONTEMPORARY DIVERSIFICATION IN COMMUNICATIONS

In the 1970s, as Nora and Minc (1978, p. 64) stated 'the IBM company [was] overflowing from the data processing field: the stakes, the scope of the debate and the nature of the competition [had] changed'. Management was exploring telecommunications, programmed learning and the electronic office, all fields in which IBM had already established a world position.

The Electronic Office

Further diversification into this field was favoured by the company's presence in the top-range typewriter market through its celebrated 'golf-ball' machine. Manufacturing and selling these typewriters yielded detailed information about the market: customer contacts allowed informed canvassing; an understanding of the problems of typing texts; and an ability to command all technological aspects of the entire printing system – the keyboards, the carriages and auxiliary equipment all being at the forefront of development. Thus selling word processing equipment poses no special market penetration problems. Not surprisingly, therefore, IBM had a greater share of the US market for these machines (73 per cent in 1978) than for data processing equipment (69 per cent in 1978) (Martin Simpson Research Associates Inc., 1979, p. 8).

Telecommunications

IBM began to produce telephone equipment with the introduction of teleprocessing. Communication between computers over distances required the development of signal converters called modulators-demodulators (modems). From 1969 IBM offered its customers a small-capacity exchange (with 200 to 800 stations) and after 1972 the more powerful 3750 PABX allowing great flexibility of use (e.g., for the 3-person conference or with portable receivers for locating people). As it can be connected to a computer, the classical telephone handset can be transformed into a terminal from which the central processor is consulted and fed with new data. But the link between computers and electronic telephony does not stop there: even the simplest and smallest exchanges must be connected to a computer and to a rudimentary logic device programmed to respond by reflex to the numerous calls. Thus it is not surprising that companies – such as the International Telephone and Telegraph Corporation (ITT) or L.M. Ericsson Telephone AB – in competition with IBM for switching centres, should also be concerned with data processing.

IBM, however, is particularly well placed on the telecommunications market. As an ex-sales director of the company in a European country has commented (Kolm, 1975, p. 496) 'for more than ten years IBM has been silently preparing new products with the aim of introducing itself into the huge telecommunications market of which the telephone is one of the most important components'. To avoid criticism from national Posts, Telegraph and Telephone (PTT) administrations, 'the company's businessmen have been encouraged to establish cooperative relationships with the technical heads of the PTTs'.

After the introduction of modems a ballon d'essai was launched, a discrete development of integrated telephone switchboards (PABX) not for sale in the US but only in some selected countries. From this was developed a much larger PABX (IBM 3750) electronic switching centre which could handle more than 2000 individual telephones and was sold officially as a PABX combination computer. The 3750, installed in all main IBM-France establishments as a connected network (see Figure 8.1), has 3 main uses:

(a) a voice function: dial or multifrequency keypad telephone sets enable oral communication between employees of the same company or with those of other organisations. Advanced telephony functions are also possible such as direct-dialling-in, automatic recall, repetition of external numbers, rapid called (8 numbers with a 1-digit code and up to 24 numbers with a 2-digit code) or a 3-person conference;

(b) a data-gathering function: low-volume data gathering operations are possible with the 3750 either from a multifrequency keypad or from a connectible terminal;

133

Figure 8.1: The Communications Systems of IBM–France, 1979. The inset shows a diagrammatic representation of the Paris area network.
Source: fieldwork

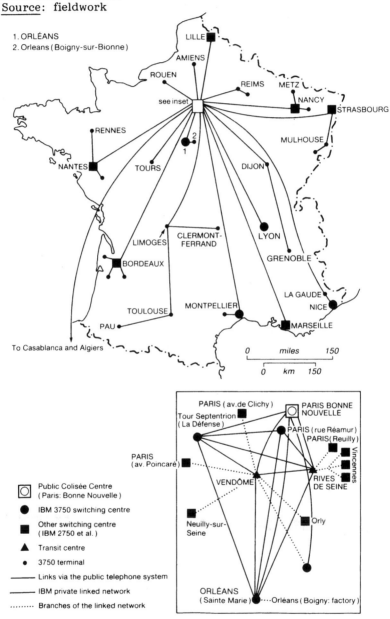

(c) a <u>control and contact</u> function: the detection, contact monitoring and command of contacts.

The French subsidiary's southern regional units, within IBM's international specialisation in R & D functions, greatly contributed to the corporation's technological progress: people at the La Gaude (Nice) centre designed many key modems; a pulse code modulation unit; a transmission control unit; a line concentrator; a vocal response unit; a private electronic switching centre; and an autonomous message switching system and numerous specialised terminals, with this type of equipment and the software components being produced at the Pompignane (Montpellier) factory.

Satellite Business Systems

The latest phase of expansion by IBM into the telecommunications field has been the introduction of Satellite Business Systems (SBS), the significance of which is 2-fold. First, use of the system internally by IBM headquarters at Armonk (New York) and setting up a worldwide system of 3 earth stations to serve 47 establishments, with 32 switching centres and 60,000 terminals, will make inter-regional access and liaison with identical technology virtually instantaneous across the globe. Second, IBM's entry into the SBS consortium (created with the Aetna Assurance Company and Comsat in 1975) manifests the corporation's interest in developing a 'competence' image for marketing space communications. Indeed, in 1979 the Japanese government considered asking IBM to provide technological know-how in the construction of a network of telecommunications satellites to cover South-East Asia, Japan, New Zealand, the western United States [and probably Australia] (Inf-Telecom, 30 August 1979, p. 2). In this way, it seems, the company in France - which stands to gain substantial business from this development and so enhance its regional impacts within France - is more concerned with the diffusion of technological support corresponding directly or indirectly to IBM 'standards' (whether they be the responsibility of the state or private consortia) than with monopolising all satellite communications directed towards intra-company communications of SBS type. The satellites in SBS, however, enable IBM to improve the mastery of its own internal network and so ensure control over the reliability of its own global communications.

The prime feature of SBS is to integrate satellite transmission (12 to 14 GHz), digital transmission, switching and processing, using relatively small earth stations (5 to 7 m in diameter) for traffic control systems and a series of telecommunications services for voice, facsimile and video transmission. The small size of the earth stations permits their installation in the user's premises if this is justified by the volume of traffic - and research suggests this to be already so among many of the 500 largest companies in the US which have spatially separated subsidiaries and operate a large volume of data and document transmission. To an important extent SBS could replace their use of telephone, telex, facsimile, mail and personal visits, but because the communications would pass directly by satellite rather than by switching centres, this is an important reason why PTT monopolies like the US Post Service or Deutsche Bundespost - often substantial local employers - are lukewarm. Only where customer traffic is insufficient will subscribers to SBS services have access to the satellite via an earth station to which they will be linked by terrestrial private or public lines.

As IBM controls 42.5 per cent of the capital of the SBS consortium, and the system, marketed in 1981, was expected to bring the corporation an annual turnover of US $1500 million by 1985 (Inf-Telecom, 13 February 1979, p. 2), competition for the US market has important implications for changes in, and adaptation of, the global regional sub-systems of the firm. According to Yves Stourdze (Le Monde, 14 December, 1978, p. 40):

> when IBM threw itself into the Satellite Business System [sic] adventure ... the manufacturer of computers had the full intention not only of dispossessing ATT of a part of its functions but also of gaining a foothold in the communications market of the top one hundred American companies. It is therefore a question of detaching from the global communications system one of the most remunerative segments and of managing it as a specific and independent market.

If IBM succeeds, the competitive displacement process will modify regional economic patterns by enhancing the market dominance of the corporation's own operating units and the economic health of their regional hinterlands in comparison with those of competitors; by weakening the national PTT monopolies, with employment, state subsidy and other implications; and by altering company organisation and job functions as the new technology displaces the old in offices and inter-establishment linkages. The convergence of telecommunications and computing technologies sharpens conflict on 2 fronts: marketing and control of equipment, and private communications services. In the latter field, for data processing alone, IBM in 1974 introduced an advanced architecture designed for centralised teleprocessing termed System Network Architecture (SNA), integrating the 35 or so access methods and 15 link control procedures used on the 200 telecommunications products which IBM then had. More recently the Advanced Communications Function (ACF) has refined SNA to take account of the multi-processor environment.

Co-existence of SNA and SBS within IBM is an internal contradiction which, in the strategic domain of telecommunications, can be understood only in terms of IBM's philosophy to encourage emulation between competing teams. It is probable that the internal conflict (SNA versus SBS) and the potential external conflict (IBM teleprocessing architectures versus national networks) explain IBM's information campaign to present SNA:

> as a collection of procedures making software and hardware mutually independent, a collection which is very open since any competing equipment may be included on condition that they respect the network protocols which are public ... In plain words, IBM-France wishes that SNA no longer be opposed either to Transpac [the French PTT's communications network] or to the user who wishes to preserve his freedom (La Lettre d'Electronique Actualites, 11 September 1979, p. 1).

The entry of IBM into the market for telecommunications which are not exclusively tied to computing is being made through SBS. In fact, private communications networks form the keystone of the new services such as electronic transfers of funds, facsimile, telephone conferences, data transmission or electronic mail. Analyses have shown that for some years ahead the volume of oral communications will far exceed the volume of data transmission; only the availability of a voice-video-data service can thus guarantee success. SBS would be profitable if, besides data and telephony, it also offered the new telecommunications services, especially the transmission of documents and teleconference facilities. It is possible that with these new services total traffic could be distributed over 24 hours. The company is thus studying the application of new methods of facsimile reproduction by digital transmissions. The prototype, already working , has attracted comment from Anderson and Kutnick (1978, p. 44):

> With product life cycles aimed at five to ten years, and an enormous R & D staff, IBM has to do something in the "in-between" time. The Research Triangle down in North Carolina has developed a prototype three second fax machine that it uses to communicate (via wide-band links) to New York. This speed is no great feat at wide bandwidths ... but IBM's toying with fax is definitely significant. Indeed, "toying" may be the wrong word. IBM has reportedly retooled some of the Copier 1's it has lying around with fibre optical tubes ... and turned them into Non-Impact Printers! These, in fact, may be the "receivers for the 3-second fax machines ... We

137

think that IBM is still trying to ascertain the potential size of the fax market before entering. The Armonk giant has a propensity for only choosing BIG markets that it can dominate.

This also illustrates the way in which another regional component of IBM has specialised in the R & D field.

If future technology indicates a very substantial weakening of the influence of the regional environment on patterns of production, management and decision-making, the use of telecommunications already enables IBM to 'internalise' or 'collapse' an apparently inter-regional urban network of establishments into a single 'central business district' and to provide service engineers wherever they may be with complete information and standarised, sophisticated 'repair tool-kits' as a result of direct access to the corporation's US facilities. This can be illustrated by reference to IBM-France.

THE TELECOMMUNICATIONS NETWORK OF IBM-FRANCE

The Telephone System

Among the various communications media available within IBM (whose international organisation is discussed later), the telephone remains widely used at the national subsidiary company level. IBM-France uses both public and private networks. It is a customer of the French PTT for:

(a) telephone calls to destinations outside its offices and factories, to customers, suppliers and smaller IBM centres (local commercial offices, equipment inspection centres, recreational centres) which have insufficient traffic to warrant the installation of a private link;

(b) data transmission (Caducée, Transpac) for commercial applications (e.g., the activity of the IBM computer centre at Neuilly-sur-Seine (Sablons) near Paris, communicating with customers of the company's Service Bureau):

(c) telex facilities (see later).

Private telephone lines, however, link the various company offices. People in the IBM offices in the Paris region containing the finance, office equipment, large systems and other divisions must be in constant communication, and a complex private network has been developed (Figure 8.1), the largest centres being linked via transit centres at Place Vendôme to the west at Rives de Seine (close to the Gare de Lyon) to the east. This structure is more economical than a star-shaped one which would not have minimised communications costs. IBM switching centres are installed at Place

Vendome (headquarters of IBM-France); Septentrion (tower block, La Défense); rue Réaumur; Rives de Seine (tower block); and Saint Jean-de-Braye (near Orléans, the adminis-trative and computing centre of IBM-France, known as Sainte Marie). These type 3750 switching centres are interconnected by special lines rented from the PTT. In addition, the Corbeil-Essonnes factory, which is also served by a 3750 switching centre, has a special link via the Place Vendôme transit centre with the entire IBM private network.

Other IBM facilities in the Paris region are connected to the network via 3 transit centres (Figure 8.1):

(a) Place Vendôme, notably the Neuilly-sur-Seine (Sablons) computer centre where the IBM 2750 switching centre system is no longer operational; the Paris (avenue Poincaré) overseas activities division where there is a non-IBM switching centre - possibly Compagnie Général de Constructions Téléphoniques (CGCT) since the building is shared with other companies; the Bois de Boulogne education centre with a 2750 switching centre; the Paris (avenue de Clichy) inspection, general staff and maintenance centre; and Orly, a centre which would normally have been linked to Rives de Seine and yet, despite the increased costs arising from greater distances, is connected to Place Vendôme on account of the quality of lines there;

(b) Rives de Seine, notably the Reuilly (Paris) inspec-tion and reconditioning centre, the Vincennes inspection centre, and the Vincennes education centre which was opened in 1979;

(c) the Sainte Marie centre at Orléans which is effect-ively part of the metropolitan system of IBM because of the huge volume of traffic it has with IBM centres in the Paris region.

The establishment of a similar network in the provinces would also have been feasible technically but IBM discarded the possibility of connecting the provincial centres with the Paris region and with each other on grounds of cost: the long distances separating the centres (which raises the costs of renting private lines); the relatively low volume of traffic; and the more specialised functional structure of these centres because, in contrast with the multiple-use IBM buildings in the Paris region where people must communicate frequently with each other on a variety of matters, the provincial centres have only simple or more intermittent and routine needs for liaison. A factory with production problems, for example, requires more frequent liaison with another factory (e.g., Bordeaux with Montpellier) than with a commercial office. Similarly, a commercial office needs to be connected with commercial departments but not with manufacturing plants. These 3 factors combined to encourage IBM-France to opt for the use of the Colisée network offered by the PTT so that in practice all IBM users in the provinces are linked via the Paris exchange Bonne Nouvelle – the Colisée transit centre. Furthermore, the IBM-France private network of the Paris region is also accessible from Colisée thus enabling communication between the provinces and Paris (Figure 8.1).

The telephone network integrates this French subsidiary: any company telephone can be used to call any other telephone whether it is situated in the same building or elsewhere in France without using the public toll network. The subsidiary thus operates as if it consisted of a single centre; the calls are always internal ones using the company's own network and the public network need be used only when it is required to call external correspondents or very small IBM units.

La Gaude Research Centre

The incorporation of this centre into the international organisation exemplifies IBM's precocious industrial and tertiary decentralisation policy and its contribution to the evolution of sophisticated telecommunication links between specialised, dispersed units. The spatial development of IBM establishments has moved through 3 stages: the location of its first overseas factories in metropolitan economic centres (e.g., Paris in 1922) near customers; suburbanisation of expansion after the Second World War (e.g., Corbeil-Essonnes in 1955) in response to rising urban land values and congested sites; and decentralisation of growth to provincial centres, starting in France with the choice of La Gaude (Nice) in 1960, a move ahead both of other corporate and of French government policies for such dispersal. Subsequently IBM constructed establishments in Montpellier (1964), Orléans (1965 and 1966) and Bordeaux (1970 and 1979).

In a sense, decentralisation was easier in the case of the international centre set up at La Gaude to advance telecommunication research because its relationships have been (and are) mainly with other IBM research centres in the US and Europe, not with Paris. Indeed, the international scope of the La Gaude centre may be judged by the fact that, of the 1000 or so letters leaving the laboratory each working day during 1984, between one-third and one-half were addressed to foreign destinations. An analysis of 854 letters sent outside France during a sample of 2 days showed that 40 per cent went to the US followed by West Germany, UK, Sweden, the Netherlands and Switzerland, mainly as a result of the presence of important IBM research laboratories in these countries (Mazataud, 1978). This predominance of the US is significant, and is true also of telex messages. According to Mazataud (1978) the proportions of the telex characters respectively transmitted from, and received by La Gaude, were 34 per cent and 41 per cent (US) and 56 per cent and 59 per cent (Europe). The destination of telephone calls also reveals the international role of the La Gaude centre, despite dominant use of this medium (75 per cent of all calls) to destinations within France: of the remaining quarter, almost one-fifth were destined each for the US, West Germany and the UK while 15 per cent went to Sweden. Clearly the lower proportion of US contacts by telephone reflected the steeper rise in costs with distance by comparison with those for mail.

Telex communications also point up the hierarchical arrangement of the functions of individual IBM centres and their contributions within the contexts of national subsidiaries to the hierarchical rank of those subsidiaries in Europe. In 1979 La Gaude received or sent 4.5 million telex characters – 12 per cent of the 37 million flowing through IBM-France – very significantly more than that of the Belgian subsidiary of IBM (3.7 million), which not only meets commercial needs but also the demand stemming from the widespread use of computing equipment. That the large German and Dutch subsidiary companies generated 25 and 9.5 million characters, respectively, gives a clue to the significance of La Gaude and IBM-France.

Message Transmission

IBM's Telecommunications and Information System (TIS) consists of 3 networks, respectively, of terminals, file transmission and message transmission. In France, the network of terminals corresponds to the convergence on Paris of 19 long-distance province-to-Paris links and of 30 links within the Paris region. File transmission is carried out by teleprocessing data contained in a magnetic tape which, in February 1981, involved 7 centres, the 4 factories, La Gaude and the 2 administrative offices. The message transmission network again depends on a network of classical teletypes, 140 to 150 (telex) teleprinters located in IBM offices, which will be replaced by teleprocessing via the network of terminals, so introducing the capability of using an intra-company word processing system. Thus IBM seems poised to launch itself into the top-range electronic mail market – telecommunications media connecting word processors equipped with computer elements – and to unleash a new generation of information processing equipment, so tightening inter-regional information linkages. These are already interwoven into a complex international network now to be discussed.

INTERNATIONAL ORGANISATION AND NETWORK ARCHITECTURE

Three-Dimensional Organisation

IBM has a 3-dimensional international organisation: global, 'continental' and national. At the global level are activities which, according to IBM, cannot be multiplied because of their cost or their particularity. An example is the research carried out by several units in the world like La Gaude or the North Carolina centres: the project plans start out from the central organisation and the results end up there. Other functions such as production are organised at the continental level while marketing and servicing are largely national.

Two main geographical-economic action spaces form the respective domains of IBM-USA, which operates solely in the US, and the IBM World Trade Corporation (WTC), a wholly controlled subsidiary of the former and which coordinates most corporate activities outside the US. IBM-WTC has itself been split into 2 distinct branches since 1974: WTC Europe-Middle East-Africa (EMEA) and WTC Asia-Latin America-Far East (AFE) (see Figure 8.2). IBM manufacturing policy within each of these 'continental' sub-groups rests on 2 basic principles: autonomy (production for the market concerned); and rationalisation and specialisation (all production units work for the continental sub-group market to avoid duplication). This policy differs from that traditional among many other multinationals in which national subsidiaries produce for their own market. It is probably fair to suggest that IBM's leadership in this respect was facilitated by internalised perfection and profit margin-less supply of equipment for its own intra-corporate communications.

The essential characteristic of IBM's teleprocessing is its great versatility. A basic constraint was built in when the teleprocessing network was designed: every terminal installed for the company's internal communications had to be suitable for all uses. Thus, any terminal can access any application on condition only that the user possesses the necessary access keys authorising him to consult a particular set. Hence the network is standardised and low-cost and incorporates both a flexibility potential and a high level of reliability – yet another manifestation of the spirit that guided the design of the convertible 360 range of computers. Once more it shows IBM's concern to ensure that the international organisation is independent of national and regional contingencies (Bakis, 1977).

The Network

The strong points of the network are the concentrators (a term used in the systems rather than the equipment sense): the computer centres linked to the IBM network and its

Figure 8.2: The IBM Information System.
Source: fieldwork

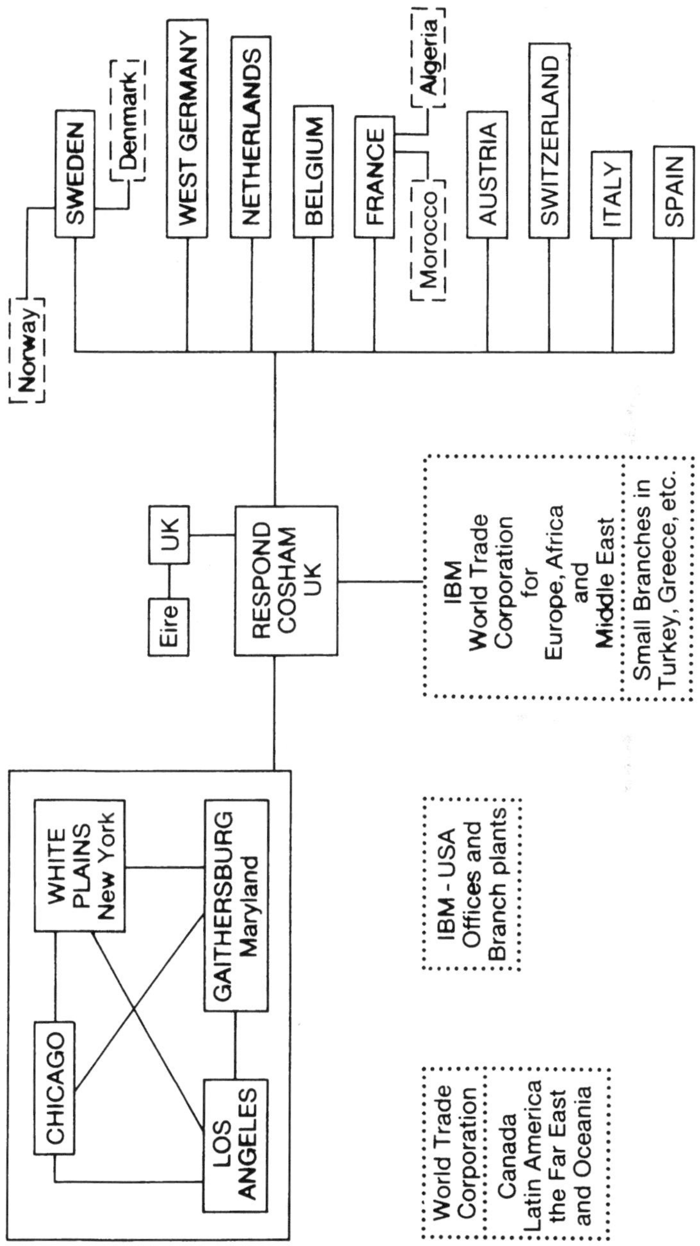

access points. Thus within IBM-France the Sainte Marie centre, near Orleans, receives communications from commercial office terminals and factories in the regions of France and, via Casablanca and Algiers, from its 'offshore' Moroccan and Algerian market areas (Figure 8.1 and 8.3). As Figure 8.3 shows, the various major national subsidiary centres handling sufficient sales in Europe are, in turn, linked to the Cosham centre (Portsmouth area, UK) which is connected to the IBM-USA and IBM-WTC-AFE networks. The principal concentrators in the US (White Plains, Gaithersburg, Chicago and Los Angeles) connect the terminals of the 'domestic' company as well as those of subsidiaries and their commercial offices in Latin America, Canada, Far East and Oceania. The link with Cosham, and thus with the network of the IBM-WTC-EMEA, is assured by the White Plains installation.

The UK centre is distinct from Cosham and comes under the control of 'RESPOND', a branch of IBM-Europe set up under British law and distinct from IBM-United Kingdom. The network access points are not necessarily located on the territory of the national subsidiary in which the centre is situated. For instance, the Austrian centre also handles orders from Yugoslavia, Hungary and other East European countries, the Norwegian and Danish agencies are connected to the Stockholm centre, and Eire is linked to the IBM-UK centre (Figure 8.2). Thus, even the smallest IBM marketing and servicing regions can be connected to the corporation's data processing system by a single terminal.

Within each subsidiary, however, the network has further regional ramifications which are illustrated by the situation in IBM-France. The company's data processing may be divided into that used for internal IBM management and that sold to external users as a bureau service by the 'Computer Centre'. Intra-IBM data processing may be further disaggregated into the TIS, charged with the control of a series of general order, factory and laboratory applications. Although these 3 categories are distinct, factories and laboratories also use the TIS for all non-specific applications necessitating data centralisation. Thus, the rules being the same for the entire firm, the TIS is responsible for the pay of IBM personnel, the operating units simply feeding in the required data.

Half the teleprocessing of IBM-France is localised in the Paris region, a quarter in Montpellier, and other significant amounts in Orléans and La Gaude (Table 8.1). In addition, scattered small sites throughout France are also concerned with teleprocessing, particularly the regional headquarters in Lyon, Marseille, Toulouse, Nantes, Lille and Strasbourg, and the offices in Grenoble, Bordeaux and Nancy. This pattern is not surprising since the IBM-France network centres on the Rives de Seine computers, with a convergence of 19 long-distance liaisons in France and around 30 special liaisons in

Figure 8.3: Primary and Secondary Communication Linkages between IBM factories in Western Europe.

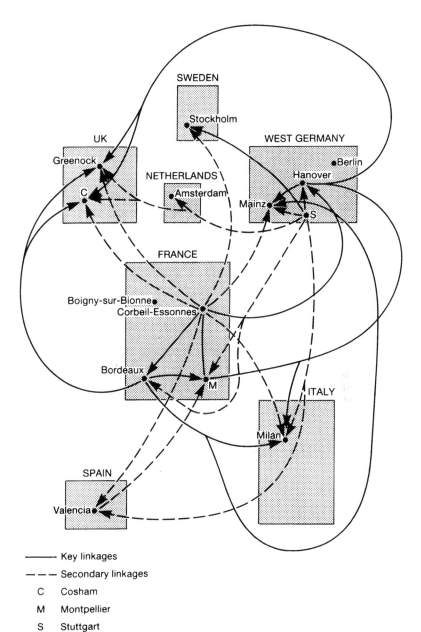

——— Key linkages

— — — Secondary linkages

C   Cosham

M   Montpellier

S   Stuttgart

the Paris region. Thus from any 3270 terminal, wherever it might be situated (in a commercial agency, administrative department, factory or research centre), access can be gained to all applications if the user has the necessary authorisation. The general network thus comprises access points by Visual Display Unit (VDU) and teleprinter terminals and of special links connecting the sites to the network nodes which assure either network management, as at Rives de Seine, or applications processing.

DATA PROCESSING APPLICATIONS AND THE SPATIAL DIVISION OF LABOUR

Without taking account of sub-contracting to service companies, it is possible to distinguish 6 types of data processing organisation in present-day industrial corporations. The first, and simplest, is centralised computing at company headquarters. The second involves the autonomy of various units in computer facilities. Third is relative autonomy whereby different establishments possess significant computer capability but are connected to headquarters by teleprocessing links for higher order data processing when necessary. The fourth type comprises distributed processing with people working in different units to carry out on-line operations with headquarters computers containing centralised data or, the fifth, with data distributed among several sites. The sixth type consists of several interconnected company networks having different types of organisation and requiring large-scale use of sophisticated telecommunications. Many multinational corporations operate the fifth type of system, but the teleprocessing network architecture of IBM belongs indisputably to the last type.

Applications
The telecommunications and information system network carries messages relating to several distinct applications. In Europe the 4 major centres are Cosham (UK), Uithoorn near Amsterdam (Netherlands), Sainte Marie (Orléans) and Orly (Paris). Rives de Seine is a message switching and routeing centre.

The following applications, discussed later, are controlled at Cosham: the RETAIN data base for maintenance, and the Field Instruction System (FIS) educational aid, and Advanced Administration Systems (AAS) for commercial services (orders, changed delivery dates, type of order). Uithoorn controls quite different applications: ERIF, the data base for the documentation on equipment being marketed, and HONE, an aid to commercial services in the design of customer-system configurations. Various applications are

Table 8.1: The approximate use of teleprocessing by IBM-France units.

Applications	Location	Per cent
Information systems		25.00
	Rives de Seine (Paris)	6.25
	Orly (Paris)	6.25
	Orléans (Sainte Marie)	12.50
Factories		50.00
	Corbeil-Essonnes	c. 24.50
	Montpellier	c. 24.50
	Bordeaux (Canéjean)	<1.00
R & D Laboratories		6.25
	La Gaude (Nice)	6.25
Computer centres		18.75
	Boulogne (Paris)	6.25
	Orléans (Sainte Marie)	12.50
Total		100.00

Source: Fieldwork

processed at Sainte Marie: some relate to IBM-France (such as data about finance and personnel), others concern international affairs, such as the administration of orders in liaison with manufacturing units and for the connection to RETAIN. Two applications processed at Orly concern inspection (distribution of spare parts, dispatching calls for maintenance inspectors) and distribution (collection of inspection reports, planning the activity of inspectors in terms of their specialities and timetabling constraints). Work relating to the different applications can call on data coming from Cosham, Uithoorn, Sainte Marie or Orly and the system can, without difficulty, call on data from the US by means of telecommunications satellite connections between Cosham and White Plains or between Cosham and Boulder (Figure 8.2).

It is, however, with production, marketing and servicing applications in particular, illustrating the local and regional links through the international system, that the remainder of this paper is concerned.

FACTORY SPECIALISATION WITHIN WORLD-REGIONAL MARKET AREAS

IBM's manufacturing organisation is rooted in the 2 basic principles of unique product design for all world markets and production by 3 autonomous world-regional markets: the United States and Canada; Europe-Middle East-Africa; and Asia-Latin America-Far East. Thus each product is manufactured in 3 different factories except where this is uneconomic for reasons of scale. If, for example, the top-of-the-range computers are only made in the US, this, according to the company, is because the European demand does not justify the manufacture of a sufficient number of units.

Within each of the 3 world-regional markets, there is very substantial division of labour between IBM factories. Establishments specialise not on the manufacture of a given type of computer but on particular assemblies (such as printers, VDU screens, disc units) while one plant co-ordinates, assembles and controls the quality of specific equipment. Hence, within North America, the Boca Raton factory in Florida was responsible in the 1970s for checking the complete 360/20 system, producing the central processing unit, assembling the 360/20 computer and testing various elements produced in other IBM factories in the US, notably Burlington (Vermont) and East Fishkill (New York) which supplied electronic components; Endicott (New York) for line-printers; Rochester (Minnesota) for card readers; Kingston (New York) for store and electrical supply systems; and San José (California) for model 20 disc control units. Other factories regularly or occasionally supplied smaller components and were thus attached to this linkage network, especially those at Boulder (magnetic stores), Brooklyn (New York: cables), Poughkeepsie (New York: central processing units for the 360/40, 50 and 195 and disc units) and Raleigh (North Carolina: terminals and peripheral devices). At zonal or 'continental' level the interdependence of plants is very great and may be further illustrated by the secondary and primary relationships among the European factories within IBM-WTC-EMEA (Skhrak, 1978) given in Figure 8.3). This close relationship, involved in the production of the 360 series computers since 1973, became even more pronounced since the introduction of the latest 370 range in 1979.

The local or sub-regional multiplier effects of these linkages is often substantial for around each IBM production unit are numerous sub-contracting companies which, together, often employ about the same size workforce as the main factory itself. This sketch thus shows the network in the 1970s to be not just the expression of the convergence of products at a point; the origin of each of these lines was itself a reception centre for elements of which the production process has been fixed by IBM (see Fredriksson and

Lindmark, 1979). The international IBM framework within which each national 'grouping' or set of plants operates, however, sets important goals at the national level to which the functions, scales and linkages of the individual plants contribute. One explanation of the international specialisation pattern lies in the company's desire to achieve the best possible balance of payments of the customer countries, especially those with the biggest markets. The sale of IBM equipment on these markets constitutes an expansion of the volume of imports. To reduce its 'foreign company' character and to make itself more readily acceptable by national administrations, IBM management makes productive investments, installing and expanding its industrial facilities only in those countries with a sufficiently large demand. The development of subsidiaries and plants is thus determined by the turnover achieved. By the same token, IBM has not sought to open factories in countries where labour is relatively cheap such as Singapore, Taiwan or South Korea nor, therefore, to engage in intra-corporate displacement of jobs. Thus, when deciding to increase its investment in Europe, the company did not envisage development in Eire despite the attraction that this country has had for the electronics industry in recent years, but favoured Spain (Valencia) where a substantial part of the rapidly expanding computer market is under the company's control.

This policy, therefore, has required dispersal of factories and judicious choice of the functions of each of them so that the value of the products permits the closest possible balance between IBM imports to, and exports from, any one country. Such a policy, however, offers major advantages for the company (and its constituent units and sub-contractors) in increased security and stability and reduced sensitivity to business cycles, currency exchange fluctuations, labour unrest and even nationalisation. Within the framework of nation states, prolonged problems of these kind would lead to only a short-term interruption in production at IBM because it can rapidly restructure its world network. To effect such restructuring IBM is really a rational technical unit, comprising an international distribution of 'responsibilities' and of specific 'missions' which meet well-defined tasks. Interdependence of production units naturally brings a multitude of relationships between establishments: for the movement of hardware at the different stages of manufacture; for information exchanges by telex or teleprocessing, or for exchanges of personnel assuring close liaison between 2 series of operations. Indeed, this offers flexibility and IBM does not view its productive network as being static but rather as representing a given stage in an evolving situation: changes do not affect factory locations but the nature of products being manufactured at them. The company has of course considered the corrective actions that would be needed to counter any unexpected problem affecting a particular establishment. While waiting for the resumption of temporarily interrupted production, the corporation can usually step up to maximum capacity at factories in the US or WTC factories and that of their respective sub-contractors and so effect short-term supply across world-regional production-system boundaries.

Rationalised Marketing
When an agent of the company receives an order anywhere in IBM-WTC-EMEA space, all the factories concerned must supply components to meet it. A rational sales administration to follow up orders enables IBM to optimise its production. The application, known as AAS, creates a link between the regional sales engineer and the computer centre managing the European-based (EMEA) order book.

In practice the salesman enters his order on a 3270 terminal. After a dialogue with the computer, the order (if correctly entered) is accepted and registered, allowing time saving since all errors and omissions in the formulation of the order - incompatibilities between equipment units composing a system, forgotten items (e.g., colour) and the desired delivery date - are avoided. This phase is carried out between the IBM agency, say within the area served by IBM-France, and the Sainte Marie centre. Each evening, the day's orders are sent to Rives de Seine and then on to Cosham. This centre, responsible for the whole EMEA area (Figure 8.3), in turn retransmits the order to each of the IBM European factories concerned. Thus, all the parties are informed of the tasks to be accomplished and, if possible, the delivery dates to be met.

A new phase in the processing of the order then comes into play. Staff at the various factories react by informing Cosham whether they can meet the request: one unit may put back the delivery date, another might announce that it will be ready earlier. Each promises to meet the data fixed by itself. The Cosham centre can then reply to the commercial agent who in turn informs the customer of the proposed delivery date. Before the implementation of the AAS, between 20 and 25 days were necessary simply to register the order. The immediate correction of errors, the request for additional details if the order is incomplete, the transmission and processing by the intermediary of the network have enabled IBM to reduce this delay significantly: the customer is informed of IBM's proposed delivery date at worst within a week and at best the day after placing the order.

Another important advantage for IBM is the parallel reckoning as to the scheduling of 'customer returns'. Frequently the person placing an order is already using hired IBM equipment: often a new order implies its recovery. The

AAS has permitted the management of available equipment on a European scale: if someone orders a 370-148 while presently using a 138, this implies a substitution and that a 138 will, after reconditioning, be available for use elsewhere. IBM thus satisfies customers while cutting costs and avoids waste of both production capacity and space to stock surplus equipment. By knowing the details of equipment to be recovered, IBM has been able to limit its production to equipment that is really necessary. Moreover, the equipment recovery procedure is valid not only for complete systems but also for their sub-units: several hundred magnetic tape units have thus been recovered from returned systems and are available for use in the latest ones. As far as possible, however, matching supply and demand is effected within national market areas, but not infrequently international movement of recovered equipment may benefit users in small regional markets.

Maintenance

IBM often announces worldwide the marketing of a new product 'x', even though initially it may concern a quite specific market, with all customers being informed at the same time. This has 2 major implications. First, sales engineers must be rapidly brought up to date with appropriate training on the equipment type announced. The heavy demand in the brief period between the announcement and the start of marketing and installation has led IBM to develop computer-ised distribution of commercial information (ERIF). Second, training courses must be provided about the use and main-tenance of the new equipment, involving theoretical instruc-tion by remote learning using FIS followed by face-to-face practical training. While the commercial agents need the documentation provided by the ERIF data base, the mainten-ance inspectors need to know the equipment sufficiently well to effect any repairs. The after-sales maintenance of all equipment presents the company with a problem which it has solved by an aid known as RETAIN. A further aid assists the commercial structures to determine, by teleprocessing, the configurations of the systems that customers want: for instance, HONE permits studies of traffic and load.

It has been pointed out (IBM Magazine, 1978(3), p. 32) that:

> There is another side to the computer innovation coin: the obsolescence of products and, consequently, of knowledge. The readjustment of the technical know-how poses a formidable question to the Inspection depart-ment: how to insert a continuing and homogeneous training in a multitude of professional lives scattered over the four corners of the commercial horizon?

This problem raised in a company publication was, naturally enough, solved by the use of computers: FIS is in effect a network-wide training-course bank. One of its major advantages is that it allows self-learning by working at a terminal and the centralised distribution of teaching throughout the company irrespective of the location of the establishments. Courses, newly created or updated, are distributed around the world, especially between laboratories and factories: for instance, IBM-France contributes some 5 per cent to this process. Thus no servicing region, whether in Africa, Asia or the US, should be significantly different in maintenance skills although 'density' on the ground of IBM-personnel, as with equipment installed, varies widely.

The RETAIN Network
Maintenance is a sensitive issue in all industrial organisations but it is critical when the equipment is hired and involves computers since the customers are other business organisations placing a premium on costly productive time lost. To preserve or to foster a good image among customers, unreliable or faulty equipment must be repaired and service restored in the shortest possible time, as the corporation itself acknowledges:

> In making itself more and more indispensable to the life of a company, computing creates the need for its unconditional reliability. Accustomed to the convenience of abundant and immediate information, users show themselves to be naturally demanding. Any slight impairment to the service and, moreover, any temporary interruption for technical reasons, is seen as a particularly prejudicial privation. In the corridors of the data processing division, impatience undergoes a metamorphosis and becomes urgency. The Inspection Department must always demonstrate immediate competence (IBM Magazine, 1978(3), p. 28).

It follows from the dimensions of these networks, function and generation differences, the size of the installations and the technological complexity which evolves at the speed of the succession of marketing announcements that neither one man nor even a small team can possess the range of skills necessary to maintain the computers and systems for which they are responsible. The difficulty is accentuated because

> inspectors now find themselves in the presence not only of a greater variety of products but also of constructions in which hardware and software are integrated in a technical whole, the detailed knowledge and understanding of which is beyond the human memory. Pre-

ventive and curative maintenance demand of inspectors a more and more pronounced overall knowledge (IBM Magazine, 1978(3), p. 28).

Paradoxically, reliability itself renders opportunities for an inspector to acquire personally the particular experience necessary to solve certain improbable problems. Reliability is improved by the inclusion in the systems of self-monitoring and security procedures. The company thus points out (IBM Magazine, 1978(3), p. 28) that

> the progress achieved in security which benefits the users, renders strangely but logically more difficult the diagnostic approach and therefore the role of the inspector. Since they cannot encompass the entire field of knowledge, the skills of individuals must from now on rely on the experience of the collective.

The principle behind the RETAIN network introduced in the early 1970s is simple - a common technical data base remotely accessible by a communications network on the global scale and capable of regular updating. One data bank is situated at Boulder in the US and a second in Cosham in the UK; they are identical as a result of daily transmission of update information. To this data base are connected, directly, laboratories and factories and, indirectly, the inspectors responsible for maintenance through an inspection support centre located in most national subsidiary companies (Figure 8.4). Thus each support centre is connected to the data base and, via a battery of terminals, the RETAIN data may be consulted by maintenance inspectors anywhere in the field.

When an inspector cannot identify the original cause of breakdown he communicates the characteristics of the problem to the specialist at the regional maintenance centre. If the difficulty cannot be solved at this stage, the regional inspector will interrogate RETAIN from his VDU terminal by using successively posed key-words. After a question and answer session allowing a diagnosis to be made, RETAIN provides a detailed account of the causes and technical characteristics of the solutions. If no RETAIN solution can be found, the specialists alert the expert inspectors of the factories or laboratories. The difficulty is then handled at this higher level and may be put to the team responsible for designing the equipment. The results of this analysis are then stocked in RETAIN to make them available for the solution of a similar problem should it recur.

This call on the company's competence (living skills for new problems or memorised data for problems which have already been solved) is backed by a call on all the information available on the machine concerned, including the equipment installed at the customer's site where the new type

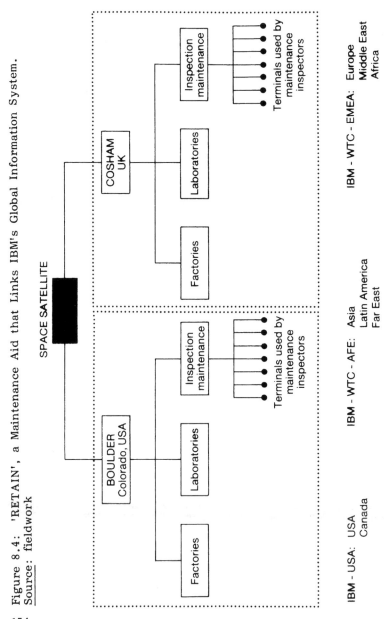

Figure 8.4: 'RETAIN', a Maintenance Aid that Links IBM's Global Information System.
Source: fieldwork

154

of fault occurred. Thus Robert Charbonnier, a head of the inspection department of IBM-France, is reported as saying (IBM Magazine, 1978(3), p. 30) that

> the computers sold and installed in the premises of our customers do not for this reason cease to live in the laboratories and factories, where expert inspectors make a synthesis of the behaviour of our equipment under real conditions and introduce, on the request of the Inspection department, desired modifications to hardware or software. Retain thus stocks in the files of its data banks, all changes in technical characteristics and all diagnostic propositions and solutions the circumstances of which have been reported. Retain data, whatever its nature, is continually revitalised. The experience of individual inspectors or of a local group necessarily becomes collective and international. In this way, continually updated and immediately accessible technical know-how is available at all points of the network.

In this way, the breakdown of a computer of an average-size company in, say Limoges, can lead to the mobilisation of data bases, laboratories and factories in several countries, not only within IBM-WTC-EMEA but in all 3 IBM world-regions. It is an operational method which tends to eliminate the creation of national or regional enclaves by sharing experience globally.

Besides its use in curative maintenance, RETAIN may also aid in preventive maintenance for which consultation of very advanced technical information is indispensable: by the exhaustiveness of its files it facilitates the general application of systematic modifications to products whenever this is necessary (IBM keeps track of its rented equipment and maintains it at the same technical level as the equipment of the same category being provided to new customers). RETAIN thus enables each maintenance inspector to be connected to a multiple-skill base common to all inspectors, raising professional security. Again Charbonnier is incisive (IBM Magazine, 1978(3), p. 30):

> For the Company, it is incontestably a kind of world-wide insurance and like the technical expression of its traditional commercial philosophy! Through Retain, IBM is able to guarantee maintenance at the same level and of the same quality throughout the five continents. But the Retain network may also be a certain illustration of the future of data processing: its quiet aptitude for the better communication of the living know-how of human skills.

TELECOMMUNICATIONS AND THE GLOBAL FIRM

Note that the new data processing leans heavily on the use of telecommunications networks - like that called télematique by Nora and Minc (1978) in their report to the French government or that which already existed under the name of téle-informatique (teleprocessing). The utility of RETAIN to IBM is obvious: it raises profitability, reduces breakdown periods, improves the efficiency of its rented equipment in other organisations, and enhances the IBM image.

REGIONAL IMPLICATIONS OF INNOVATIONS

Innovations in electronics, computing and telecommunications have direct and indirect effects on corporate organisation. Even though the teleprocessing network is installed and the principal applications are specified, the lack of information means that their impact must be inferred from various indicators. The RETAIN system implies that the maintenance inspector faced with a difficult breakdown in some provincial backwater is not alone in restoring the system to working order: he can call on worldwide expertise. Combined with the AAS, rationalising production and stocks, it reduces the regional configuration of the company to the optimal areas for speedy maintenance and minimum cost of equipment delivery. Telecommunications and data processing have, however, created or facilitated greater international cohesion and contemporary innovations - rapid telecopy (facsimile), tele-conference and electronic mail - and can assist multinational organisations to become even more internationally orientated. The shortening of 'communication lines' will mean a greater international division of service-type work, reducing the importance of the regional environment, but technology only creates possibilities and the shape of a network, like the mode of its operation and the nature of its applications, remains dependent on 'strategic' or political decisions of the company.

The employment impacts of computerisation are a very sensitive issue and potentially can have great future effects upon the scale and structure of jobs in regions with the highest concentrations of service jobs, namely metropolitan areas and their central business districts. Data is very hard to obtain but it seems that in IBM the number of people directly employed in registering orders has not increased since the introduction of the AAS information system in the early 1970s, yet the volume of orders registered and the administrative workload (related to the multiplication of operations necessary for the sale of data processing equipment in the 1970s) has increased very considerably: now, instead of ordering 1 machine, a company can order a complete system including perhaps 30 VDU terminals, each of which may be required at a different location on different dates. If the terminals are not all of the same type or model, arrangements are even more complicated and the administrative workload becomes greater without necessarily involving any higher charge to the customer. As IBM has to absorb such costs, it becomes more advantageous for the manufacturer to deliver only a big computer (the central unit of the IBM 3033, for instance) or to rationalise further its regional marketing and maintenance organisation. These courses have been avoided by using the AAS system which has reduced labour costs per unit sale.

Telecommunications are also, of course, at the heart of the debate as to whether less developed regions in countries (or less developed countries in a global context) can benefit significantly from decentralisation of administration, R & D and other non-manufacturing functions.

In the first stages of its development, computing acted as an instrument in the service of centralisation to minimise costs of data processing. Not surprisingly, until 1972 the Paris region had up to 62 per cent of all the computer terminals installed in France (Bakis, 1978). Initially, teleprocessing did not lead to spatial dispersion, but centralisation often proved incapable of providing users with the right information at the right time in a simple and practical way; this generated opinion in favour of the geographical decentralisation of responsibilities. Users want to obtain information more simply without having to peruse huge listings or to acquire special computer know-how. It has therefore been necessary to rethink the relations between user and computer, a task made easier by the technological revolution of the past 15 years. Yet continuity of centralisation can occur both in the ex-headquarters of computing and in new decentralised establishments, grouping certain skills in a few places, and can be reinforced by the wide-scale use of teleprocessing media. Perhaps, therefore, the tools of 'decentralisation' are in the process of introducing a reinforced centralisation of global control while taking from the local levels their initial relative autonomy.

It appears that the IBM network across the world is a prefiguration of this type of technological decentralisation-centralisation. Initially the sales surface area in the Paris region led the company to consider expanding its premises there to meet demand. However, the DATAR (Délégation à l'Aménagement Régional et à l'Action Régionale) planning authority, to which the IBM plan was put, asked the company to decentralise its activities before granting permission for the extension of its administrative premises in the Paris region. This stimulated between 1960 and 1966 the establishment of the research centre at La Gaude, the computer assembly factory at Montpellier, the punched card and stationery factory at Boigny-sur-Bionne and the administrative centre of the French subsidiary at Sainte Marie. To operate them smoothly, telecommunications media had to be developed. Further decentralisation has been undertaken since 1966, with a new plant in Bordeaux (Canéjean) and transfer of further Parisian production functions there in 1979, and with successive extensions at La Gaude, Montpellier, and Sainte Marie.

Telecommunications and teleprocessing have certainly accelerated the trend for regional company functions to become part of a dual organisational hierarchy. Upon the territorial divisions of a multinational company are often superimposed another series of functional divisions, and this is particularly true of IBM. These divisions can be so inter-woven that one person (e.g., the manager of the factory at Montpellier) can, at the same time, form part of a hierarchy relative to the national subsidiary company to which he belongs (IBM-France) and also of a hierarchy relative to his position in the whole company's framework (IBM-Europe). It might be said that it is the functional division which actually gives IBM its multinational character since it is by this means that geographically distinct establishments function as a coherent whole in the framework of a given project. The adoption of advanced telecommunications media - making IBM an 'advanced edge user' - allows the international operation of manufacture, sales and research functions to be particularly efficient. A worldwide cohesion of activities can emerge as a sub-product of the use of advanced telecommunications media, but only further research can indicate whether they have an induced effect on organisations or whether they simply play an accompanying role to corporate mutations or evolutions caused by other factors.

PAPER TIGER OR TELEPROCESSING TYRANT?

This study of IBM's internal communications shows the essential role played by teleprocessing. Alongside older communications media, such as mail, face-to-face meetings, telephone and telex, teleprocessing has occupied a most important place in the international organisation of the company. Use of this medium for 'on line' applications or for the transmission of files and the massive use of data pro-cessing without telecommunications (transport of magnetic tapes) has probably enabled IBM to master space to survive since it grouped sites in numerous towns, regions and even countries, and contributed, through its control and efficiency of information, to its technological leadership in, and dominance of, many regional markets. The importance of the telephone network to IBM-France has also been demonstrated: the network creates the potential internal unity within the subsidiary by enabling each person to call any other person anywhere in IBM-France, just as if they were in the same building, by dialling a 6-digit extension number.

Despite data deficiencies, stemming from the caution of IBM, it has been possible to expose 3 impacts of teleprocessing: greater cohesion of production, sales and maintenance; increased productivity enabling the information system to bear a heavier administrative workload for marketing decentralised computer systems; and the diminution of autonomy among subsidiaries. All have contributed to both lower costs or substantial profits and increased interdependence of regional conditions across international frontiers.

The chapter may lead to the hasty conclusion that IBM is a supremely well-made organisation where everything is consistent and well thought out. But Le Moigne has commented (1977, p. 68) that:

> the policies of IBM are not worked out by a well oiled machine of top class managers. They are - probably - the moving result of horrible tribal clashes, and one might presume that with IBM more than elsewhere, "decisions make themselves" rather than that "they are made". It is important not to fall into the well-known misconception of victims (a misconception which makes the force of tyrants): in convincing oneself that the policies of multi-national companies are "consistent, thought out, convergent and powerful", one ends by resigning oneself to the hypothesis of the force and to the intelligence of the tyrant. But is not this hypothesis false? The tiger may not be in paper ... but its feet are certainly made of clay!

However, one must admire the internal logic, apparent consistency and organisation of a multinational company which has been able to provide itself with the means to achieve remarkable profitability. None the less, there must also be concern about the social implications at the sub-national level of an economic entity which disposes such great financial, industrial and, even more importantly, technological power. In many sovereign states, such power is counterbalanced by structural forces such as opposition parties, trade unions or public opinion. It is unclear where the forces are that play a comparable 'regulatory' role for IBM: they are certainly not to be found in the United Nations Organisation or among nations sometimes too weak or dependent to be a real interlocutor on basic questions, nor among unions of IBM workers cloistered as they are within the various national subsidiaries. Perhaps the regulatory element must be sought within IBM itself.

REFERENCES

Anderson, H. and Kutnick, D. (1978) 'What is Electronic Mail ... and Where does it fit into the Office?', Tele-communications, 12 (11), 31-56

Bakis, H. (1977) 'IBM: Une Multinationale Régionale' [IBM: A Regional Multinational], Presses Universitaires de Grenoble

Bakis, H. (1978) 'Disparités Régionales dans le Développement de la Téléinformatique française' in A. Giraud, B. Missika and C. Wolton (eds.), Les Réseaux Pensants, Télécommunication et Société, Masson, Collection Scientifique et Technique des Télécommunications, Paris, pp. 42-9

Fredriksson, C.G. and Lindmark, L.G. (1979) 'From Firms to Systems of Firms: a Study of Interregional Dependence in a Dynamic Society' in F.E.I. Hamilton and G.J.R. Linge (eds.), Spatial Analysis, Industry and the Industrial Environment: Progress in Research and Appli-cations, Wiley, Chichester, Vol. 1, 155-86

Kolm, S.-C. (1975) 'L'exploitation par l'inflation XXX - IBM ou l'émergence d'une Nouvelle Dictature', Les Temps Modernes, No. 351, 494-501

Le Moigne, J.L. (1977) 'Compte Rendu du Livre IBM: Une Multinationale Régionale de H. Bakis', Informatique et Gestion, No. 91, 68

Martin Simpson Research Associates Inc. (1979) The Office Products Analyst, 1, 8

Mazataud, P. (1978) 'Les Constructeurs de Matériel Infor-matique en France', Bibliothèque Nationale, Comité des Travaux Historiques et Scientifiques, Paris

Nora, S. and Minc. A. (1978) 'L'Informatisation de la Société [The Computerisation of Society], La Documentation Francaise, Paris

Onyemelukwe, J.O.C. (1974) 'Industrial Location in Nigeria' in F.E.I. Hamilton (ed.), Spatial Perspectives on Industrial Organisation & Decision Making, Wiley, London, pp. 461-83

Read, H. (1977) 'Foreign Policy: the High and Low Politics of Telecommunications' in A.G. Oettinger, P.J. Berman and W.H. Read (eds.), High and Low Politics: Information Resources for the 80s, Ballinger, Cambridge, Mass., 195-237

Skhrak, B. (1978) 'Intégration Industrielle des Firmes Multi-nationales', unpublished thesis Université d' Aix-Marseille II, Faculté des Sciences Economiques, Centre d' Economie et de Finances Internationales

Chapter Nine

SPATIAL AND STRUCTURAL CONSEQUENCES OF
INDUSTRIAL CHANGE: THE AMERICAN GULF
COAST PETROCRESCENT

Bernard Weinstein and Harold T. Cross

During the 1970s, the oil patch, especially the Texas-Louisiana Gulf Coast Crescent, experienced unprecedented economic boom. Driven by rising prices for oil and gas, the regional economy posted extremely rapid employment and income gains from increased exploration and drilling activity, manufacture of oilfield equipment, expansions at refineries and chemical plants and relocation of energy company offices to the Gulf Coast. Since 1980 by contrast, the regional economy has been in a tailspin: job growth has slowed markedly in all metropolitan areas; unemployment remains well above the US average despite national economic recovery. Of 106 US refineries shut since 1980, 37 are in Texas and Louisiana. Because refinery workers receive high wages, reductions have serious local economic consequences.

Contraction of the US refining industry has resulted from several factors. Anticipation of continually rising prices and demand for gasoline, combined with incentives offered by national energy policies, led to a 20 per cent increase in domestic refining capacity between 1975 and 1980, mostly in California, Texas and Louisiana. Just as this new capacity came on stream, prices and demand for gasoline and other distillates dropped, making oil refining marginally profitable at best. Indeed, a recent survey by Platts Oilgram found that the "best" profit margin among Houston-area refiners was a 64 cents per barrel loss; the worst, a per barrel loss of $4.61.

Though capacity nationwide has been reduced by nearly 2.7 million barrels per day since 1980, the 191 active refineries are currently operating at only 75 per cent of rated capacity. With most small refineries already closed or up for sale, the oil companies must now look to their larger units for further reductions in capacity to bring supply and demand more closely into balance.

Other factors point to continued decline in Gulf Coast refining:

1. recent mergers and acquisitions among the big oil companies;
2. cheaper imports of refined products;
3. OPEC and other oil exporting nations investment in new, state-of-the-art refineries and petrochemical plants that will be able to undersell US producers;
4. much less stringent environmental standards abroad.

US refining is not going out of business, but is changing its product mix and modus operandi. Future emphasis will be on products with a higher value-added than gasoline, like lubricating base oils and petrochemical feedstocks. This product realignment will be accompanied by new investments in process-control technology, automation and energy conservation. As a result, refineries of tomorrow will employ many fewer workers than the refineries of today. Employment in refining nationwide has dropped by more than 13 per cent since 1982, from 173,000 to 150,000 and by 2000 will be below 100,000. Gulf Coast communities heavily dependent on the petrochemicals should diversify.

RECENT DEVELOPMENTS IN REFINING AND RELATED INDUSTRIES

Refining and petrochemicals and related rig fabrication, work boats, drilling equipment and offshore services have entered a period of significant entrenchment.

Merger and Acquisition Activity

There has been a wave of mega-mergers in the oil industry since 1980. Table 9.1 shows how the 3 largest mergers of Texaco-Getty, Chevron-Gulf and Mobil-Superior create a new line-up in the American oil industry in revenues, reserves, production and spending. The American economy has experienced three major waves of mergers: 1895-1905; 1920-33; the third started around 1950 and is still with us. The first two were smaller and involved more horizontal mergers. The current wave has been dominated by conglomerate mergers across conventional market lines, but a resurgence of horizontal mergers occurred after 1980.

The petroleum industry, long a symbol of bigness and power in American industry, has experienced much activity. Among the 25 most merger-active firms identified by the Federal Trade Commission (FTC) between 1961 and 1968, 8 were large petroleum companies acquiring more than $6 billion of assets in this short but explosive period, second then only to the 11 conglomerates that dominated merger activity.

Hence, recent mega-mergers are not without precedent, but are a response to overcapacity caused by the 20 per cent

Table 9.1: Mergers Create a New Line-up in the US Oil Industry
(Data for 1983)

Revenues (billion $)		US Oil Reserves (liquid, billion bbls.)		US Liquids Production (billion bbls.)		Capital & Exploration Spending (billion $)	
Exxon	94.7	Sohio	2.82	Exxon	0.28	Exxon	9.0
Mobil + Superior	60.8	Exxon	2.78	Arco	0.24	Chevron + Gulf	5.8
Mobil	59.0	Arco	2.57	Texaco + Getty	0.23	Texaco + Getty	5.1
Chevron + Gulf	58.1	Shell	2.17	Chevron + Gulf	0.22	Mobil + Superior	4.9
Texaco + Getty	53.2	Texaco + Getty	2.16	Sohio	0.22	Std. Oil (Ind.)	4.1
Texaco	41.1	Chevron + Gulf	1.97	Shell	0.19	Texaco	3.8
Std. Oil (Ind.)	29.5	Std. Oil (Ind.)	1.71	Std. Oil (Ind.)	0.15	Mobil	3.8
Chevron	29.2	Chevron	1.18	Texaco	0.12	Arco	3.4
Gulf	28.9	Mobil + Superior	1.04	Chevron	0.12	Chevron	3.1
Arco	26.3	Texaco	0.97	Getty	0.10	Shell	2.8
Shell	19.9	Mobil	0.86	Mobil	0.10	Gulf	2.8
Sun	15.5	Gulf	0.79	Gulf	0.10	Sohio	2.3
Phillips	15.4	Unocal	0.66			Unocal	1.8
						Conoco	1.7

Source: Oil and Gas Journal, September 10, 1984.

increase noted above in the 1970s, itself a "corrective" of a situation involving the smallest growth of any region in the world during the 1961-72 period. The lack of domestic refining capacity has been seen as a major cause of the mid-1970s fuel oil and gasoline shortages. In retrospect, given current overcapacity, this low rate of growth was appropriate and not an over reaction to short-run demand.

Increasing firm size has been another motive for merger and offers new economies of scale to Mobil, Chevron and Texaco to make refineries of merged companies more profitable and exploration efforts potentially more productive. Table 9.1 shows no drastic changes in the largest oil companies ranking. To avoid anti-trust problems and make full use of their enlarged marketing power, the newly merged companies are expected to sell or close many of their service stations and several refineries. Advocates of economic efficiency see this as a restructuring process that will enhance the profitability of an American oil industry faced with a world oil glut and intense international competition. Because utilisation rates of refineries are crucial to their profitability, such streamlining can only enhance profitability. The country's refineries are currently running at only 75 per cent of capacity. Buyers of surplus refineries and petrol stations may be hard to find. Texaco has been unable as yet to find buyers for a Getty refinery in Kansas and 2,300 Getty petrol stations in 15 states. Chevron is being required by the FTC to spin-off about 4,000 Gulf stations in six Southeastern states (Kentucky, Tennessee, Alabama, Mississippi, Louisiana and Florida), and has already sold a large Gulf refinery. Meanwhile, the number of US petrol stations declined from 263,000 in 1977 to under 209,000 in 1984.

While the oil industry may be unique in merger size, further acquisition can be justified because concentration ratios (i.e., the per cent of shipments accounted for by the largest manufacturing companies) were relatively small compared to motor vehicles, steel, aircraft, photography and electronic computing equipment. The raison d'etre for these mega-mergers in the oil industry then can be attributed to overcapacity: companies are trying to get access to lower cost reserves and excess capacity implies that there must be rationalisation in the industry.

Changes in Refining Capacity: 1975-80 and 1980-84

Restructuring has become a euphemism for industrial shrinkage. Policymakers and media give far more attention to the impact of restructuring in decline or stagnation than they do under conditions of growth. Joseph Schumpeter argued that mergers are part of the "process of creative destruction" as an industry evolves along a life cycle of growth and change. That the 1980s heralded a new era in the life cycle of the petroleum industry, an era very different from the 1970s growth phase, manifests itself in refinery shutdowns, idle capacity, acquisitions and mergers.

The 1975-80 period saw an increase of 38 refineries in the USA, 11 located in Texas, another 11 in Louisiana; increased refining capacity by nearly 3 million barrels per calendar day (B/CD), 32 per cent of this in Texas alone. The 1980-84 period (Table 9.3) saw 106 refineries closing across the country, 23 of these in Texas, another 14 in Louisiana. Most of the 29 inactive refineries in the United States in 1984 are small, with capacity under 50,000 barrels per calendar day, and are in The Gulf States and California. Nationally, crude oil refining capacity has dropped from 17.8 million barrels per calendar day (B/CD) to 15.1 B/CD since 1980, 32 per cent of that reduction occurring in Texas and Louisiana. Most dramatic was the recent layoff of over 1,200 workers, supervisors and managers at Texaco's huge Port Arthur refinery, about 40 per cent of its employment - additional to 2,000 jobs already lost in 1980-83. Formerly rated at 402,000 B/CD capacity, the streamlined operation is now rated at only 200,000 B/CD.

When refining capacity declined in the USA, 23 petrochemical plants were downgraded on the Texas Gulf Coast, implying partial or complete closure. Local petrochemical companies were also involved in 41 acquisitions and 16 joint ventures. But the greater activity involved upgrading existing facilities, i.e., on-site expansion of existing operations rather than building new plants. The Texaco 1983 Annual Report cites the Getty acquisition as part of a massive programme to upgrade its worldwide manufacturing system. Since early 1981, the company eliminated excess, noncompetitive capacity and upgraded remaining capacity by a $2.7 billion investment programme including 10 major construction projects. In 1983 the Chief Executive Officer of Texaco referred to an investment of $2 billion in its Port Arthur refining complex since its inception (1902), the largest investment by the company in any location.

Recent Trends in the Oilfield Equipment Industry
The recent decline in real value of production by the oilfield equipment industry coincides closely with worldwide drilling activity. Yet its future prospects do not depend solely upon stable or rising oil prices: US producers, who export about 54 per cent of their output, face stiff competition in overseas markets while home drilling activity will be strongly influenced by proposed tax revisions. Despite sparse comparable international data, the US market share of worldwide exports is upwards of 60 per cent so long term prospects are tied to both foreign drilling levels and to US competitiveness. During the high drilling demand period (1978-82), the US

apparently increased its foreign market share in terms of the value of US exports of oilfield machinery per operating foreign rig (in so far as this is a true measure of demand), or at least maintained it. Only the coincidence of increasing competition in a declining drilling market and the rising dollar value made US firms lose ground to foreign competitors in 1983 and 1984. The long term key to retaining a competitive edge is technology. US oilfield equipment is "state-of-the-art". Moreover, as ever more inhospitable sites are drawn into production (offshore, deep drilling, "Artic" production), the need for higher technology goods will increase. Fortunately, a 1985 study by the US International Trade Administration found no evidence of declining R & D expenditures during the recent decline in drilling activity. However, there is increasing quality and quantity of foreign competition. Experience gained in North Sea exploration and production has, in some oilfield equipment (notably seismic surveying), made French and British quality rival the US. Moreover, the number of foreign competitors is rising as a result of both a desire to avoid the vagaries of currency fluctuations through establishment of foreign subsidiaries and to raise "local content" in oil producing countries. For the first time, Saudi Arabia is demanding joint ownership of oilfield service operations and wants foreign firms to make products like rock bits, valves and oilfield tools locally. All this will shrink the world market share of US producers despite their technological sophistication.

A similar situation exceeds in rotary rig activity in the US averaging about 60 per cent of worldwide non-communist oil-well drilling, the overseas and US markets being equally important. The driving force behind this market is the US drilling activity levels which will increase partially because the severe drop in 1983 may have been an overreaction and recent federal lease sales and mergers temporarily depressed US activity. Moreover, two Congressional tax reform proposals, and the Treasury Department reform package, include repeal of percentage depletion allowances and current expensing of intangible drilling costs. Industry estimates project the net impact of such changes would send the US active rig count to under 1,900. Based on historical rig count-oilfield machinery manufacturing employment levels, this could reduce employment in the industry by about 8,500 jobs, 65 per cent of which would be lost in Texas.

UNDERLYING CAUSES OF STRUCTURAL ADJUSTMENT
IN THE USA

Causes of structural change in the oil industry are several and complex. However, most recent changes may be attributed largely to two forces that influence both producers and refiners: (1) changing international and domestic supply-demand relationships and (2) domestic public policy decisions. The more important continues to be the marketplace. The consequences of a changing oil industry for the Gulf Coast economy are simply a local playing-out of events that precipitated elsewhere.

Structural Change in Domestic Oil Production

The major influence on domestic oil production beyond all doubt is the international market price for crude oil - the OPEC "benchmark price" or the price for "Saudi Light". The former has been on a roller-coaster ride: from 1976 until 1981 it rose sharply to US $35 per barrel reflecting OPEC success in supply control, but since then it has fallen almost as sharply to just over $27 per barrel with some analysts forecasting a further decline to $10 per barrel as the cartels lose control over world oil supplies and prices.

Though rising oil prices harmed the national economy as a whole, they tremendously stimulated those states with substantial oil reserves, notably Texas, Louisiana, Oklahoma, Alaska and California where exploration and production became more profitable, encouraging a flurry of drilling activity. Between 1978 and 1981, for example, the number of active drilling rigs nationwide increased by almost 1,000 per cent, while real capital outlays for exploration and drilling more than doubled. The Federal Government's decision to deregulate oil prices contributed to this surge of activity, of course, but the major influence was the rapid increase in the OPEC benchmark price.

Short-term and long-term oil price influences differ since the former involve something that is known, the latter expectations. While short-term profitability is affected most directly by short-term fluctuations in the benchmark price, decisions concerning investment of capital in drilling and exploration are influenced more strongly by the anticipated long-term trend in prices. Upon the recommendation of many industry analysts and economists, enormous capital resources were committed to exploration and production during the late 1970s in the expectation that oil prices would continue to rise indefinitely, so fuelling rapid growth in drilling-related manufacturing producing oilfield equipment, drilling rigs and process control instruments. A large proportion of Gulf Coast manufacturing employment is concentrated in such industries.

Rising oil prices in the late 1970s also encouraged substantial exploration and drilling outside the United States, particularly in the North Sea. OPEC nations continued to expand production and other developing nations, like China, turned to exploration and drilling to enhance their meagre foreign currency earnings. As more nations became oil producers and supply increased at prices below the OPEC benchmark, US exploration and drilling shifted progressively from a regulated market which encouraged survival of marginal producers (who could pass prohibitive production costs on to consumers through the "fixed" price) to a deregulated market which tends toward efficiency, driving out marginal producers. Evidence of this lies in the fact that domestic drilling activity has returned to its 1978 level and real capital expenditures have declined by almost 30 per cent.

Structural Change in Domestic Refining

Similarly, domestic refining is undergoing structural change precipitated largely by the changing market for refined products. On the supply side, domestic refiners have been buffeted by increasing offshore competition; on the demand side, consumer purchases of refined products have been shrinking, disproving the assumption that the demand for refined products would increase despite increases in their price.

Increasing oil prices encouraged OPEC nations to develop integrated oil industries which produce and process crude oil. In every instance, they sought to increase their foreign currency earnings (especially US $) by capturing a share of the refined products market. For them, foreign currency earnings are critical for development projects. Having raised the expectations of their populations, many governments not unwisely perceive such earnings as the key to their survival. Although little planned capacity is yet operational, its impact will be great before 1989 because it is highly automated and possesses a critical advantage over American refiners whose labour costs are increasingly the only variable cost which can be controlled. Moreover, political constraints encourage developing nations to input raw materials to their refineries at below cost to maintain operations at full capacity.

Some measure of the potential impact may be gained from the beating American refiners have taken since 1980 from refiners in Western Europe and the Caribbean. Almost 50 per cent of the demand for refined products is for gasoline, and US gasoline imports from those regions have grown annually from 4 per cent of domestic consumption in 1981 to 11 per cent in 1985. Some increase is due to the strength of US $ but mostly to the growing uncompetitiveness of American refiners who have lost comparative advantage: it is more expensive to produce gasoline in the USA than elsewhere because domestic refineries are comparatively old and labour-intensive. Furthermore, more refiners are competing for a smaller market as higher oil and refined product prices did discourage demand, largely through conservation. Industry analysts predict gasoline demand will be 25 per cent below the 1984 level by 2000.

EMPLOYMENT CONSEQUENCES OF RESTRUCTURING

Every metropolitan area along the Gulf Coast has experienced large declines in manufacturing employment since 1980, with losses ranging from 4.8 per cent in Lafayette to 33.3 per cent in Lake Charles (see Table 9.2). Clearly Beaumont-Port Arthur metropolitan statistical area (MSA) has suffered declines in both total non-agricultural and manufacturing employment. Houston and Victoria MSAs also lost significant manufacturing employment as did Galveston-Texas City and Corpus Christi on a smaller scale. Aside from Beaumont-Port Arthur, the other Texas Gulf Coast MSAs have posted small increases in total non-agricultural employment since 1977.

Manufacturing employment in the Golden Triangle (Beaumont-Port Arthur MSA) decreased by 32 per cent from December 1981 through December 1984 in the 42 largest industrial plants. Texas Employment Commission statistics for total manufacturing employment in this MSA reflect a 29 per cent decline for the same period. Table 9.3 shows employment trends in the surveyed firms aggregated by geographic area and industrial sector. Decline cannot solely be attributed to structural change in the oil industry. The USA underwent a major recession in 1981-82, with a significant local impact. Falling crude oil prices and uncertainty about future prices affected the Offshore Services and Ship Repair/Rig Fabrication sectors as oil exploration activities in the Gulf of Mexico declined in 1983. Shipbuilding and repair (SIC 3731) has been in a depression worldwide. These two of the local economy have lost 69.1 and 76.4 per cent respectively, of their December 1981 employment compared with 30.7 per cent in Oil Refining/Related Activities and 16.3 per cent in Petrochemicals. Little of these declines is likely to be recovered. Between 1970 and 1980 the Golden Triangle's population growth rate of 8.0 per cent was the third lowest of Texas' 26 MSAs and grew more slowly than any other medium-sized metropolitan area in the entire US Sunbelt during the 1970s. Between the April 1980 census and July 1, 1982, population in the Golden Triangle grew by more than 12,000 persons, or 3.3 per cent, but was the fifth lowest of the state's metropolitan areas.

Though population and employment growth have been weak since 1970, personal income growth has remained strong, matching or exceeding the national average. Both per capita income and median family income in the Beaumont-Port Arthur MSA were well above Texas averages in 1980, its poverty rate was more than two percentage points below the state rate. The future outlook is less than rosy. Most of the area's refineries and petrochemical plants are operating well below capacity and return to full production is not anticipated. Furthermore, petrochemical production is moving increasingly offshore, suggesting there will be little new construction in

Table 9.2: Employment Data – Gulf Coast MSAs.

(Thousands)

	1977		1980		Dec. 1984		% Change 1980–Dec.1984	
	Total Non-Agr.	Mfg.	Total Non-Agr.	Mfg.	Total Non-Agr.	Mfg.	Total Non-Agr.	Mfg.
Texas								
Beaumont-Port Arthur	142.8	40.0	148.7	38.5	141.0	30.5	-5.2	-20.8
Houston	1,173.6	195.1	1,439.3	240.2	1,539.7	197.2	7.0	-17.9
Galveston-Texas City	65.3	11.9	70.3	11.4	72.0	10.1	2.4	-11.4
Victoria	N.A.	N.A.	27.1	3.5	28.4	2.9	4.8	-17.1
Corpus Christi	104.3	13.1	124.7	16.1	131.0	14.7	5.1	8.7
Louisiana								
Lake Charles	54.0	11.3	66.3	13.5	58.0	9.0	-12.5	-33.3
Lafayette	58.1	3.2	78.8	4.2	90.4	4.0	14.7	-4.8
Baton Rouge	176.6	23.8	203.9	25.9	214.8	22.2	5.3	14.3
New Orleans	455.5	51.2	499.4	53.5	506.9	40.2	1.6	24.9

Source: Supplement to Employment & Earnings, States & Areas, Data for 1977–80, Bureau of Labour Statistics, Sept. 1981; Louisiana Department of Labor; Texas Employment Commission.

Table 9.3: Employment Trends in the Golden Triangle.

	No.of Firms (12/84)	Dec. 1981	Dec. 1982	Dec. 1983	Dec. 1984	12/81-12/84 Jobs Lost Number	%
I. Geographic Area							
Beaumont	18	13,930	10,896	10,887	10,715	3,215	23.1
Orange	8	8,535	5,049	4,589	4,660	3,875	45.4
Port Arthur	7	11,391	9,353	7,858	6,772	4,619	40.5
Mid Jefferson Co.	6	3,365	3,087	2,842	2,716	649	19.3
Silsbee	3	2,172	2,078	1,901	1,895	277	12.8
Total	42	39,393	30,463	28,077	26,758	12,635	32.1
II. Industrial Sector							
Oil Refining/Related Activities	8	13,087	11,528	10,371	9,065	4,022	30.7
Petrochemicals	16	10,751	9,998	9,353	9,002	1,749	16.3
Offshore Services	5	3,075	812	555	951	2,124	69.1
Ship Repair/Rig Fabrication	3	5,840	1,594	1,343	1,378	4,462	76.4
Paper/Forest Products	4	2,782	2,730	2,686	2,607	175	6.3
Others	6	3,858	3,801	3,769	3,755	103	2.7
Total	42	39,393	30,463	28,077	26,758	12,635	32.1

Source: John Gray Institute, Lamar University, Beaumont, Texas.

the Beaumont-Port Arthur MSA. As a result of a 40 per cent decline in the number of active drilling rigs in Texas since December 1981, demand for drilling machinery, pipe and oilfield services has dropped, substantially affecting many firms in the metropolitan area. Other major industries, such as steel, rubber and shipbuilding, are also in secular decline. At least $100 million of annual purchasing power has disappeared from the Golden Triangle (Beaumont-Port Arthur) economy as a result of Texaco's 1983 plant closure and, because of the strong linkages between refining and other industries and services, additional income and employment will be lost across Texas and elsewhere.

Much the same can be said of trends in the Galveston-Texas City, Houston and Corpus Christ MSAs, though Victoria is exceptional in its greater service sector growth. The economic outlooks for Galveston-Texas City and Corpus Christi may not match Texan growth. Two industries, petrochemicals and refining, are unlikely to expand; nor, therefore, is another significant local activity, construction, though, by contrast, the growth in health, education and tourism could bring job stability to Galveston. Greater Houston has less economic vitality than in 1980: substantially diminished population and income growth rates are being paralleled by net employment gains only in low-wage services which tend to mask large high-wage job losses in over-concentrated energy-related manufacturing. Thus the city's economy is being transformed by long-term structural changes, not simply temporarily depressed by short-term cyclical forces; because the MSA is hub of a larger energy-based regional economy experiencing these changes, which are vastly different from more diversified north and central Texan MSAs, Greater Houston's economic development community must revitalise the area with a broader manufacturing base.

The 5 Texas Gulf Coast MSAs have had variable unemployment rates. Beaumont-Port Arthur (recent peak in 1983 15.4 per cent; January 1985 13 per cent) and Galveston-Texas City (14.3 per cent; 12.0 per cent respectively) MSAs endured higher peak unemployment levels than the other 3 (10.0-12.2; 6.2-9.0) and have been unable to reduce their rates as much as the others.

The remaining 3 Gulf Coast MSAs in Louisiana - Lake Charles, Lafayette and Baton Rouge - have all registered substantial high-wage job losses in oil-related manufacturing which are not compensated by gains in low-wage service sector employment. As elsewhere in the Gulf, their petrochemical plants and refineries are operating well below capacity, and a return to full production is highly unlikely given the worldwide glut of oil and feedstocks, emerging offshore competition and the strong dollar, while in Lafayette there were also substantial job losses in oil and gas extraction, oilfield equipment manufacturing and the offshore shipping fleet.

THE NEED FOR A GRASSROOTS INDUSTRIAL POLICY

Recently, arguments about industrial change have focused on whether or not it threatens the future well-being of a city's, region's or the nation's economy. At one extreme, industrial change is viewed as a crisis: contraction of basic industries and the accompanying dislocation of workers are cited as evidence of the economic system's inability to effect efficiently and equitably a transfer of productive resources from declining to growing activities. More government intervention is required to resolve the crisis, and it has elicited a broad range of proposals variously described as "national industrial policy", "reindustrialisation policy", or "national sectoral policies". Lester Thurow, Robert Reich, and Felix Rohatyn argue for a revitalised Reconstruction Finance Corporation, Barry Bluestone and Bennett Harrison for central planning for nationalised industries, Gail Schwartz and Pat Choate for a permanent linkage between business and government, while the National Infrastructure Advisory Committee proposes a "national infrastructure fund".

At the other extreme, the problem of structural adjustment is minimised in the cynicism of Herbert Stein, Charles Schultze, Robert Crandall, and, most notably, Richard McKenzie, who, along with the Heritage Foundation, has waged a persistent "guerilla war" against national industrial policy through a steady stream of papers and the recently released Blueprint for Jobs and Industrial Growth. They claim the American economy has succeeded in adapting to a more competitive international environment and that any structural dislocations of people and property have arisen largely out of the failures of Keynesian demand-management policies pursued by the federal government since 1960.

Although they differ in both diagnosis and prescription, the two prevailing perspectives are the product of the neo-classical paradigm that has dominated American economic thought for the past half-century: that the US economy, in its "normal" state, is a closed system in equilibrium. Yet the neo-classical paradigm has constrained the industrial policy debate to pedantic arguments over the efficacy of intervention to return the economy to "normalcy", bringing to mind Thermistocles who said "I cannot fiddle, but I can make a great state from a little city"! Rather than focusing on policy initiatives to restore equilibrium, the debate might more appropriately consider the relevancy and desirability of pursuing that end. If the neo-classical view is replaced by one of the economy as an open system in dynamic dis-equilibrium, the notion of equilibrium as an achievable policy goal becomes irrelevant. The disequilibrium perspective has an intellectual history in the long-wave and business-cycle theories of Kondratieff and Schumpeter and has found more recent expression in industry and regional life-cycle theories. These theories explicitly reflect the choices of individual entrepreneurs registered in bulk in the marketplace. On a grander scale, Schumpeter's theory of "creative destruction" and the broader product cycle theories at the aggregate level suggest an open, not closed, economy that is characterised by incessant structural change.

The dynamic perspective establishes industrial change as a natural, indeed necessary, market process as opposed to an economic crisis demanding new governmental intrusions. Dislocations of workers and other productive resources that necessarily accompany structural change are seen not as evidence of market failure but, rather, as symptoms of an economy in the process of renewal, though the process may be painful. Because any form of intervention in the economy distorts the price signals that allocate productive resources among competing opportunities, costs and benefits cannot be evaluated with any degree of objectivity, despite the best traditions of neo-classical welfare economics. The implementation of either a "national industrial policy" or the modification of existing regulations, trade barriers, and subsidies that serve to protect certain industries necessarily entails the adoption of particular social and political agendas. The policy alternatives offered by the neo-classical paradigm, therefore, amount to nothing more than the allocation of sacrifice among winners and losers and and smack of an elitist corporate statism.

To the extent the industrial policy debate really reflects an over-whelming concern with adaptation to the new realities of the competitive marketplace, why not start from the bottom up instead of the top down? Why not consider a "grassroots" approach to industrial change that emphasises individual choice and the pursuit of new opportunities instead of the allocation of sacrifice? Grounded in a view of the economy as a dynamic system characterised by the break-up of established patterns of production and trade and the exploitation of new opportunities, the grassroots approach calls for a highly decentralised response to industrial change based on cooperative efforts by business, labour, industry and education at the local or regional level. The over-arching purpose of such an approach should be to foster an economic climate that encourages innovation and adaptation in response to an ever changing and increasingly competitive environment.

More clearly, perhaps, the grassroots approach is a legitimate extension of the cycle theories of industrial change usually ignored by neo-classical economists preoccupied with temporal concerns. Regions and localities should specialise in the production of commodities in which they have relative cost advantages and exchange them in the marketplace for products in which they have relative cost disadvantages. Recognising that terms-of-trade may have shifted, and, indeed, will continue to do so, each community must reassess its comparative strengths and weaknesses and pursue industrial and human resource development strategies that conform to these new realities.

Specifically, the grassroots approach should address three areas of importance to the long-term economic well-being of communities. First, efforts should be undertaken at the local level to promote greater economic diversification so that the community will be less vulnerable to the vicissitudes of the business cycle. Universities, for example, should assist local businesses and Chambers of Commerce in identifying opportunities for new and expanded ventures. Objective analyses that pinpoint an area's comparative strengths and weaknesses in geography, transport, infrastructure and human resources, and profiles of its existing industrial structure and backward and forward linkages, are a necessary prerequisite to systematic industrial recruitment or indigenous growth efforts. Many cities in the Sunbelt which have successfully expanded and diversified their economies - Dallas, San Antonio, Phoenix, Durham-Raleigh-Chapel Hill and Tupelo, to name a few - have spent a great deal of time and effort establishing solid working relationships with their local universities. University business and economics faculties should consider adopting the "extension service" concept of their cousins in the fields of agronomics and agricultural economics and provide small businesses with technical and managerial expertise and continuing education.

All too often the indigenous growth of small businesses is inhibited not by a lack of ideas, but by an ignorance of the mechanics of business management. Here too, universities should encourage small business development and entrepreneurship by bringing together potential entrepreneurs and venture capitalists. A leader in this field is the Institute for Constructive Capitalism at the University of Texas at Austin, whose director, George Kozmetsky, has become a travelling evangelist for entrepreneurship, preaching the virtues of small business development at the local level.

Second, both labour and management should work closely to reduce unnecessary, and ultimately harmful, conflict that adds to the turmoil already caused by structural change. Again, the academic community can make a positive contribution by heightening the public's awareness of labour-management issues and by providing a forum where all sides may be heard in an atmosphere of fairness and restraint. This is, perhaps, the most important component of the grass-roots approach since the industries most affected by industrial change have tended to be older manufacturing industries characterised by a fairly high degree of unionisation. The contraction of these industries over the past few years has been accompanied by a string of wage and work-rule concessions unparalleled in the modern history of labour-management relations. As a result of two years of concession bargaining in steel, autos, rubber and other major industries, the 1983 average contract wage settlement in the USA worked out to a mere 1.7 per cent, far below the increases recorded in the late 1970s.

Recent labour-management-university cooperative efforts in Southeast Texas can serve as a model for other areas of the nation hard hit by recession and structural change. The "Golden Triangle" has been a notable exception to the image of a prosperous, non-unionised "Sunbelt" and has suffered from a poor labour-management climate in recent decades. In fact, during the 1970s, strike days lost per worker in the Golden Triangle averaged 3.2 annually, a rate nearly eight times the national level. High rates of absenteeism and grievance filings also plagued area industries. Today the situation is much improved. No major strikes have been called in nearly two years; absenteeism is practically non-existent. Many industrial plants are reporting declines in grievances received and cases arbitrated, and several of the construction trade unions have accepted wage freezes. This change is dramatically highlighted by the successful conclusion of negotiations between the Oil, Chemical and Atomic Workers International Union (OCAW) and the oil industry earlier this year. For the first time in twenty years, agreement was reached without a strike and with moderate wage and benefit increases more or less in line with settlement patterns in other major industries.

Two factors conspired to bring about industrial peace. The first was the US economic recession and structural adjustment problems in the oil industry outlined above. But a second factor contributing to successful bargaining was the establishment of a cooperative, as opposed to adversarial, negotiating environment between labour and management well in advance of the contract deadline fostered by conferences, seminars and publications intended to: (1) increase the public's awareness of economic and competitive factors and their impact on collective bargaining; (2) improve individual and institutional relationships while honing the skills of the parties involved in negotiation; and (3) channel information to those directly involved with the bargaining.

Finally, the grassroots approach to structural adjustment must address the critical issue of human resource development. Industrial change invariably displaces workers and alters long-term employment prospects for a given region. Therefore, business, labour, industry and education must work diligently to train and retrain workers for tomorrow's jobs. Labour unions must expand and broaden apprentice programmes that focus on providing industrial workers with generic skills that can be transferred to new tasks. Business and industry must increase their investment in human capital through on-the-job training and advanced job-skills programmes. Universities can contribute to the adjustment process through continuing education programmes that emphasise vocational skills and rehabilitation and by sponsoring seminars for shop stewards, foremen, and managers to improve in-plant communication and supervision.

Moreover, business and education should work together to revise professional curricula in business, economics, and engineering programmes to better reflect the changing needs of the labour market. The University of Alabama, for example, has pursued a much publicised and highly successful programme of providing engineering and business students with internships on the shop floors in many of the state's industrial plants while Lamar University in Beaumont, Texas, has received substantial cooperation from the oil industry in establishing one of the most advanced CAD/CAM laboratories in the USA.

All these measures are directed at improving an area's business climate. Because they rely on voluntary initiatives by business, labour, industry and education, they are far more realistic and infinitely more desirable than the worn-out policies and programmes suggested by the neo-classical paradigm. The "grassroots" approach explicitly recognises a characteristic of industrial change that interventionists often choose to ignore – that basic economic activity in a particular location cannot be forced. Or, as Alfred Marshall so eloquently pointed out, that the spirit of enterprise is something in the air of a place, and the air may go stale. Rather than implement costly new programmes or modify existing ones that cannot halt or even mitigate industrial change, it would be far better to allow old structures to wither away and let new patterns of production and trade emerge on the basis of the uncoerced preferences of producers and consumers at the local and regional level. Intervention increases the likelihood of poor public sector investments that may serve only to prop up declining or stagnant industries, cities and regions. Not having to personally bear the risk or accept the responsibility for investment decisions, interventionists may make choices on the basis of personal, social or political agendas, with tax-payers at large bearing the cost. Should productive citizens in Tupelo, Mississippi be required to subsidise workers at an increasingly uncompetitive steel mill in Pittsburgh?

There is no defensible moral justification for such an arrangement. But unable to make their case on the grounds of efficiency, interventionists usually fall back on the "fairness" argument, asserting new policies, programmes and institutions are needed to bring about a more "just" allocation of resources. But what is "fair" about forcing citizens to expend resources in a manner they would not voluntarily choose? Why, to slightly rephrase the question, should tax-payers be compelled to support collectively a social and political agenda they might not choose to support individually? "Fairness", despite various philosophical contortions or collectivist pedantry is a highly subjective notion that is a function of individual preferences and not necessarily societal norms. The belief that some sort of national industrial "fairness" policy can be designed and implemented from the top down ignores the dynamics of the marketplace, national and international, and runs the risk of undermining individual prerogatives and local choice. A bottom-up "grassroots" approach holds greater promise for facilitating the structural adjustment process while at the same time promoting national economic efficiency.

Chapter Ten

ORGANISATIONAL AND REGIONAL CHANGES IN INDUSTRIAL
SYSTEMS: INTEGRATION OF THE OIL INDUSTRY INTO AN
ADVANCED ECONOMY

Eirik Vatne

Understanding present turbulence and socio-economic change
is still based on rather weak theoretical foundations. Neither
orthodox market economic theory nor Marxian theory have
developed satisfactory explanations of how and why economic
actors behave as they do, and what influence this has on
spatial development. It is necessary to develop a dynamic
theory based on empirical knowledge which is dialectic and
not static, stochastic and not deterministic. A promising
contribution to this important task by Nelson and Winter
(1982) should be of interest to geographers studying
industrial systems. They emphasise institutional factors, large
corporations as a dynamic force in development, technological
change, accumulation and the understanding of competition in
a not-so-perfect world.

In 1976 Ian Hamilton called for focus on multiregional or
transnational corporations as managers of new and complex
industrial systems (Hamilton, 1976a). McDermott and Taylor
(1982, p. 204) conclude that "attention in the future may
need to be directed more towards the network of interacting
organisations than towards individual organisational structures. Linkages, then, should be treated as points of intersection between organisations through which power relations
are established and played out."

The aim of this chapter is to examine how transnational
corporations organise industrial networks, which roles these
organisations play and what is their economic rationale.

INDUSTRIAL MARKETS AND ORGANISATIONS

Heterogeneous Markets and Networks
Orthodox understanding of competition in factor and product-
markets is that goods and services sold or bought in the
market are homogeneous. Many suppliers deliver identical
products to the market and all customers behave identically
vis-à-vis the products they demand. Under these conditions

179

prices would be the only information a firm needs to purchase goods and transactions would be conducted under certainty, the products being standardised and it would be easy to change suppliers.

An opposite view is that products and services traded in modern society are heterogeneous. For a range of standardised consumer-goods and services the assumption of homogeneity holds, but not for the majority, and combination, of goods and services traded between firms in the intermediate industrial market. The inputs in a complex industrial product or service involve many dimensions. The decision what to buy, and from which firm, is a difficult one, where price is only one of the pieces of information needed in the procurement process.

Many reasons explain development towards heterogeneous markets. One is the heterogeneity of human capital itself: differentiated organisation affects productivity. From this perspective firms are a surrogate for a market for their use of inputs. Another reason is the ever-increasing specialisation among firms leading to exploitation of economies of scale, increased efficiency, making them complementary and forcing them into integrated systems (Fredriksson & Lindmark, 1976). A third mechanism behind market heterogeneity is the law of "small number bargain". Few actors in segments of the market combined with uncertainty, complexity and human opportunism will increase the cost of doing transactions in the market and force firms to integrate in some way (Williamson, 1975).

Hägg and Johanson (1982) mention other more specific reasons for heterogeneity in intermediate markets. Firms in such markets are often strongly orientated by their own technology or even by the raw materials they use. Technology requires both machinery and people to operate it. The markets for machinery and, more widely, technology are highly heterogeneous. Many different machines and techniques exist to produce the same output, but with different factor combinations. Once made, investment in technology is often fixed and binds the firm to one type of technology for a certain time, often to one particular supplier. Because different firms invest at different points of time this creates heterogeneity in the market. Many plants today comprise highly sophisticated and complex technology. Over time this machinery is partly changed incrementally, involving new innovations and adjustment. This learning-by-doing process is influenced by a complex mix of different heterogeneous variables - different problems to cope with and different people to solve them.

Whatever reason for heterogeneity, it involves more than just a difference between suppliers or buyers. It also implies that various combinations result in segmented transactions to make them perform and manage to work together. This has important implications for how industrial markets are organised.

Organising Transactions

The above relates to transactions between legally independent organisations. The same argument can be used to understand the development of large multi-plant and transnational firms. Williamson (1981) argues that a firm should be understood more as a governance structure trying to economise on costs of doing transactions and less as a production function. Thus firms and markets should be treated separately as alternative governance structures. Organisational innovations such as the large multiregional corporations are, in his view, first of all designed to economise on transactions costs and not for anti-competitive purposes.

Transaction cost theory provides a powerful explanation of how and why transactions are organised in intermediate markets. Williamson argues that the market is typified by heterogeneity. Individual actors in the market have bounded rationality, the environment is characterised by uncertainty and few actors. This transaction environment creates opportunism among individual actors and, through this, closure of information channels, adding to uncertainty (Williamson, 1975). Opportunism produces transaction costs since uncertainty implies that not all information is trustworthy: some is meant to be disinformation. In such a world firms have to investigate, formalise agreements, double check, play safe and still run a risk. All this costs money and takes time.

How transactions are organised - in a classical market, inside networks of legally independent firms or through vertical integration and full internalisation - will depend on the attributes of the transactions. Of special interest are: the frequency with which transactions recur; the uncertainty to which transactions are subject; the degree to which transactions are supported by durable, transaction-specific investments (Williamson, 1979).

Based on these three variables a simple two-by-three matrix could be put together which describes six types of transactions (Figure 10.1).

To these six types of transactions Williamson adds three broad types of governance structures: one is non-transaction specific, a second semi-specific, a third highly specific.

Figure 10.2 shows a classical market, has a non-specific governance structure, dealing with standardised or homogeneous goods or services. Alternative purchase and supply arrangements are easy to work out, transaction costs are low and an entrepreneur only has to consult his own experience in deciding to continue a relationship or to change to another supplier.

Another type of governance structure is required when the transaction is no longer homogeneous or readily available

Figure 10.1: Illustrative commercial transactions (Williamson, 1979, p.247).

| | | Investment Characteristics | | |
		Nonspecific	Mix	Idiosyncratic
Transation	Low	Purchasing standard equipment	Purchasing customised equipment	Constructing a plant
Frequency	High	Purchasing standard material	Purchasing customised material	Site-specific transfer of inter-mediate product across successive stages

Figure 10.2: Matching governance structures with commercial transactions. (Williamson, 1979, p.253).

| | | Investment Characteristics | |
		Nonspecific	Mixed	Idiosyncractic
Transaction	Low	Market	Trilateral governance (Project organisation)	
Frequency	High	Governance	Bilateral Governance (Joint venture)	Unified Governance (Hierarchy)

in a market. Uncertainty and opportunism increase with occasional transactions of mixed or highly idiosyncratic kinds. Specialised investments needed to do transactions are vulnerable to change. Opportunity cost is much lower in alternative uses. To transfer assets to another firm would pose difficulties in asset valuation. In this case market relief is unsatisfactory: to set up a specific organisation to handle occasional investments will often involve prohibitive costs. Because the transaction is heterogeneous contracting is needed to take care of contingencies and policing to control the performance through to completion. In this case an intermediate institutional form is required. Trilateral governance implies that a third-party assistance must handle transactions, resolve disputes and evaluate performance instead of strict reliance on contracting. In the oil industry trilateral governance is a normal organisational structure when highly specific investments like offshore platforms are being built. Engineering consultants operate as third parties between the oil companies and the fabrication yards.

When mixed or idiosyncratic investments are necessary and transactions are recurrent, a specialised governance structure is needed. The transactions are non-standardised which makes reliance on market governance hazardous. Recurrent transactions permit the cost of specialised governance structures to be recovered, thus reducing opportunism and extensive contracting. Highly specialised investments require extensive specialisation by human and physical assets, their transaction not involving any obvious scale economies released through interm-firm trading that they buyer or seller is unable to realise through vertical integration. Thus WIlliamson argues that such transactions will be internalised. This sort of governance exists in the primary sector of the oil industry.

In cases of mixed investments the degree of specialisation is not so extensive. Outside procurement may be favoured by scale economy and cost control considerations. If so, some sort of contractual agreement has to be reached, both parties having an incentive to sustain the relationship because of bilateral dependence through specialisation. Because both are involved in a long term relation under uncertainty, flexibility is of crucial importance. To write a comprehensive contract under such circumstances, where all relevant future contingencies pertaining to the supply of goods or services are described and discounted with respect to both likelihood and futurity, is often impossible prohibitively expensive. In this case bilateral governance in a joint venture has to be built on trust.

All these governance structures appear in intermediate markets, but with a historical trend towards more investment-specific transactions through specialisation so that more transactions are internalised or organised inside networks and fewer transactions take place in a pure market situation.

LARGE CORPORATIONS AS ORGANISERS OF ECONOMIC ACTIVITIES

Large vertically-integrated corporations become big first of all, therefore, because they operate in segments of industrial markets where transaction-specific investment is high, transactions recurrent and logistics crucial. Internalisation enables these companies to economise transaction costs and operate more efficiently than a production system under market governance could do. Other important factors behind vertical integration are the quest for monopoly gains and the imperative of technology. But, as Williamson argues:

> "These mainly have a bearing on market shares and on the absolute size of specific technological units, but the decisions to make or buy, which determine the distribution of economic activity as between firms and markets, and the internal organisation (including both the shape and the aggregate size) of the firm are not explained, except perhaps in trivial ways, in these terms" (Williamson, 1981, p. 1537).

Large vertically-integrated corporations usually organise the production and marketing of mass-produced and often complex industrial outputs where scale-economies in one or several technological separable units are present. They usually take direct charge of R&D, assembly and marketing and several important units where highly transaction-specific investments are needed and vulnerability to disturbance is high. Besides what is integrated into the hierarchical governance structure of the firm, they also control a large production system as buyers or sellers of a substantial amount of intermediate products or services. For instance, more than 50 per cent of inputs to a modern car come from outside the car manufacturer, mainly from a few large producers of mass-produced components and equipment and a large number of smaller subcontractors delivering customised products and services (Frediksson & Lindmark, 1979).

A highly successful corporation in the capitalistic world would be able to use all types of governance structures for specific transactions, economising on transaction costs by externalising or internalising transactions in accordance with the nature of the service or product. In this respect a large corporation is as much a planner and coordinator of industrial activities, as a producer of industrial output. Thus large corporations build up extensive industrial networks for: recurrent supplies of semi-specialised products; occasional supplies of products and services which involve transaction-specific investments; and occasional and recurrent supplies of standardised products and services where there are no transaction-specific investments involved. Through these linkages they control inter-organisational networks where dependence could be mutual or singular.

Economising on transaction costs in an unpredictable world demands stability and development of mutual trust between buyer and seller. Opening up information channels and developing confidence are essential before transaction-specific investments and specialisation between firms will occur and this takes time. Two organisations have to adapt to each other by a learning-by-doing process, even for standardised products supply. This demands stability and heavy investments in external relations from both sides, with obvious implications for the possibility of new firms entering intermediate markets. To develop linkages in the segment of the market under market governance would be easier than in the more specialised segments where near and even long-standing contact with the buyer would be important. the power relations between firms would also be different depending on the market segment in which they operate. Under market governance the buyer has a significant possibility to control performance and change to another supplier, which leads to stiff competition and greater difficulties in realising a good profit on the transaction. Under an intermediate form of governance there will be mutual interest in keeping both parties satisfied.

Both in Marxian and his institutional economic theory the emphasis is on the large corporation as the "leader of the game". In Marxism economies of scale lead to large corporations, monopoly capitalism and the final destruction of the market economy follows a dialectic, but deterministic process. Traditional equilibrium theory interprets this process towards monopoly power as a market failure and deviation from static efficiency in which prices are close to marginal production cost.

Institutional economic theorists partly build their analysis of large firms on the ideas of Schumpeter. The same dynamics of competition, innovation and monopolisation will lead to "creative destruction" and new vitality and economic growth: a dialectical evolutionary, but stocastic process. Some companies will be more innovative than others, able to make use of economies of scale in R&D, production, distribution and management and by this earn a super-profit which gives larger forms greater capabilities for risk spreading and finance. Thus large corporations have an important role to play as progressive forces in economic growth and change. By the power they possess in the market, they are able to make a superprofit which destroys static efficiency. Most of this is ploughed back again into research and productive investments and paid back to society by their dynamic progressiveness through technological innovations and more efficient organisation of economic activity (Schumpeter, 1950).

This rather positive attitude towards large firms and transnational corporations as innovators and organisers of industrial production stands in sharp contrast to much analysis of large corporations in orthodox market theory and in almost every other discipline in social sciences. The glorification of free market competition and stigmatisation of oligopoly competition has created a climate in which critical analysis of large corporations and transnationals is often based on a very crude understanding of their role in economic development. Much emphasis has been laid on the power the multi-regional and transnational corporations have over national governments (Barnet & Müller, 1975), how they

185

manipulate markets and create hidden coalitions and monopoly power (Sampson, 1975), how they affect regional development both in developed countries (Holland, 1976) and developing countries (Amin, 1976). These corporations use space actively as a way of coping with ever-changing economic forces; and they create a new regional dimension of division of labour (Taylor & Thrift, 1982) which has obvious effects on where capital is accumulated (Lipietz, 1980).

Empirical work on multinational oil companies' operations in the UK and Norway indicates their power and influence on government and on local industry (Vatne, 1984). Yet more sophisticated analysis of large and multinational companies' role in economic and regional development is necessary, incorporating potential progressive dimensions.

INDUSTRIAL NETWORKS IN THE OIL INDUSTRY

Structure

The petroleum industry's prime activity is to explore and produce oil and gas from reservoirs underground, transport the product normally as crude oil to a refinery, process it and supply it to end-consumers as petrol, heating oil or gas, or derivates. As far back as Rockefeller and the Standard Oil Company in the USA the most successful companies operated these separate technological units in an vertically-integrated manner.

Transactions in the primary sector are recurrent and supported with highly idiosyncratic investments with few alternative uses. Thus transaction cost theory predicts a unified governance structure inside an organisation, though this does not imply that vertical integration is the only way to organise primary oil business activity as local conditions could change the outcome.

To study interorganisational production networks one must examine other parts of the industry where transactions are occasional or transaction-specific investment is of semi-specific nature. Exploration, drilling, construction of pipe-lines, production and refining facilities are all executed occasionally in the life of a larger oil company, though more frequently in major companies. Under these conditions a well defined network of legally independent and specialised firms has developed which in many respects functions as a closed, monolithic network organised form above with very strong links between organisations. Behaviour inside networks is influenced by the technology and historical evolution of such networks. Oil production started simultaneously both in the USA and Russia but American corporations mainly dominated the 19th century industry. Later Dutch, British and French capital joined in. Present-day "majors" Exxon (Standard Oil of New Jersey), Mobil, Socal (Chevron), and newly fused

Texaco and Gulf (American), Royal Dutch Shell (Dutch/ British), British Petroleum and the French CFP all have roots in the pioneering period when fierce competition was followed by cartel agreements, monopoly power, state intervention and imperialism (Sampson, 1975).

Ownership of mineral sources belongs to the owner of the land in the United States and this made it fairly easy to enter the industry. The number of operators, fast growth of the market, the domestic base, and a young and developing industry found a good environment in which to forge a specialised support industry. At the start oil companies did their own exploration and drilling, even refinery construction (Pratt, 1980). Entrepreneurs, mainly experienced oil workers and managers, soon took over drilling, tool manufacturing, well-services, construction of pipelines and production facilities. Thus, accompanying the process of vertical integration in the primary sector was an opposite, less pronounced trend toward a form of disintegration. Strong backward linkages developed from the oil companies to a variety of specialised, independent supply firms.

The European oil industry developed quite differently. Mainly operating abroad in colonies, it had to have strong links with the home government or ruling class in foreign countries where ownership of mineral resources usually belongs to the state. Operating overseas in the non-industrialised environment was a further hindrance to the development of many small-scale operators and may be the reason why European firms failed to develop an independent support industry. Apart from the French oil industry - which developed an integrated industry under state ownership - British and Dutch firms have depended on American support and oil technology to such a degree that many think the oil industry was an American 'invention' (Odell, 1983).

After World War II many countries have tried to develop an indigenous oil industry based on national technology. The Communist bloc has more or less succeeded in this task. So have France and Italy. Several South and Central American nations and Japan are reducing their dependence on US technology and companies (Cortes, 1976; Anez, 1978). State intervention has been a necessary condition in all of these cases.

Yet still it is only American and French oil firms which have developed integrated national support covering most international operations necessary to produce petroleum. Ties between oil and support companies have developed over many years through heavy investment of time, money and human capital by both parts. Technology in much of the oil industry develops as a learning-by-doing process, another factor for cooperation and strong links between companies.

Organising Procurements

The State owns the oil and gas resources on both the Norwegian and British continental shelves. The rights to explore and develop these resources are given to oil companies, normally in joint ventures because of the large amount of capital needed and the high risk involved. The owners of a licence bought in an auction or given under other regulative terms choose one - usually an experienced oil company - to act as an operator. It is the operator's responsibility to organise exploration, development and production. This way this is done differs between oil companies. Major companies with recurrent development projects off-shore tend to develop specialised services inside the firm such as the processing of seismic data, basic design of platforms, supervision of construction. Smaller companies only occasionally engage in off-shore development and depend on outside help. But the main pattern is that oil companies do not engage in occasional activities, holding a tight grip on planning, supervision and control, concentrating on long term production and maintenance of the different structures.

The buyer can choose to handle procurement of products and services himself or delegate it to a main contractor or a third party. Usually it is a mix of all three types, depending on the kind of product or service in question. Figure 10.2 shows that, usually, standard equipment and services will be supplied through sales from a supplier under normal market conditions. Typical examples would be tools, pipes, valves, drilling mud, steel or general commodity items. Often, purchases of smaller, standardised products are organised by the procurement department in the oil company acting as operator; that department in larger firms keeps an archive of potential suppliers.

Regarding procurement of larger, more complex products or services, market governance is not good enough. As theory states, more heterogeneous goods or services will demand another governance structure. The need for trans-action-specific investments, the time elapsing between ordering and delivery, the possibility of change underway, the problem caused if delivery is not on time or at the standard of quality specified - all create uncertainty and require opening up information channels. Purchases of this type include steel jackets, platform frames, different modules from power-station to accommodation facilities or long-term services like catering, transport or diving and pipe-laying or custom-made items. Under these conditions the two parties will be more dependent on each other the more transaction-specific investments have to be made in physical equipment, in streamlining the organisation, in developing mutual external linkages. Interdependence will be the greater the more the transaction involves development of new technology, which it often does in the high-technology part of the off-shore supply market. Trilateral governance is common to solve the problem of capacity and contingency when investments are very complex or during the construction of a huge production platform. An experienced engineering or consulting organisation is brought in to assist the oil company with project management, design, procurement and control of performance on site. Usually consultants are large specialised organisations with long experience and strong links to the oil companies.

If the operator is more experienced and doing large scale development more frequently, there will be a tendency towards a bilateral governance structure where the oil company will take charge of more of the management and direct transactions with suppliers. As Table 10.1 shows, the procurement department will emphasise more traditional market criteria when buying homogeneous supplies: availability, price and service are important attributes. They will be open to all producers of such standard items if they can compete, but even here the purchaser has a set of potential suppliers in his vendors' list which is very much coloured by the cultural background and experience he has. Satisfactory relations are not easily broken up. Even for standardised commodities there will be transaction costs involved in building up a new information system of potential suppliers when a company moves its operations to another region. At least it will take time to build new lists.

Table 10.1: Criteria used by oil companies when evaluating tenders for homogeneous and heterogenous supplies respectively.
Source: Johansen, 1983, p.66.

Homogeneous supplies	Heterogeneous supplies
(small orders)	(large orders)
1 Availability - prompt delivery	1 Keep to technical specifications - quality in production
2 Price	2 Organisational competence
3 Service and follow-up	3 Experience from earlier deliveries
4 Experience from earlier deliveries	4 Trust and near contact to the operator
5 Trust and near contact to the operator	5 Price

EVOLUTION OF NATIONAL NETWORKS TO SERVICE NORTH SEA DEVELOPMENT

Because most oil companies or engineering consultants are American and with their operations mainly in the USA, their information systems are mainly built up at the US head office. Thus one expects that American companies dominate the vendors' list even for items which are not oil specific. Their earlier operations abroad, mainly in non-industrialised countries, further favoured the established network.

This pattern is even more pronounced for heterogeneous items. In this market many items are of a one-off type, specially designed for one purpose, usually with the large oil companies doing basic design 'in house' and leaving detailed engineering to a smaller consultant. A smaller oil company could leave everything to an engineering consultant. A consultant delivers a very complex product where cooperation with the operator is very close. Under such circumstances it is important to share a common technical culture and as a consequence they choose those trained by American consultants.

Oil platforms or refineries are very complex engineering tasks. To manage the construction, fabrication is split into smaller units or modules. The task of designing is given to one specialised organisation, fabrication to several specialised firms because of the complexity, volume of the work and time limits. The designer is responsible for the integrated entity, fabricators only for small units constructed according to given specifications. American consultants and oil companies have designed for the North Sea and American-trained engineers use specifications built on US standard and measures which differ from European ones. This difference in technical culture between American designers and European manufacturers puts added communication and production costs on European tenders (Stinchcombe, 1979).

Thus long-standing relations between organisations are favoured; and early entry into a heterogeneous market is important for first mover advantages. Not surprisingly then, the start of oil development in the North Sea saw a very low national share in the supply market (Table 10.2). In 1972 the UK share was only 25-30 per cent (IMEG, 1972), in the Norwegian sector only 28 per cent in 1975 (Berrefjord and Heum, 1983). One reason for the low domestic share of this large market was obviously the lack of domestic experience of, and willingness to learn in this particular business. Yet, even taking account of this, Table 10.2 gives strong support to the argument that a national network of suppliers develops around oil companies and other large companies, more so for heterogeneous items than homogeneous. Under American or French control a large share comes from the home base, but figures for the Frigg field also show that the Norwegian share

Table 10.2: Share of supplies in the development of two early fields in the Norwegian sector (in per cent).
Source: Johansen & Vea, 1983.

Development Stages:	Ekofisk	I	Frigg II	III
Norway	17	17	33	53
France	–	37	39	29
USA	55	16	13	6
UK	5	22	7	6
Italy	10	–	–	–
Netherlands	9	–	–	–
Others	4	8	8	6
	100	100	100	100
Owners	US, F,I,N		F,N	
Operator	US		F	
Eng. consultant	US			

has risen over time as a result of changes in government policy.

Although domestic shares were originally low in both countries, the composition of these supplies was different. Norway had, through its strong maritime tradition in ship-building and shipping, a set of risk-willing entrepreneurs with established links to oil companies. They saw the market potential in the off-shore supply market and turned early to designing, building and operating support vessels, seismic ships and semi-submersible drilling rigs. British supplies were composed more of standard products from existing producers and deliveries from American subsidiaries operating in Britain (Cook and Surrey, 1983).

An extra problem, adding to difficulties facing domestic industry when it tries to enter the supply market, is the power-relation between a most professional, important purchaser and small fabricators. First the oil company or its consultant undertakes most higher-level work like design, purchasing, management and control-functions, leaving only welding to the yard which earlier designed its own products. The fabricator has to open up his organisation to the buyer and let outside controllers look into the organisation both beforehand and during the production period to control the performance and quality continuously. They are held respon-sible for delays, cost-increases and quality even if the problems are caused by outside events. To act against this is

191

a very complicated and costly contractual procedure before they can hope to change the contract. The right to innovations developed by the manufacturer under the project belongs to the oil company. On top of this, the contracts normally used are written by the legal department in the oil company according to American legal practice which is distinctly different from Norwegian practice (Berrefjord and Heum, 1983).

The separation of design, control and fabrication has caused special problems for many companies. Most fabricators in Norway have earlier been shipbuilders. Integration into the off-shore construction business has demanded a specialisation and fragmentation of firms. Engineering procurement and design tasks have been organised in separate firms located near the oil companies' head office. Fabrication is all that is left to the yards, together with a large bureaucracy to handle control functions. Fabricators are normally located along the coast in more marginal regions. Through the integration process a more vulnerable structure has been formed, subject to outside decisions and less able to operate flexibly.

GEOGRAPHY AND INDUSTRIAL SYSTEMS

Geographers have been preoccupied with the growth of the multi-regional corporation (Thomas, 1980) and the regional separation of headquarters, R & D departments and production plants (Watts, 1980). This separation has resulted in division of labour between regions, inside national states and between nations (Massey and Meegan, 1982). Externally-controlled branch plants in marginal regions are a product of this process and can even destroy the hope for indigenous growth and autonomy (Firn, 1975). Entry of multinational corporations can do the same (Hamilton, 1976b).

Surprisingly few studies have analysed the whole industrial network multinationals often control, the main emphasis being on intra-organisational behaviour and relations with the outside world, a sort of inside-out approach. Some studies have emphasised how multi-regional corporations link with local industry (McDermott, 1976), with a selection of subcontractors (Susman and Schutz, 1983) or with their differing task environments (McDermott and Taylor, 1982). Very few examine the network of organisations involved in industrial output, the power-relations inside such networks or regional production networks.

This is even more astonishing since the solid base of 'growth pole' theory emphasises the Schumpeterian understanding of entrepreneurs' and large firms' roles in a dynamic economy and the influence these organisations have on their business environment through inter-activity linkages (Perroux, 1950).

Traditionally geographers have studied the market governance structure of neo-classical location and the unified governance structure inside industrial organisations in the geography of enterprise. As Vea (1984) recommends, it would be wise to start thinking about organisational forms in industry as distributed along a continuum from simple small scale market adjusters to strong interfirm relations and large integrated hierarchies. All forms of governance structures usually co-exist, but their importance may vary. To understand better the relations between these structures and organisations - where growth impulses originate, how they spread through interfirm relations and what implication the division of labour has on accumulation - is critical to an understanding of what determines regional development.

The division of labour inside multi-locational corporations uncovers general processes which also are active inside larger production systems. The core of such a production system would be the large corporation as organiser of a complex set of production units inside or outside the organisation. Around this core is a set of firms with strong and mutual dependence on the large corporation, operating in a heterogeneous market where investment in open information channels demands stability. Extensive exchange of information and mutual development of products, services or markets often demands a common commercial/technological culture, physical proximity and leads to development of national (regional) networks. Such networks are part of the technological and commercial base that shapes many multinationals and any multinational corporation doing business abroad usually brings with it this network of firms (Hamilton, 1976b).

Outside this base of firms is a range of different suppliers operating under more 'normal' market conditions - selling homogeneous products or services in competition with other firms. In these markets it is not necessary to invest so much in mutual trust when the transaction-specific investment is non-existent and alternative supplies can be arranged. Price is of crucial importance and thus production tends to be located in more peripheral or marginalised regions.

Thus, when production systems are studied from a geographical perspective, it is not only necessary to study industrial systems as material-processing or information processing. Inter-organisational theory stresses the decision-making system and by that the power-relations inside inter-organisational forms. Large corporations play a role not only as production and marketing units, but also as organisers and distributors of work and capital.

The same division of labour, as within a multi-plant organisation between the corporate headquarters, specialised design or research organisations and more standardised production satellites, can be observed inside inter-organisational production systems where core firms are planners, controllers and designers, the peripheral firm producers under strong control from the core. Development and change in regional industrial systems from this perspective express the dynamism of production systems under different governance structures due to transaction-specific factors. How such systems develop over time and in space, how power is distributed inside the system between organisations, regions, what kinds of mechanisms generate growth, and how accumulation is distributed, are all questions which remain inadequately answered.

REFERENCES

Amin, S. (1976) Unequal Development, Harvester Press, Brighton

Anez, C.M. (1978) International Transfer of Technology for Oil and Gas Exploration and Production with Special Reference to the Venezuela Oil Industry, Ph.D. thesis, University of Sussex, Falmer

Barnet, R.J. and Müller, R.E. (1975) Global Reach. The Power of the Multi-National Corporations, Cape, London

Berrefjord, O. and Heum, P. (1983) Olje-Politikk. Oljepolitikken og Leveransespørsmålet, Tiden, Oslo

Cook, L. and Surrey, J. (1983) 'Government Policy for the Off-Shore Supplies Industry. Britain Compared with Norway and France', SPRU Occasional Paper Series No. 21, Science Policy Research Unit, University of Sussex, Falmer

Cortes, M. (1976) Transfer of Petrochemical Technology to Latin America, Ph.D. thesis, University of Sussex, Falmer

Firn, J.R. (1975) 'External Control and Regional Development: The Case of Scotland', Environment and Planning, 7, 393-414

Fredriksson, C. and Lindmark, L. (1976) Nationella och Lokala Productionssystem - en Strukturstudie av Svenskt Näringsliv., Inst. för Företaksekonomi. Umeå University, Umeå

Fredriksson, C.G. and Lindmark, L. (1979) 'From Firms to Systems of Firms: A Study of Interregional Dependence in a Dynamic Society' in F.E.I. Hamilton and G.J.R. Linge (eds.), Spatial Analysis, Industry and the Industrial Environment Volume 1: Industrial Systems, Wiley, Chichester, pp. 155-186

Hägg, I. and Johansen, J. (eds.) (1982) Företag i natverk - ny syn pa Konkurranskraft, Studieförbundet Näringsliv och Samhäll, Stockholm

Hamilton, F.E.I. (ed.) (1976a) The Organisation of Spatial Industrial Systems, London School of Economics, London

Hamilton, F.E.I. (1976b) 'Multinational Enterprise and the EEC', Tijdschinft voor Economische en Sociale Geographie, 67, 258-78

Holland, S. (1976) The Regional Problem, MacMillan, London

IMEG (International Management and Engineering Group of Britain Ltd.) (1972) Study of Potential Benefits to British Industry from Off-Shore Oil and Gas Resources of the UK, HMSO, London

Johansen, E. and Vea, E. (eds.) (1983) 'Utvinningstempo og Norsk Industri', Report No. 33. The Institute of Industrial Economics, IIE, Bergen

Johansen, E. (1983) 'Hvordan oppna Leveranser til Oljevirksomheten?' in T. Reve (ed.), Leveranser til Oljevirksomheten. Strategi og Styrino, Universitetsforlaget, Bergen

Lipietz, A. (1980) 'The Structuration of Space, the Problem of Land, and Spatial Policy' in Carney, Hudson and Lewis (eds.), Regions in Crisis, St Marins Press, New York

Massey, D. and Meegan, R. (1982) The Anatomy of Job Loss. The How, Why and Where of Employment Decline, Methuen, London

McDermott, P.J. (1976) 'Ownership, Organisation and Regional Dependence in the Scottish Electronics Industry', Regional Studies, 10, 319-335

McDermott, P. and Taylor, M. (1982) Industrial Organisation and Location, Cambridge University Press, Cambridge

Nelson, R.R. and Winter, S.G. (1982) An Evolutionary Theory of Economic Change, The Belknap Press of Harvard University Press, Cambridge, Mass.

Odell, P.R. (1983) Oil and World Power, Penguin, Harmondsworth

Perroux, F. (1950) 'Economic Space: Theory and Applications', Quarterly Journal of Economics, 64, 89-104

Pratt, J.A. (1980) The Growth of a Refining Region, Jai Press Inc., Greenwich, Conn.

Sampson, A. (1975) The Seven Sisters. The Great Oil Companies and the World They Made, Hodder and Stoughton, London

Schumpeter, J. (1950) Capitalism, Socialism and Democracy, Harper and Row, New York

Stinchcombe, L.A. (1979) 'Delays and Project Administration in the North Sea', Report No. 14. The Institute of Industrial Economics, IIE, Bergen

Susman, P. and Schutz, E. (1983) 'Monopoly and Competitive Firm Relations and Regional Development in Gobal Capitalism', Economic Geography, 161-178

Taylor, M. and Thrift, N. (eds.) (1982) The Geography of Multinationals, Croom Helm, London

Thomas, M.S. (1980) 'Explanatory Framework for Growth and Change in Multi-Regional Firms', Economic Geography,

195

56, 1-18
Vatne, E. (1984) 'Integration of the Oil Industry into an Advanced Economy. Organisational and Regional Changes in International and National Industrial Systems', Discussion Paper No. 7/84. The Institute of Industrial Economics, IIE, Bergen
Vea, E. (1984) 'Spatial Analysis of Industrial Organisations: An Inter-Disciplinary Perspective', Discussion Paper No. 3/84. The Institute of Industrial Economics, IIE, Bergen
Watts, H.D. (1980) The Large Industrial Enterprise: Some Spatial Perspectives, Croom Helm, London
Williamson, O.E. (1975) Markets and Hierarchies: Analysis and Anti-Trust Implications: A Study in the Economics of Internal Organisation, Free Press, New York
Williamson, O.E. (1979) 'Transaction-Cost Economics: The Governance of Contractual Relations', The Journal of Law and Economics, 22, 233-262
Williamson, O.E. (1981) 'The Modern Corporation: Origins, Evolution, Attributes', Journal of Economic Literature, XIX, 1537-1568

Chapter Eleven

SPATIAL IMPACTS OF ORGANISATION CHANGE
IN HUNGARIAN INDUSTRIAL ENTERPRISES

Györgyi Barta

In Hungary, especially since the early 1960s, development and
expansion of industry led to a cyclically-repeating process of
concentration of enterprise organisation with multi-plant
enterprise organisation becoming the main form. Resultant
spatial separation of parent companies from their branch
plants brings about new problems and types of relationship.
Differences of interests arise, yet branch plants have much
less chance of asserting their claims owing to their dependence on the parent. Branch plant autonomy is limited. Thus,
industrial development of an area can be influenced by a
structure comprising mainly branch plants belonging to
distant parent companies and also independent, locally-
managed industrial enterprises. Spatial analysis of Hungarian
industrial organisation is still in an initial stage. A
countrywide examination is now under way to reveal which
towns can be considered industry-directing centres and what
kind of attraction these centres have.

ECONOMIC PROCESSES SHAPING INDUSTRIAL
ORGANISATION

Enterprise organisation and its spatial dimensions in Hungary
were shaped by economic and political measures which con-
tradicted each other until the late 1960s (Berend, 1979). The
new economic mechanism was introduced in 1968, and opened
up a wider scope for business activities of enterprises,
expanding their independence in investment. Yet between 1973
and 1977 strong central efforts were made to restrain
economic reform, especially by a series of enterprise
amalgamations designed to reinforce central government
control.

Economic and Industrial Decentralisation
Two decisive sources of industrial investments should be
analysed in Hungary: the central State budget; and the

197

resources of state and cooperative industrial enterprise. The proportion of central state investments has been declining since 1968 to the point where in the 1970s enterprises account for about 54-56 per cent of all state and cooperative investments in industry (Fodor, 1982). Yet in the 1960s and 1970s enterprise investment to expand production met with difficulties in big cities because of shortages in labour supply. This was especially acute in Budapest where the lack of space and administrative controls on industrial expansion and labour immigration were added constraints. By contrast, there was plenty of labour in industrially underdeveloped and mostly agricultural areas, provincial towns and villages, which during these 15 years thus attracted hundreds of larger and smaller plants (Barta and Enyedi, 1981).

Spontaneity was typical of their spatial dispersion: the process was not planned territorially. Classical location theorists have argued that transport was the major determinant of plant location. However, in the 1960s and 1970s, the Hungarian transport tariff system had a minimal effect on the choice of branch plant location. Tariffs were increased only recently – indeed, after large scale industrialisation had occurred. More important, industrial enterprises charge the consumers with increased costs of production and transport.

Although transport costs did not directly influence the distance between the parent and enterprise and its branch plant, there is a marked correlation between the distance of branch plants from their parent companies and the frequency of branch plant occurrence. In the years 1970-75 half of the 300 plants opened in villages in Hungary were located less than 50 km from parent companies, a further 20 per cent no more than 100 km away. The average distance separating these 300 branch plants from their parents was 77 km. Thus distance was an important motive for the parent, indicating that access is a fundamental requirement in choosing plant location. Access not only depends on distance and transport facilities, but also on telephone and telex connections and personal local knowledge. In addition, however, the distance at which a branch plant is located from the parent also depends on the industrial 'capacity' of the headquarters' settlement of the parent and its surrounding settlements and on the industrial development potential of the parent enterprise. In Budapest, for instance, there was such an acute labour shortage that enterprises established branch plants at more distant points. Only 25 per cent of the branch plants set up between 1970 and 1975 by Budapest parents were within 50 km from the capital, a further 20 per cent within 100 km; 55 per cent were located further away.

Regional policy and planning neither established guidelines and governance of this process, nor did it reckon with the degree, directions and motives of dispersion. Only later was it evaluated and criticised. Many experts agree that the location of branch plants in large numbers, stimulating wide-spread small town and village industrialisation, was a harmful spontaneous process from the industrial development view-point, which frittered away investment and diffused out-of-date industry of low standard to rural areas. As rural industrialisation was virtually without any conceptional foundation it was consequently quite accidental. What kind of industrial structure emerges and whether a kind of division of labour is formed among the branch plants established in certain settlements were all questions unanswered prior to the initiation of the process. In the event, separation of pro-duction facilities led to great increases in transportation, so raising production costs.

Experts dealing with regional and settlement development have primarily emphasised the beneficial effects generated during industrial decentralisation and industrialisation of small towns and villages. The living conditions of people in industrialising settlements certainly improved, infrastructure development accelerated, and industrial dispersion made a great number of settlements small "growth poles".

Both these two extreme views contain real, indisputable elements (Enyedi, 1980). Yet decentralisation was dictated by the Hungarian economic conditions and mechanisms of the time. Continuous forced growth, investment constraints, cheap labour, the lower priority accorded to efficiency, the deformed price system, all shaped industry in those years. The spatial dispersion of industry was merely connected with the development of national industry and primarily served industrial enterprise interests (Szegö, 1976). Social aspects such as creating employment, only played a minor role.

Amalgamations of Enterprises

This practice of locating industry undoubtedly led to spatial centralisation as the number of control centres hardly increased, while plants were widely dispersed in the country.

The process of enterprise amalgamations, having been renewed after 1945, also increased the territorial central-isation of industry, though in another way (Inzelt, 1978; Laki, 1982). After all, each enterprise could undertake the location of industrial plants, so long as it possessed adequate funds. Yet amalgamations are started by administrative decisions. In selecting the acquiring and acquired enterprises not only did the market conditions (specialisation, capital, skills, production capacity) but - sometimes more effectively - the directive political and power factors play the more important part. Amalgamations were most often initiated by large enterprises. In the long run the process increased the number of the really powerful industrial centres and weakened the independence of former industrial centres. The growth and decline of enterprise amalgamations reflected different economic periods. From 1962 to 1964 the number of industrial enterprises decreased by nearly a third, but by 1967-68 this process had stopped and was even slightly reversed. Then after 1972 amalgamation recommenced, reaching a peak in 1976-77, and showed the strength of central power. Since 1979 the process has slackened. Yet it is also clear that centrally-initiated counter-processes, such as the disintegration of mismanaged large enterprises and unprofitable trusts, were also attempted.

As periods of industrial expansion and amalgamations of enterprises more or less overlapped, a very strong and in many cases unequal competition developed for labour in certain areas. This became clear-cut especially at the beginning of the 1970s, when all labour reserves were exhausted throughout the country. As a consequence, the size structure of the companies changed considerably (Révész, 1978). The proportion of the enterprises employing fewer than 100 workers declined from 15.7 per cent in 1965 to 10.7 per cent in 1970 and 6.6 per cent in 1980 (Table 11.1). It is clear, too, that there was an increase in the number of large enterprises.

Since 1980 these tendencies have begun to be reversed and the proportion of enterprises in every size category employing up to 2000 workers increased. Most amalgamations occurred in the engineering and light industries, especially in cosmetics, chemicals, insulating materials, silk, olive, confectionary, rubber, and in the cement and lime industries.

Changes in the Form of Ownership
Changes in ownership cannot be separated from the previous phenomenon. In Hungary industrial enterprises are state- and

Table 11.1: Size Structure of Enterprises in State Industry.

Size groups of manual workers (persons)	1970	1973	1975	1978	1980	1980
0 - 100	10.7	10.5	9.1	6.7	6.6	7.4
100 - 1000	53.9	54.5	54.3	47.9	49.9	50.5
1000 - 2000	15.8	15.8	16.2	20.7	20.5	21.6
2000 - 5000	14.3	14.0	15.3	18.6	17.5	16.2
5000 -	5.3	5.2	5.1	6.1	5.5	4.3
	100.0	100.0	100.0	100.0	100.0	100.0

Source: Statisztikai Evkönyv 1982 (Statistical Yearbook 1982), Central Statistical Office, Budapest, 1983.

CHANGE IN HUNGARIAN INDUSTRIAL ENTERPRISES

Table 11.2: Distribution of Industrial Enterprises by Form of Ownership, 1965-1982 (percentages).

	1965	1970	1975	1980	1982
Ministerial	30	32	34	38	43
Local councils	20	18	16	12	10
State	50	50	50	50	53
Cooperative	50	50	50	50	47
Soc. Ind. total	100	100	100	100	100
According to the number of employees					
Ministerial	80	78	78	81	80
Local councils	9	9	8	6	6
State	89	87	86	87	86
Cooperative	11	13	14	13	14
Soc. Ind. total	100	100	100	100	100

Source: Megyei Statisztikai Evkonyvek (County Statistical Yearbooks), Central Statistical Office, Budapest.

cooperative-owned. The private sector is insignificant, in 1980 producing only 0.7 per cent of gross production, and employing 2.8 per cent of all industrial employees. The state-owned enterprises are under the guidance of either ministries or the county and town councils (Table 11.2). Most of the acquiring enterprises were controlled by the ministerial sector and while amalgamations mostly occurred within the same ownership type, quite an important change was brought about by the takeover of some council-owned industries by enterprises in the ministerial sector. Out of 325 council-owned enterprises in 1970, only 133 remained in control in 1982. Nearly 70 per cent of the acquisitions took place in the same county, i.e., both the acquiring and the acquired enterprise were located in the same county; a fact, however, which showed the active participation of the local councils in supporting these processes. One reason for the lack of concern showed by the councils was probably that most local enterprises, which by their specialisation were performing mostly service functions, operated rather more often at a loss than at a profit. County and town councils established industrial enterprises to reduce the labour surplus of their territories. The financial resources of the councils proved to be too limited to invest adequately in their enterprises. There was also a lack of professional administration and competence which further

Table 11.3:   Size Structure of Enterprises in Cooperative
Industry, 1973-1982 (percentages).

Size groups (the number of manual workers)	1973	1975	1978	1982
- ,100	41.4	36.4	13.9	11.0
100 - 1000	58.1	63.0	83.2	86.7
1000 - 2000	0.5	0.6	0.5	2.0
2000 - 5000	-	-	0.4	0.3
	100.0	100.0	100.0	100.0

Source: Statistical Yearbook 1982, Central Statistical Office,
1983.

disadvantaged their enterprises. Thus the councils, in having
seemingly removed hidden or perceptible unemployment, were
then at pains to get rid of their enterprises. Clearly the
decrease in council-owned industry led to the emergence of
dependency of the counties on distant industrial centres and
to the decline in the role of local management in directing
industry on its own territory (Román, 1978; Szegö, 1976).
      After 1972 similar processes occurred in the cooperative
industry, though for other reasons. Cooperatives attempted to
raise their prestige by enlarging plant sizes in an attempt to
defend themselves effectively against state-owned large enterprises by developing monopoly in certain product lines (see
Table 11.3). Concentration within the cooperative sector
resulted from the merger of smaller cooperatives into larger,
stronger ones (Varga, 1979). Another process of concentration followed from a decline in the industrial service network: multi-plant cooperatives and council enterprises often
closed some of their plants. Indeed, between 1965 and 1980,
10 per cent of the plants of cooperatives and 40 per cent of
the branch-plants of enterprises owned by local councils
ceased to operate. Physical closure generally only involved
the small plants with 5-20 workers, the larger ones employing
50-200 being reorganised, incorporated, and their specialisation changed but not liquidated (Schweitzer, 1982).

TERRITORIAL CENTRALISATION IN INDUSTRY

Until the mid-1970s spatial decentralisation took place: the
proportion of employment and output in Budapest decreased
while the industrial significance of the provinces, towns and
villages increased. The gap between industrially developed

and underdeveloped regions narrowed (Table 11.4). In the same period the spatial decentralisation of industrial production was accompanied by a cyclically fluctuating, but permanent, territorial centralisation of industrial enterprise control. The result of these two processes was the increasing separation of the place of production from that of administration. One expression of this was that multi-plant enterprises multiplied but more plants belonged to the same enterprise. Between 1965 and 1980 the average number of plants owned by one enterprise increased from 5.8 to 6.4. Some industrial centres thus extended their influence over a number of counties or even throughout the country.

Table 11.5 shows the great difference in size between Budapest and other Hungarian cities. But it also indicates that these towns organise and carry out a great part of their industrial activity outside their city, and, in some cases, especially Budapest, the greater part of employment in their own enterprise being located outside the town. The changes during the 10 years in this respect divide the larger cities into two groups, except for Székesfehérvár where the out-of-town industrial activity remained insignificant. Enterprises in towns industrialised previously (Budapest, Győr, Miskolc) have more branches spread in out-of-town areas. Cities having a briefer industrial past (Debrecen, Nyiregyháza, Kecskemét) could still expand within the city, mainly because the increase in population in these cities (22-53 per cent) exceeded that (2-8 per cent) of the former group.

Resolutely-directed relocation of industry or the spontaneous moving out from the capital (Simon, 1976) or other bigger cities are not a specifically Hungarian phenomenon. Between 1972 and 1982 the number of industrially employed in Vienna decreased by 26 per cent, so that it is not so surprising that in Budapest in the same period industrial jobs decreased by 35 per cent, yet only a small part of this could be explained by relocated industry. By contrast, nearly a half million industrial jobs could be relocated from Paris into the French provinces (Bastié, 1973).

Probably such a level and permanent increase of organisational centralisation in one city within a country, as Budapest in Hungary, is a rather rare phenomenon in the world. The change of industrial structure in big cities such as the development of new branches, relocation of traditional branches, enterprise centralisation - which is also widespread in developed countries, if not on such a level as in Budapest - increased the concentration of white-collar workers. The control centres of the industrial enterprises can more easily tolerate the greater or smaller distances from their own branch plants than separation from the intellectual climate and commercial-cultured environment localised only in big cities.

A link can be traced between the proportion of cadres taking part in management and the economic independence

203

CHANGE IN HUNGARIAN INDUSTRIAL ENTERPRISES

Table 11.4: Territorial Decentralisation of Industry 1965-1982 (percentages).

Type of Region	Number of Industrial employees		Fixed assets stock		Production*	
	1965	1982	1965	1982	1965	1980
Budapest	41.1	24.3	30.8	22.3	36.2	25.1
Country	58.9	75.7	69.2	77.7	63.8	74.9
Towns**	37.6	49.4	45.7	56.7	-	-
Villages	21.3	26.3	23.5	21.0	-	-
Undeveloped regions***	24.9	37.3	16.9	28.9	22.8	37.2
National	100.0	100.0	100.0	100.0	100.0	100.0

* Territorial distribution of the production in an approach counted by various methods: in 1965 on the basis of corrected national income, in 1980 on the basis of net national product (Bartke, 1971; Barta, 1973, 1977; Nemes Nagy, 1984).
** Excluding Budapest.
*** The area of the Hungarian Great Plain and South-Transdanubia (about half of the country.

Source: Territorial Statistical Yearbooks 1965, 1982, Budapest Statistical Yearbooks 1965, 1982, Central Statistical Office, Budapest.

level of a region (Planque, 1983). Similar analyses were also carried out in Hungary by Futó-Csillik (1985), though he divided Hungary only into two areas, Budapest and the provinces. Instead of the "directing force" he used the proportion of white-collar workers within industrial employment. The independence index was counted on the basis of the proportion of plants whose headquarters are also in provincial cities. The conclusion was that in Hungary, too, the independence and the intellectual significance of the provinces decreased in the period under survey (1971-82). That analysis touches on the problem originating in the overcentralised structure of the economy: the directing centre taps the intellectual capital of the provinces, which would otherwise be a basic condition of their further development. Thus despite the reduction in spatial differences in production, the most dynamic control elements of industry remained in Budapest. Even though industrial control also increased in some other cities, its significance fell far behind that of Budapest. A perceptible differentiation has come about among the counties according to the scale of their dependency. It is strongest in counties in neighbourhood of the

CHANGE IN HUNGARIAN INDUSTRIAL ENTERPRISES

Table 11.5:   Industry Locating Activity of the Big Cities of Hungary (over 100,000 inhabitants), 1972 and 1982.

Towns	1	2		3		4	
	1982	1972	1982	1972	1982	1972	1982
Budapest	2064	431	536	51	81	47	43
Miskolc	211	47	49	48	65	3	4
Debrecen	205	43	44	42	39	2	3
Szeged	175	49	67	43	58	2	2
Pécs	173	59	63	71	65	3	3
Györ	127	73	75	37	67	3	4
Nyiregyháza	115	65	48	70	45	1	1
Székesfehérvár	108	27	27	11	13	1	1
Kecskemét	100	59	37	80	60	1	1

1   Population of the cities in 1982 (000s).
2   Number of settlements outside the town where the parent companies of the town have branch plants.
3   Proportion of employees in branch plants outside the town as a percentage of those employed in the parent companies of the town.
4   Proportion of employees in towns and their attraction areas together (to the industrial employees of the country).

Source: Industrial plant data 1972, 1982 (aggregated from the non-published data of the Central Statistical Office).

most significant industrial centres, especially Budapest, and the recently industrialising areas of west Transdanubia.

RESEARCH NEEDS

The dispersion of industrial production in Hungary in the 1960s and 1970s was accompanied by a very remarkable territorial centralisation of control functions. In future the task of research is to examine whether the centralised industrial structure hinders the development of industry itself or balanced socio-economic progress of the provincial areas of the country. This is not at all a simple task, since the answer to this question lies inside the multi-plant industrial enterprises. It may be uncovered by exploring the existing differences of interest between the parent companies and their branch plants. But this kind of information is usually kept a well-guarded enterprise secret, as all over the world.

CHANGE IN HUNGARIAN INDUSTRIAL ENTERPRISES

REFERENCES

Barta, Gy. (1973) 'Magyarország Gazdasági Fejlödése 1960-tol 1970-ig Megyei Osszehasonlitás Tükrében' (Economic Development of Counties in Hungary from 1960 till 1970), Földrajzi Ertesitö, 2-3, 215-38.
Barta, Gy. (1977) 'A Területi Gazdasági Különbségek Változása 1960-1975 Között' (Change of Regional Economic Differences between 1960 and 1975), Teruleti Statisztika, 5, 377-391.
Barta, Gy. and Enyedi, Gy. (1981) Iparosodás és a Falu Atalakulása (Industrialisation and the Transformation of Villages), Közgazdasági és Jogi Könyvkiadó, Budapest.
Bartke, I (1979) 'A Gazdaság Területi Szerkezetének Atalakulásáról' (On the Change of the Regional Structure of Economy), Gazdaság, 4, 66-83.
Bartke, I (1971) Az Iparilag Elmaradott Területek Ipari Fejlesztésének Föbb Közgazdasági Kérdései Magyarországon (Main Economic Problems of Industrial Development of Industrially Undeveloped Areas in Hungary), Akademsei Kiadó, Budapest.
Bastie, M.J. (1973) 'La Décentralisation industrielle en France de 1954 a 1971', Bulletin Association Géographes Francais, 408-9, 561-8.
Berend, T.I. (1979) A Szocialista Gazdaság Fejlödése Magyarországon 1945-1975 (Development of Socialist Economy in Hungary 1945-1975), Kossuth Könyvkiadó, Budapest.
Enyedi, Gy. (1980) Falvaink Sorsa (The Prospects of our Villages, Magvetö Kiadó, Budapest.
Fodor, L. (1982) Lépéskényszerben a Magyar Ipar (Hungarian Industry under Pressure of Change), Kossuth Könyvkiadó, Budapest.
Futo, P. and Csillik, P. (1984, typescript) Budapest Ipara Nemzetkozi Osszehasonlitasbán (Industry of Budapest in an International Comparison), Városépitesi Tudományos és Tervezö Intézet, Budapest.
Inzelt, A. (1978) 'A Vállalati Centralizációról' (On Enterprise Centralisation), Gazdaság, 2, 58-77.
Laki, M. (1982) 'Megszűnés és Osszevonás' (Liquidation and Amalgamation), Ipargazdasági Szemle, 1-2, 242-9.
Nemes Nagy, J. (1984) 'Az Ipari Nettó Termelés Területi Arányai és Osszefüggései a Területfejlesztéssel a Nyolcvanas Evek Elején' (Regional Distribution of Industrial Netto Production and Connections to the Regional Development at the Beginning of the 1980s), Teruleti Statisztika, 1, 1-12.
Révész, G. (1978) 'Iparunk Vállalat és Uzemnagyság Szerinti Szerkezete' (Size Structure of Industrial Companies and Branch Plants), Gazdaság, 3, 55-75.

Román, Z. (1978) 'A Magyar Ipar Szervezeti Rendszere' (Organisational System of Hungarian Industry), Ipargazdasági Szemle, 3, 7-51.

Schweitzer, I. (1982) A Vállalatnagyság (Size of Enterprises), Közgazdasági és Jogi Kiadó, Budapest.

Simon, A. (1976) 'A Fövárosi Iparkitelepitési Határozatok Végrehajtása' (Realisation of Decisions for the Relocation of Capital Industry), Területi Statisztika, 5, 518-523.

Szego, A. (1976) 'A Területi Erdekviszonyok, a Központositott Ujrafelosztás és a Területi Igazgatás' (Regional Interests, Redistributional System and the Regional Management), Szociológia, 3-4, 420-42.

Varga, Gy. (1979) 'Vállalati Méretstruktura a Magyar Iparban' (Size Structure of Hungarian Industrial Enterprises), Gazdaság, 1, 26-44.

Chapter Twelve

CONTROLLING THE TERRITORIAL PRODUCTION
COMPLEX CREATION PROCESS IN THE USSR

Mark Bandman

Territorial-production complexes (TPCs) have already shown
themselves to be a progressive form of spatial organisation of
productive forces in solving regional intersectoral problems of
national rank (Bandman, 1984). In the last decade the complexes in the eastern USSR, such as Bratsk-Ust' Ilimsk, West
Siberia, South Yakutsk, South Tadzhik, Sayany, Pavlodar-
Ekibastuz, and those based on the Kursk Magnetic Anomaly
and Timan-Pechorsk area of the European USSR, have
provided the main increases in the production of oil, electric
power, coal, iron ore and related manufactures (see also
Gorkin and Smirnyagin, 1979).

PLANNING PROCESSES

Putting into practice the new, simultaneously intersectoral and
regional form of social production requires a high level of
management organisation. It is difficult to ensure the sub-
ordination of the interests of all those engaged in the TPC
creation to the solution of a specific regional problem of
national rank within the framework of existing systems of
sectoral or territorial planning management decisions. Recent
congresses of CPSU have given priority to TPCs and made
them subjects of forward planning. Many Soviet scientific
institutions have focused their research on the improvement of
that planning and its implementation, including the Institute
of Economics and Organisation of Industrial Production
(IEOIP) of the Siberian Branch of the USSR Academy of
Sciences in Novosibirsk.

The TPCs are subjects of national planning and control,
their development elaborated within the framework of the
Automated Planning Computing System (ASPR) of the USSR's
State Planning Committee (Gosplan). Priority TPCs are
planned in the following stages: pre-planning considerations
and planning; forecasting the TPC formation scheme, long-

term planning of the general TPC design, formation and evolution; and five-year and annual plan implementation.

The plans for TPC formation and evolution are directives, specifically setting targets, inputs, responsible institutions and persons, and time frames harmonised with the corresponding sections of the USSR state plans, the sectoral and territorial plans. The TPC planning, in comparison to the sectoral approach, should enable the achievement of an additional return due to the optimum pattern and spatial evolution of the TPC, the rational national use of all resources.

The main estimates for the priority TPCs for the decade to come are included in the main economic and social development directives of the Soviet Union. The five-year and annual TPC format in plans as a whole are incorporated as a specific section in the corresponding national economic and social development plans of the respective Union Republic and province. Targets for energy priority TPC are specified in the plans of ministries, departments, and provinces (territories, Autonomous Soviet Socialist Republics) as a special item and included in all indicators of the corresponding sectoral and territorial plans. TPC planning does not replace or duplicate the economic and social plans of a province (territory, ASSR) within which the complexes have to be created as those are plans for solving a specific regional problem.

The TPC plan documents have specific features to differentiate them from sectoral plans of ministries by the limited dimension of the TPC's region and from territorial plans of the sectors (for territories, ASSR) by limited parameters within the area under consideration and the vague boundaries of the region where the problems have to be solved. TPC plans also consider together all production units irrespective of their rank and the department to which they belong and all measures necessary for achieving goals irrespective of the place where they have to be carried out. TPC plans also determine the time span within which the planning decisions for the individual units have to be carried out; and these may not coincide with the existing periodisation of the State plans.

The operation period for bodies controlling a specific complex is determined by the time during which the problem under study has to be solved or by the period during which that problem is assumed to be extremely important to the entire Soviet economy. The main task of the TPC control bodies is to ensure a proportional and balanced TPC creation process to achieve the goals set with the least amount of all kinds of inputs. All the TPC control bodies should be legally formalised, operate in accordance with the legal norms set for them, and base their activities upon the pre-planning and planning documents approved for a specific complex. The TPC control bodies should possess resources and be fully responsible for their decisions.

Two TPC control levels are specified: in the centre (in Moscow) and directly in the region where the complex is created. Between the control bodies of these two levels direct forward and backward linkages are obligatorily established. Some governmental functions and rights should be delegated to the higher-level bodies and their representatives.

It is necessary to approve the institution of head organisations for each TPC: the general customer (the USSR State Planning Committee), the general drafter of the TPC formation scheme and development programme (the Council for Development of Productive Forces of the USSR State Planning Committee or, on behalf of Soviet Gosplan scientific research institutes of the State Planning Committees of union republics or other scientific institutions); the drafter of the general TPC project (one of the USSR Gosstroy's leading institutions); the general contractor (one of the construction ministries); the general supplier of equipment and of some kinds of materials (the USSR State Planning Committee); the customers of individual construction items (ministries and departments); the unified customer of the social infrastructure (a territory, provincial executive committee of the People's Deputy Councils, or ASSR Council of Ministers); and the chief scientific institution (an institute of the USSR Academy of Sciences or an institute of the department responsible for the TPC).

The TPC control bodies may not in any way duplicate or replace territorial and sectoral control bodies which usually operate within the provinces (territories, ASSR). Their competence and rights are limited and related to the problems only of the on-going control of the design and fulfilment of the preplanning documents and plans of the TPC formation. In all the other respects the area of the complex is managed by the executive committees of the provincial (territorial) Councils of People's deputies or of the ASSR's Council of Ministers, ministries and departments.

The TPC control system should be flexible with regard to the structure and form of interaction both within the TPC and the organisations of the complex. In determining the structure the specific nature both of the problem (the objective of the TPC creation) and region where it has to be solved should be taken into account. An important feature of the system of control bodies as proposed by the TPC Section of the IEOIP system is that most of its elements are not new, but hitherto the activities of relevant organisations have been insufficiently clearly specified.

THE DIVERSITY OF SOVIET TPCs

There are no identical TPCs, and probably there never will be any. The differentiation of the TPC control systems is mostly affected by the following: (1) the nature of the problem (Kursk Magnetic Anomaly and Angara-Yenisey problems) for whose solution the TPC was created; (2) the pattern of the exporting sectors (oil, gas, coal, iron ore, machine-building, energy-consuming production units, electric power generating) to other regions; (3) the complexity of the internal pattern of the TPC (multi-purpose and or single purpose complexes); (4) the location pattern (a single complex or several complexes in a Union Republic, a number of openly connected or a system of mutually connected TPCs); and (5) specific, natural, economic, and geographical conditions of the region where the TPC is created.

The pattern of control bodies of the TPC outlined above mainly corresponds to the structurally complex multi-goal TPCs which are being created in developing and pioneer economic development regions (Middle-Ob, Sayany, Bratsk-Ust' Ilimsk, Lower-Angara, etc.).

The control body structure of the single-goal TPCs (South-Yakutia TPC in the initial formation phase, the TPC in the Kursk Magnetic Anomaly) may be more simplified. The functions of the authorised agent of the USSR Council of Ministers Presidium Commission may be entrusted to the head industry's deputy minister whose authority should be considerably enlarged, and a direct linkage ensured with the corresponding USSR Council of Ministers Presidium Commission. A different control body pattern seems to be needed for the TPC based on the Kursk Magnetic Anomaly which is being formed, in contrast to the other TPCs, not only as a result of the very intensive expansion of one sector (steel) but also in a developed region.

A question as to what control pattern will be adequate for a set of TPCs to be created within one administrative and territorial division: Middle-Ob' and North-Tyumen' TPCs within the Tyumen' province; Sayany, Central-Krasnoyarsk, Lower-Angara, North-Krasnoyarsk TPCs within Krasnoyarsk territory; and probably the Pavlodar-Ekibastuz and Mangyshlak TPCs in Kazakhstan. In this case no standard is possible, two versions of the solution are likely to exist depending on how close the interlinkages of the TPCs prove to be. If an individual TPC is created within one administrative division to solve different problems, the TPCs are not closely interrelated and then the construction is carried out by different general contractors (as is the case of the Pavlodar-Ekibastuz and Mangyshlak TPCs), or the formation period differs (North-Krasnoyarsk and Sayany, Central-Krasnoyarsk or Bratsk-Ust' Ilimsk and Upper-Lena TPCs), and the above specified fundamental control pattern of the TPC creation may be retained.

Should the complexes form a system of interlinked TPCs, even if they embrace adjacent areas of neighbouring administrative divisions (Middle-Ob' TPC within sections of Tyumen' and Tomsk provinces), then it seems to be necessary to locate some of the control agencies, mainly those coordinating intercomplex relations, in the most appropriate local administrative centre. This should be so especially when TPCs engaged in solving one or several closely related problems, such as the creation of the oil and gas industry in bases in Tyumen and Tomsk or of the energy-consuming enterprises using thermal and hydroelectric power, compete for preference in the creation of units of the specialised sectors, in allocating resources or in employing the construction materials, energy, transport and communications.

The foregoing are proposals of the TPC formation Sector of the IEOIP intended to improve the TPC creation-control process. Probably these proposals will be specified more precisely in the future to accommodate the different points of view stated in the specialised literature and in the press.

REFERENCES

Bandman, M.K. (ed.) (1984) Regional Development in the USSR, Pergamon, Oxford.
Gorkin, A.P. and Smirnyagin, L. (1979) 'A Structural Approach to Industrial Systems in Different Social and Economic Environments' in F.E.I. Hamilton and G.J.R. Linge (eds.), Spatial Analysis, Industry and Industrial Environment: Vol. 1 Industrial Systems, Wiley, Chichester, pp. 25-36.

Chapter Thirteen

THE REGIONAL DIVISION OF LABOUR:
MACHINERY MANUFACTURING, MICROELECTRONICS
AND R & D IN JAPAN

Kiyoji Murata and Atsuhiko Takeuchi

Japan's machinery industry, once considerably behind those of the USA and Europe, developed rapidly in the 1960s and 1970s. As Tables 13.1 and 13.2 show, the annual growth rate of the machinery industry was 18.77 per cent in the 1960s, declining in response to the world's business recession in the 1970s as is indicated by the annual growth in exports which dropped from 24.6 per cent in the 1960s to 18.9 per cent in the 1980s.

Rapid growth in production and exports of machinery were supported by conscious introduction of foreign technological knowledge and investment in equipment. The economic white paper of 1956 emphasised the necessity for promoting innovation and for catching up with the European countries and USA. Many basic machinery technologies were imported in the 1960s and energy-reduction technologies in heavy and chemical industries were developed after the oil shock. Conservation of energy and rationalisation of production process were realised by the introduction of central control systems and factory automation. Reduced dependency on material-type production such as petrochemicals and steel required a switch over to new types of growth industry, so stimulating the strong desire to innovate and promote the development of micro-electronics based industry. The application of integrated circuits (ICs) in watches and clocks, cameras, radios and television sets was promoted and production of electronic desk-top calculators, general-purpose computers, numerical-control type machine tools and industrial robots was established and is running smoothly.

World Microelectronics-based Industry
The world output of integrated circuits (ICs) in 1982 was US $9,930 million which meant the near doubling of growth between 1978 and 1982. As Table 13.3 shows, Japan's output of ICs ranks next to the USA, accounting for US $2,950 million or 30 per cent of world output. The growth of MOS

213

Table 13.1: Shipments of Machinery Industry (in 1,000 million yen).

	1960	1970	1980	Annual Growth Rate 1960-70 (%)	1970-80 (%)
Manufacturing Industry	15,578.6	69,034.8	214,700	16.05	12.02
Total of Machinery Industry	3,993.7	22,304.3	68,264.0	18.77	11.84
General Machinery	1,205.0	6,802.8	17,600	18.90	9.97
Electrical Machinery and Appliances	1,291.6	7,330.5	22,235	18.96	11.74
Transportation Equipment	1,325.0	7,275.8	24,954	18.57	13.11
Precision Machinery and Apparatus	170.5	891.7	3,458	17.99	14.51
Weapons	1.6	3.5	17	8.14	17.12

Source: Census of Manufactuers; various years, Tokyo.

Table 13.2: Exports of Machinery (in 1,000 million yen).

	1960	1970	1980	Annual Growth Rate 1960-70 (%)	1970-80 (%)
General Machinery	79.8	722.2	4,090.9	24.64	18.94
Electrical Machinery and Appliances	93.2	815.0	5,135.4	24.22	20.21
Transportation Equipment	155.8	1,239.3	7,761.8	23.04	20.14
Precision Machinery and Apparatus	34.6	226.1	1,413.9	20.65	20.12
Weapons	–	.1.2	14.6	–	28.39
Total	363.4	3,003.8	18,416.6	23.52	19.89

Source: Trade of Japan – various years, Tokyo.

215

Table 13.3: Output of Integrated Circuit (IC) Manufacturing Industry of the World (in million US $, percentages).

		1978		1982		Annual Growth Rate 1978–1982
All IC	USA	2,660	(52)	5,010	(50)	17
	Japan	1,240	(24)	2,950	(30)	24
	13 European Countries	1,060	(21)	1,690	(17)	12
	Other Countries	140	(3)	280	(3)	18
	Total of the World	5,100	(100)	9,930	(100)	18
MOS IC	USA	1,330	(56)	2,740	(53)	20
	Japan	660	(28)	1,740	(33)	27
	13 European Countries	360	(15)	680	(13)	17
	Other Countries	20	(1)	50	(1)	26
	Total of the World	2,370	(100)	5,210	(100)	22
Bipolar IC	USA	1,330	(49)	2,270	(48)	14
	Japan	580	(21)	1,210	(26)	20
	13 European Countries	700	(26)	1,010	(21)	10
	Other Countries	120	(4)	230	(5)	18
	Total of the World	2,730	(100)	4,720	(100)	15

Source: Japan Association of Micro-Electronics Based Industry Trend of the World Micro-Electronics based Industry, 1984.

Note: 13 European Countries are West Germany, France, UK, Norway, Sweden, Denmark, Finland, Netherlands, Belgium, Luxemburg, Switzerland, Italy and Spain.

ICs (metal-oxide-semiconductor integrated circuits) was high, mainly to cope with the increase in demand because they have the merit of high agglomeration with smaller electricity consumption.

Looking at machinery and appliances, there are considerable differences between different types of manufactured goods (Table 13.4). Japan has a large share only in household and general consumption items, while that of the USA is big both in industrial use machinery and parts. Of the 13 European countries, the output of West Germany is top with US $20,294 million (27.6 per cent), followed by France with US $14,338 million (19.5 per cent) and the UK with US $14,265 million (19.4 per cent).

REGIONAL CONCENTRATION IN JAPANESE MICROELECTRONICS-BASED MACHINERY INDUSTRIES

The Japanese machinery industry can be viewed in terms of: (1) the distribution of factories, persons engaged and output; and (2) the regional shares of research and development, production, distribution, information and subcontracting. The concentration of high-technology industry is analysed first taking into account changes in the distribution of all machinery industries. Figure 13.1 provides the geographic framework for the ensuing analysis.

Changes in the Distribution of Machinery Industries

The machinery industry was overwhelmingly concentrated in the three large metropolitan regions, Tokyo (Kanto), Osaka (Kinki) and Nagoya (Chukyo), while the share of output in other regions was small until the first half of the 1960s (Figure 13.2). Thereafter, especially in the 1970s, the decentralisation of manufacturing industries was promoted by central and local government, which provided inducements for investment in provincial areas. As a result, persons engaged in Tohoku, Kyushu and Tokai regions increased while the share of the Tokyo and Osaka metropolitan regions decreased (Table 13.5 and Figure 13.3).

Though three large metropolitan regions have reduced their share somewhat, they still account for 60 per cent of persons engaged; Southern Kanto, including Tokyo, still employs 30 per cent and retains its predominant position. Looking at changes in distribution of large scale factories with 500 persons and more, Table 13.6 shows that the growth and regional shares of Tohoku, Northern-Kanto and Tokai were remarkable. The increase of large-scale factories in these regions is mainly accounted for by the location of new branch factories by multi-plant enterprises. Thus, during the past twenty years, inducements to machinery industries to

Table 13.4: Output of Micro-Electronics Based Industry of USA, 13 European Countries and Japan.

	Output (million dollar, %)				Annual Growth Rate	
	1975	1980	1981	1982	'75-82	'80-82
(USA)						
Industrial Use Machinery and Appliances	27,759 (52.9)	69,768	79,929	88.800 (56.9)	18.1	12.8
Household and General Consumption						
Machinery and Appliances	5,224 (31.1)	10,883	11,670	11,197 (31.9)	11.5	1.4
Parts	9,286 (44.6)	24,739	25,240	26,119 (48.5)	15.9	2.8
Total	42,269 (46.9)	105,390	116,839	126,116 (51.5)	16.9	9.4
(13 European Countries)						
Industrial Use Machinery and Appliances	19,950 (38.0)	58,385	52,122	51,289 (32.9)	14.5	-6.2
Household and General Consumption						
Machinery and Appliances	6,118 (36.5)	10,974	8,630	9,102 (25.9)	5.8	-8.9
Parts	7,729 (37.1)	15,984	13,235	13,039 (24.2)	7.8	-9.7
Total	33,797 (37.5)	85,344	73,987	73,530 (30.0)	11.7	-7.2

(Japan)							
Industrial Use Machinery and Appliances	4,775	(9.1)	12,613	14,761	15,894	(10.2)	18.7	12.3
Household and General Consumption								
Machinery and Appliances	5,430	(32.4)	13,005	16,682	14,804	(42.2)	15.4	6.7
Parts	3,826	(18.4)	11,683	14,879	14,665	(27.2)	21.2	12.0
Total	14,031	(15.6)	37,301	46,322	45,363	(18.5)	18.3	10.3
(Total)								
Industrial Use Machinery and Appliances	52,484	(100.0)	140,766	146,812	156,083	(100.0)	16.8	5.3
Household and General Consumption								
Machinery and Appliances	16,722	(100.0)	34,862	36,982	35,103	(100.0)	11.1	0.3
Parts	20,841	(100.0)	52,407	53,354	53,823	(100.0)	14.5	1.3
Total	90,097	(100.0)	228,035	237,148	245,009	(100.0)	15.4	3.7

Source: Trend of the World Micro-Electronics Based Industry, 1984.

Figure 13.1:   Japan - Prefectures, Regions and Main Cities.

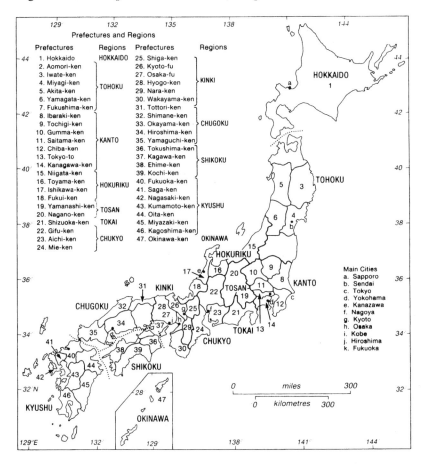

establish in provincial regions achieved an increase in their regional share, though the three large metropolitan regions still dominate. The actual state remains practically unchanged in Japan.

Distribution of Microelectronics-based Industry

Though the growth of the microelectronics-based industry only took place during the last fifteen years, it has greatly influenced not only the machinery industries but many other sectors of manufacturing, too. As Table 13.7 shows, the overwhelming majority of factories is located in three main regions, Kanto (with Tokyo as its centre), Kinki including

220

Figure 13.2: Distribution of Machinery Industry, 1980.
Source: Census of Manufacturers.

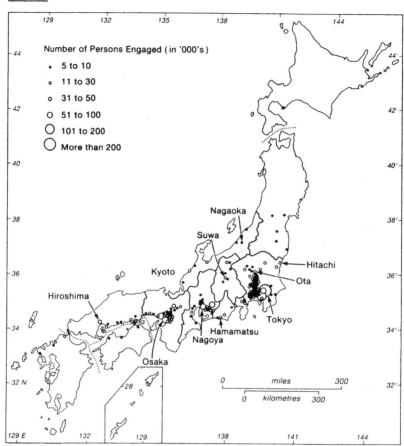

Osaka, and Chukyo including Nagoya. The concentration in
Southern Kanto - Tokyo metropolitan region is remarkably
high. ICs production accounts for less than half of all
factories in Japan but 70-90 per cent of factories assembling
and finishing products like industrial robots, computers,
medical equipment, aircraft and space equipment, and optical-
fibre communications equipment are located in the three main
metropolitan regions. The distribution of the production of
three commodities - ICs, computers and industrial robots -
will now be discussed (Table 13.7 and Figure 13.4).

ICs which saw rapid growth during the last ten years
are mainly produced in big factories which have mass-

221

Table 13.5: Changes in the Distribution of Persons Engaged in Machinery Industry.

	1960	(%)	1980	(%)
Hokkaido	13,592	(0.0)	24,188	(0.7)
Tohoku	40,150	(2.0)	221,696	(6.3)
Kanto	896,158	(44.0)	1,330,953	(37.8)
Southern Kanto	789,430	(38.8)	1,024,071	(29.1)
Hokuriku	71,945	(3.5)	145,791	(4.1)
Tosan	57,917	(2.8)	172.215	(4.9)
Tokai	70,969	(3.5)	179,282	(5.1)
Chukyo	221,148	(10.9)	460,830	(13.1)
Kinki	448,280	(22.0)	565,342	(16.0)
Chugoku	111,733	(5.5)	215,241	(6.1)
Shikoku	26,955	(1.3)	58,500	(1.7)
Kyushu	78,359	(3.8)	149,717	(4.2)
Total	2,037,206	(100.0)	3,523,755	(100.0)

Source: Census of Manufacturers.

Table 13.6: Changes in Distribution of Large Machinery Factories (500 or more workers).

	1960		1980	
Hokkaido	2	(0.4)	5	(0.5)
Tohoku	11	(2.2)	40	(4.2)
Kanto	215	(43.6)	386	(40.9)
Southern Kanto	190	(38.5)	301	(31.9)
Hokuriku	20	(4.1)	27	(2.9)
Tosan	16	(3.2)	41	(4.3)
Tokai	16	(3.2)	51	(5.4)
Chukyo	58	(11.8)	125	(13.2)
Kinki	106	(21.5)	161	(17.1)
Chugoku	26	(5.3)	48	(5.1)
Shikoku	6	(1.2)	15	(1.6)
Kyushu	17	(3.4)	45	(4.8)
Total	493	(100.0)	944	(100.0)

Source: The Central List of Factories in Japan.

Figure 13.3: Number of Persons Engaged in Machinery Industry and Rate of Increase, 1960-1980.
Source: Census of Manufacturers.

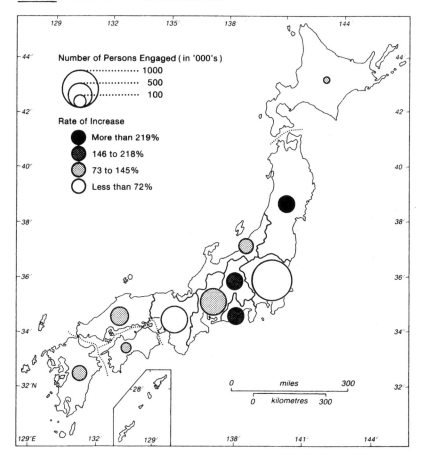

production systems. The manufacturers are well-known: general electrical machinery and appliance producers such as Hitachi, Toshiba, and Mitsubishi; communications equipment manufacturers such as Nippon Electric Co. (NEC), Fujitsu and Oki; and household electrical machinery and appliances manufacturers such as Matsushita, Sanyo, Sharp and Sony. Manufactured ICs are mainly used as parts for assembling finished products in their own factories. In addition, Seiko, the biggest watch manufacturer in Japan and the world, established a microelectronics-based printer and computer manufacturing department in 1965 making ICs for its own

223

Table 13.7: Distribution of Micro-Electronics Based Industry, 1982.

(Number of Factories)

	IC	Industrial Robot	Computer	Medical Equipment	Aircraft	Space Apparatus	Optical Communication Equipment
Hokkaido	2 (1.89)		9 (9.68)	2 (4.35)		1 (1.27)	
Tohoku	14 (13.21)						
Kanto	32 (30.19)	33 (53.23)	64 (68.82)	29 (63.04)	48 (61.54)	54 (68.35)	17 (77.27)
Southern Kanto	20 (18.87)	29 (46.77)	54 (58.06)	24 (52.17)	41 (52.56)	49 (62.03)	15 (68.18)
Hokuriku	5 (4.72)	1 (1.61)	4 (4.30)	1 (2.17)			
Tosan	9 (8.49)	4 (6.45)	3 (3.23)	3 (6.52)	1 (1.28)	2 (2.53)	1 (4.55)
Tokai	1 (0.94)	3 (4.84)	4 (4.30)	1 (2.17)		1 (1.27)	
Chukyo	1 (0.94)	10 (16.13)	3 (3.23)	7 (15.22)	19 (24.36)	2 (2.53)	1 (4.55)
Kinki	11 (10.38)	10 (16.13)	4 (4.30)	2 (4.35)	10 (12.82)	14 (17.72)	2 (9.09)
Chugoku	0 (0.00)						
Shikoku	1 (0.94)	1 (1.61)	2 (2.15)	1 (2.17)		2 (2.53)	
Kyushu	30 (28.30)					3 (3.80)	1 (4.55)
Total	106 (100.00)	62 (100.00)	93 (100.00)	46 (100.00)	78 (100.00)	79 (100.00)	22 (100.00)

Source: Research Materials of Japan Industrial Location Center.

Figure 13.4: Distribution of Main Factories of Selected Micro-electronics Based Industry, 1982.
Source: Research Materials of Japan Industrial Location Center.

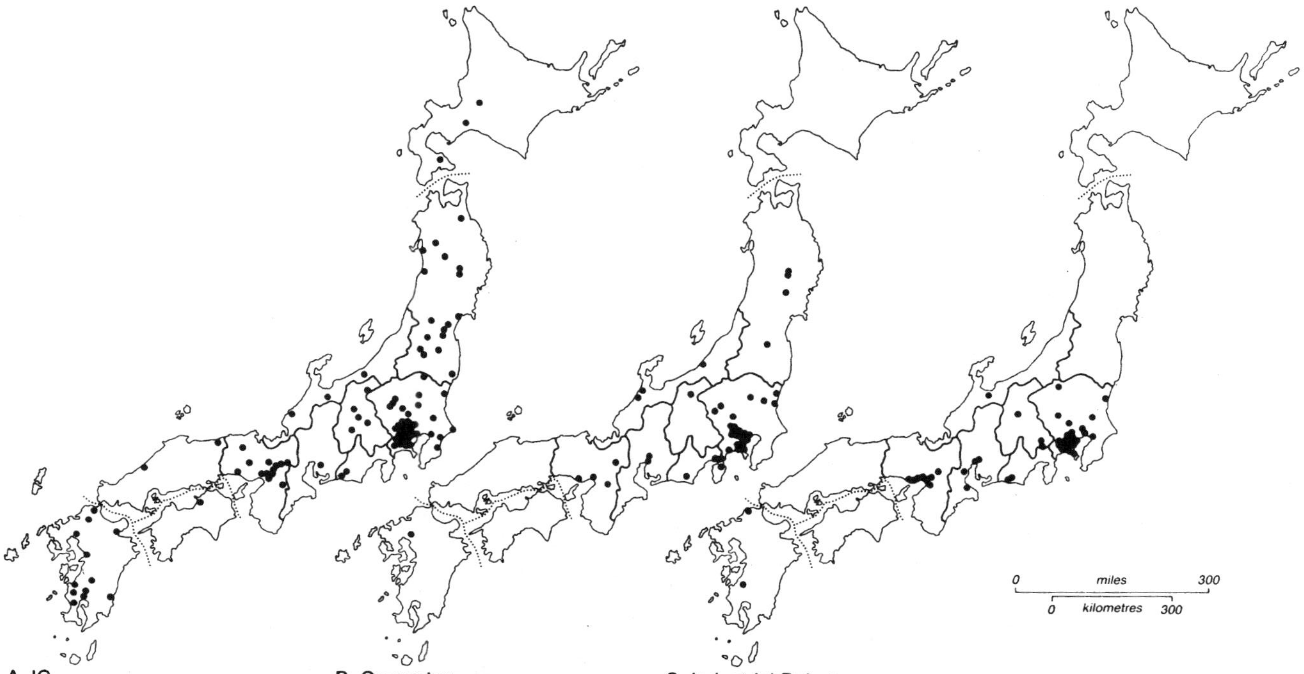

A. IC

B. Computer

C. Industrial Robot

miles 300

kilometres 300

requirements. Yamaha, the musical instrument manufacturer, also make ICs for its own needs. On the other hand, there are some manufacturers who specialise in IC production. Among them is Rohm, a well-known IC manufacturer which has its main factory in Kyoto, 7 branch factories in Japan and 6 subsidiary factories in the USA, Europe and Asia. Rohm manufactures 700 kinds of high quality semiconductors and supplies products to more than 70 domestic and overseas general microelectronics-based machinery and appliances manufacturers.

More than half of the IC manufacturing factories are located in provincial regions; 30 factories, or 28 per cent, are located in Kyushu which is called "Silicon Island". Tohoku has 12 factories, or 13 per cent. The factories in the provincial regions mainly produce SSIs (small-scale ICs), MSIs (middle-scale ICs) and some factories began to manufacture LSIs (large-scale ICs) and VLSIs (very large-scale ICs) in recent years. On the other hand, factories located in big metropolitan regions, especially Tokyo, are main factories and also operate as pilot plants closely connected with research and development functions.

The number of general purpose computers installed in Japan in 1978 was 23,942 compared with 57,954 in the USA but the production output of computers is not big, Japan having a 7 per cent share of the world market in 1981 compared with a 77 per cent share for US producers. Production of general purpose computers started at the end of the 1950s and increased rapidly in the 1960s. The third generation computer was developed and on-line information systems spread rapidly. Manufacturers are divided into three groups: general purpose computer manufacturers; minicomputer and small business computer manufacturers; and terminal unit, input-output unit and other parts manufacturers. Among them only six companies produce general purpose computers. As Table 13.7 shows, 64 factories, or 69 per cent of computer manufacturing factories, are concentrated in Kanto. Most factories located in provincial regions specialise in the manufacturing of many kinds of parts, and some assemble simple small scale units.

Japan's production of industrial robots has increased rapidly since the early 1970s so that it is now the foremost producer and user of robots, and the world's leading producer of computerised automation in general. Initially Japanese production was concentrated on less sophisticated first generation robots. However, substantial development in technology has been made by production companies so that the share of more sophisticated robots in total production has risen over the period 1976 to 1980. Many of the enterprises involved in robot production are large companies, mainly in the engineering sector, whose robot divisions are integrated into much larger manufacturing groups which are themselves frequent users, but have entered the industry because they view it as a high growth sector and thus as a potential source of profits. More than 60 per cent of all robots are applied to the automobile and electrical machinery industries and are mainly used for assembling, grinding and drilling, welding and spray-painting. Looking at the distribution of robot manufacturing factories, 53 factories, or 85 per cent, are located in three main regions of Kanto, Kinki and Chukyo and are connected both with R & D functions and with the supply of many kinds of parts.

THE CONCENTRATION OF RESEARCH AND DEVELOPMENT FACILITIES

There were 230,000 engineering researchers in Japan in 1981. 174,800 (76 per cent) of them belong to private enterprise institutes, 29,900 (13 per cent) to state and private universities, and 16,100 (7 per cent) to national research institutions. Of 486,400 million yen for engineering research, 287,000 million yen (59 per cent) is used in universities, 126,500 million yen (26 per cent) in national research facilities and 73,000 million yen (15 per cent) in private enterprises.

National Research Facilities
Of 14 machinery-related national research facilities, 9 are located in the Tokyo metropolitan region, including Tsukuba situated in the outer ring about 60 Km north east of central Tokyo and named an "academic town" or "science city". Tsukuba academic town was constructed according to the renewal plan of inner Tokyo; a state university and 45 large-scale and high level national research facilities were moved there from inner Tokyo during 1971-1980. The Space Research Institute and Metal Material Research Institute are still located in Tokyo and 6 large-scale research facilities of public corporations such as the National Railway (JNR), Telegraph and Telephone (NTT), Broadcasting (NHK), International Telegraph and Telephone (KDD) with 4,300 researchers and 91,000 million yen research funds.

Of 149 universities with faculties of technology and engineering, 88 (59 per cent) are concentrated in the three main metropolitan regions, especially in Southern Kanto. The Tokyo metropolitan region has a remarkably big concentration (see Table 13.8), with the highest level of research facilities and is the largest core of research and development in the microelectronics-based industry. There are many joint research groups of researchers in universities, national institutions and the research and development laboratories of private enterprises in that region.

Table 13.8: Distribution of National Research Institutes and Universities of Machinery Related, 1981.

	National Research Institutes			Universities		
	Number of Institutes	Number of Researchers	(%)	Number of Universities	Number of Researchers	(%)
Hokkaido	0	0	(0.0)	7	766	(7.4)
Tohoku	1	20	(1.0)	8	802	(7.8)
Kanto	8	1,749	(90.7)	54	3,424	(33.3)
Southern Kanto	3	716	(37.1)	28	3,054	(29.7)
Hokuriku	0	0	(0.0)	7	600	(5.8)
Tosan	0	0	(0.0)	3	200	(1.9)
Tokai	0	0	(0.0)	1	131	(1.3)
Chukyo	1	20	(1.0)	13	1,020	(9.9)
Kinki	1	70	(3.6)	21	1,674	(16.3)
Chugoku	1	20	(1.0)	9	407	(4.0)
Shikoku	1	20	(1.0)	2	133	(1.3)
Kyushu	1	30	(1.6)	24	1,131	(11.0)
Total	14	1,929	(100.0)	149	10,288	(100.0)

Source: List of Research and Development Laboratories.

Research and Development Laboratories of Private Enterprises
There were 713 research and development laboratories of private enterprises with about 18,500 researchers and 337,400 million yen research funds in 1981. The machinery sector accounts for 57 per cent of the researchers and 67 per cent of research funds, the electrical machinery industry for 34 per cent and 28 per cent respectively. As Table 13.9 shows, the distribution of R & D laboratories is predominantly in two regions, Kanto and Kinki. Though Kinki has 21 per cent of these laboratories, including those of Matsushita and Sanyo, research capabilities are considerably inferior to Kanto. In Kanto, each big company, such as Hitachi, Toshiba, NEC, Fujitsu and Sony, has more than 1000 researchers in their R & D laboratories and lead the innovation in microelectronics-based industries in Japan.

Enterprises concentrated in the Tokyo region also enjoy the advantages of contacts with, and getting quick information from, universities, national research facilities, think-tanks and the other related R & D functions of the metal and chemical industries. Moreover, when joint research projects between state and private enterprises are planned, the enterprises with the main offices or main R & D laboratories in the Tokyo region have the advantages of being able to join in easily. For example, when the joint R & D project was launched for opto-electronic IC (OEIC) - which plays a basic part in the development of optical computers, optical communications and optical video discs - in Tokyo with a government budget of 18,000 million yen, 50 researchers participated from the National Electric Research Institute and 8 private enterprises of which 7 were from Tokyo; only 1 was from Osaka. The research term of this project is 8 years (1979-1987) and 270 papers have been made public and 66 patent rights have been obtained during the 4 years 1979-1983. This is only 1 example. Many big research projects are carried out in Tokyo so that to join research projects or get quick information, many enterprises in Osaka, Nagoya and other cities moved their main offices to, or established R & D laboratories, in the Tokyo region.

Scientists and Engineers
As Table 13.10 shows, there are about 67,000 scientists in Japan; 52,000 (67 per cent) of them are concentrated in the three main metropolitan regions. Southern Kanto, including the Tokyo metropolitan region, has 33,865 or 50.7 per cent, and has a good lead over Kinki and other regions. Table 13.10 shows the big concentration of engineers in the Tokyo metropolitan region, especially the remarkably big concentration of information-processing engineers. Thus, innovation supporting the development of the Japanese industry comes mainly from Tokyo.

Table 13.9: Distribution of R & D Laboratories in the Machinery Industry, 1982.

	Independent	(%)	Attached	(%)	Total	(%)
Hokkaido	0	(0.0)	2	(0.4)	2	(0.3)
Tohoku	2	(1.1)	6	(1.1)	8	(1.1)
Kanto	110	(62.5)	283	(52.7)	393	(55.1)
Southern Kanto	103	(58.5)	256	(47.7)	359	(50.4)
Hokuriku	0	(0.0)	15	(2.8)	15	(2.1)
Tosan	3	(1.7)	15	(2.8)	18	(2.5)
Tokai	2	(1.1)	20	(3.7)	22	(3.1)
Chukyo	8	(4.5)	51	(9.5)	59	(8.3)
Kinki	44	(25.0)	100	(19.7)	150	(21.0)
Chugoku	3	(1.7)	14	(2.6)	17	(2.4)
Shikoku	2	(1.1)	7	(1.3)	9	(1.3)
Kyushu	2	(1.1)	18	(3.4)	20	(2.8)
Total	176	(100.0)	537	(100.0)	713	(100.0)

Source: List of Research and Development Laboratories.

Table 13.10: Distribution of Scientists and Engineers, 1980.

	Scientists	(%)	Engineers				Information processing	(%)
			Mechanical related	(%)	Electric related	(%)		
Hokkaido	1,740	(2.6)	1,575	(1.5)	2,885	(2.7)	1,225	(1.5)
Tohoku	2,110	(3.2)	2,300	(2.2)	5,245	(4.9)	1,680	(2.1)
Kanto	37,575	(56.3)	43,960	(42.0)	47,695	(44.2)	50,420	(62.8)
Southern Kanto	33,865	(50.7)	40,155	(38.3)	42,910	(39.7)	48,310	(60.2)
Hokuriku	1,305	(2.0)	2,915	(2.8)	4,010	(3.7)	1,335	(1.7)
Tosan	695	(1.0)	1,685	(1.6)	2,390	(2.2)	735	(0.9)
Tokai	1,500	(2.2)	3,160	(3.0)	2,310	(2.1)	1,165	(1.5)
Chukyo	4,015	(6.0)	10,830	(10.3)	8,000	(7.4)	4,375	(5.4)
Kinki	10,715	(16.1)	21,480	(20.5)	19,250	(17.8)	12,665	(15.8)
Chugoku	2,925	(4.4)	8,205	(7.8)	5,775	(5.3)	2,830	(3.5)
Shikoku	935	(1.4)	2,795	(2.7)	2,805	(2.6)	910	(1.1)
Kyushu	3,220	(4.8)	5,830	(5.6)	7,615	(7.1)	2,970	(3.7)
Total	66,735	(100.0)	104,735	(100.0)	107,980	(100.0)	80,310	(100.0)

Source: National Census.

231

Universities which are the supply source of scientists and engineers are also concentrated in the three main metropolitan regions. As Table 13.11 shows, the number of both undergraduate and postgraduate students in the three metropolitan regions is big. In Table 13.11, Tokyo-to (prefecture) is separated as a sub-region of Kanto to show the outstanding concentration of universities in the capital that localises not only talent which supports the high level of research, development and production today, but also the main source supplying tomorrow's talent for industrial innovation and development.

The location of a factory in a provincial area is usually planned when the production has already been set up and running smoothly in the core metropolitan regions and the expansion of output by a mass production system is intended. Low-wage workers, reasonably-priced land and other physical and social conditions become important factors, and university graduates are not always influential in deciding location. On the contrary, graduates of local universities find it difficult to find a job locally which corresponds to their major field of study as their localities concentrate more routine mass-production functions.

TOKYO AS A LARGE CENTRE OF SKILL AND TECHNOLOGY

Groups of Skill and Technology in Manufacturing Sites

As mentioned above, R & D functions are concentrated remarkably in the Tokyo metropolitan region (Figure 13.5). Moreover, a high level of skill and technology has been cultivated by engineers and workers at the manufacturing sites of machinery manufacturers, especially in inner Tokyo. The machinery industry in this region is supported by the highest level of technology and plays the role of a seedbed for the machinery industry in Japan, though most managements are medium and small-scale because many large factories have moved to the outskirts and peripheral areas because of location controls by the government. Since Japan started industrialisation, well-known large enterprises such as Toshiba, Nissan, Isuzu, NEC and Sony have been born, developed new technology and products, and grown up in this region. Two major features can be observed:

Firstly, middle and small-scale factories with high technology supply many kinds of sophisticated parts to the big enterprises. Factories located in the outskirts of the Tokyo region assemble the finished products by depending on the parts-manufacturers groups which have their own high level of technology and skill. The manufacturing skills of the machine element, such as the spring, gear, screw and metal mould, and also the skill of processing, such as gilting, pressing, casting and heat treatment, are high and these

232

Table 13.11: Distribution of the Students of Universities with Technology Faculties, 1981.

	Number of Students Undergraduate	(%)	Postgraduate Master Course	(%)	Doctor Course	(%)
Hokkaido	2,820	(4.3)	342	(3.5)	105	(4.3)
Tohoku	4,510	(6.9)	627	(6.4)	208	(8.5)
Kanto	24,649	(37.9)	3,983	(40.7)	1,151	(47.0)
Tokyo	12,144	(18.7)	2,613	(26.7)	885	(36.1)
Hokuriku	2,930	(4.5)	602	(6.2)	15	(0.6)
Tosan	1,185	(1.8)	228	(2.3)	0	(0.0)
Tokai	455	(0.7)	98	(1.0)	17	(0.7)
Chukyo	5,490	(8.4)	861	(8.8)	147	(6.0)
Kinki	10,120	(15.6)	1,630	(16.7)	590	(24.1)
Chugoku	3,285	(5.0)	334	(3.4)	43	(1.8)
Shikoku	775	(1.2)	144	(1.5)	0	(0.0)
Kyushu	8,840	(13.6)	931	(9.5)	174	(7.1)
Total	65,059	(100.0)	9,780	(100.0)	2,450	(100.0)

Source: General List of Universities.

Figure 13.5: Concentrated area of Machinery Industry and Distribution of R & D Laboratories in Southern Kanto, 1982. Source: The Census List of Factories in Japan List of R & D Laboratory.

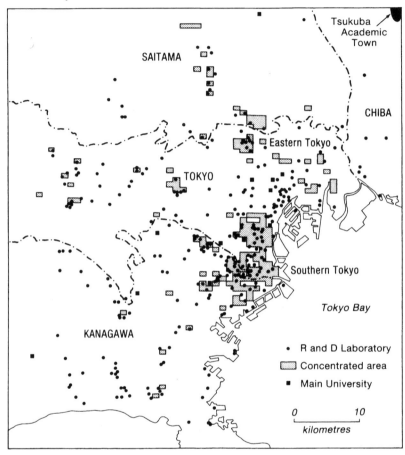

skilled processes formed the basic industry groups. These groups play an important role as the base supporting a pyramid and also have common roots with the machinery industry in Japan. In fact, the position of these basic industrial groups in this region is much higher than that of the machinery industry in general in Japan.

Secondly, in the industrial complex formed by machine and related industries, the development and production of small lots and various kinds of mechanical products is closely connected with the R & D and information functions. In fact there is no mechanical product which cannot be made in this region. Thus, the enterprises hold 42 per cent of industrial property rights of all medium and small-scale enterprises in Japan. Moreover, many enterprises specialising in various service sectors such as measuring, testing, maintenance of machines and equipment, and technology consulting are located there, also giving incentives to technological development in the machinery industry.

Concentration of Information and Information Processing Functions

Tokyo is a big information centre as well as the centre of business and manufacturing industries. The great accumulation of information and information processing functions in Tokyo strongly influences the development of high technology industries. The vast majority of machinery manufacturing enterprises have head offices in Tokyo as do foreign enterprises. These enterprises have close contacts with the authorities concerned, trading concerns, banks, think-tanks and information processing organisations. About 22,000 persons are engaged in information processing in Tokyo, 60 per cent of the total for Japan. Osaka ranks second with about 13 per cent (Table 13.12). Such rich information contributes to the concentration of high technology industries and R & D laboratories.

At Akihabara in inner Tokyo, there is a large wholesale area with more than 700 wholesale stores selling all sorts of electrical and electronics-based manufactured goods and parts. The market area served extends over the whole of Kanto and new or specific manufactured goods have a nationwide market. More than 2000 persons, including many foreigners, visit the area daily and stores have space where customers can test the apparatus and consult with specialists for advice on their needs. Manufacturers also visit the market for new information about hardware and software. Thus Akihabara has a function as a centre gathering and transferring information, in addition to its wholesale function. This aspect of Akihabara inevitably promoted the appearance of independent systems firms and more than 100 are concentrated there. Their staff include many who left big manufacturing and information service industries. They provide incentives for improving and developing both the hardware and the software of electronics-based machines and tools to meet the needs and ideas of the customers and staff of the stores. They usually cooperate with manufacturers and offer proposals about improvement and development of products or establish a manufacturing company to produce new products which they have developed.

Table 13.12: Distribution of Persons Engaged in Information Processing Industry, 1980.

	Researchers	(%)	System Engineers	(%)	Programmers	(%)	Total	(%)
Hokkaido	3	(0.1)	173	(1.3)	214	(1.1)	390	(1.1)
Tohoku	17	(0.6)	237	(1.7)	356	(1.8)	610	(1.7)
Kanto	2,254	(85.6)	9,615	(70.3)	14,316	(71.7)	26,185	(72.2)
Tokyo	2,080	(79.0)	8,274	(60.5)	11,755	(58.9)	22,109	(61.0)
Hokuriku	12	(0.5)	309	(2.3)	339	(1.7)	660	(1.8)
Tosan	7	(0.3)	97	(0.7)	168	(0.8)	272	(0.7)
Tokai	2	(0.1)	59	(0.4)	89	(0.4)	150	(0.4)
Chukyo	19	(0.7)	611	(4.5)	777	(3.9)	1,407	(3.9)
Kinki	284	(10.8)	1,759	(12.9)	2,588	(13.0)	4,631	(12.8)
Chugoku	8	(0.3)	324	(2.4)	512	(2.6)	844	(2.3)
Shikoku	7	(0.3)	137	(1.0)	151	(0.8)	295	(0.8)
Kyushu	19	(0.7)	349	(2.6)	456	(2.3)	824	(2.3)
Total	2,632	(100.0)	13,670	(100.0)	19,966	(100.0)	36,268	(100.0)

Source: Census for Selected Service Industries.

Table 13.13: Distribution of Persons Engaged in Machinery Industry, 1980.

	Engineers	(%)	Workers	(%)
Hokkaido	44,317	(3.4)	59,053	(2.2)
Tohoku	65,302	(5.0)	232,755	(8.6)
Kanto	571,860	(44.2)	921,305	(34.1)
Southern Kanto	507,827	(39.3)	682,727	(25.3)
Hokuriku	48.385	(3.7)	128,013	(4.7)
Tosan	23,997	(1.9)	135,832	(5.0)
Tokai	35,564	(2.7)	113,980	(4.2)
Chukyo	91,688	(7.1)	294,794	(10.9)
Kinki	206,041	(15.9)	414,319	(15.3)
Chugoku	75,696	(5.9)	159,096	(5.9)
Shikoku	30,540	(2.4)	64,459	(2.4)
Kyushu	100,419	(7.8)	179,138	(6.6)
Total	1,293,809	(100.0)	2,702,744	(100.0)

Source: National Census.

TOWARDS TECHNOPOLIS?

The Japanese machinery industry is concentrated in three main metropolitan areas, especially Tokyo which is the biggest, regardless of government decentralisation policies for manufacturing. The same tendency is seen in microelectronics-based industries making computers, industrial robots and medical equipment: 75-85 per cent of factories are concentrated in 3 main metropolitan areas with overwhelming prominence in the Tokyo region. On the other hand, about half of the IC manufacturing plants are distributed widely in provincial areas. A regional division of labour is formed between finished goods production and IC production.

The attraction for the location of finished goods production in the Tokyo region is the existence of external economies. High-level R & D functions, information processing and quick supply of all sorts of high quality parts locally are indispensable conditions for manufacturers. Thus the Tokyo region offers big agglomeration advantages to the production in microelectronics-based industries and more than offsets the disadvantages of high land prices, traffic congestion and housing problems. Tokyo, then, is essentially a centre of innovation, and the metropolitan area can be called the "Tokyo technopolitan area".

The IC, the basic part of electronics-based products, is first manufactured on a trial basis in a specially equipped facility close to R & D laboratories, then production is transferred to a full-scale manufacturing process in the main factory. When the stability of manufacturing technology, safety of products and demands in market are ascertained, production is transferred to a specialised factory with a mass production system. The locational characteristic of the IC is that its transportability is very great: freight costs are very low. For instance, in a case of LSI, the ratio of transport cost by aeroplane from Kyushu to Tokyo is only 0.3 per thousand of the price, i.e., negligible. So the location of an IC manufacturing plant is "ultra footloose" or "transport cost free". Thus, IC manufacturing factories with mass production systems have tended to be located where the conditions such as low price industrial land, plenty of water, labour force and other physical and social conditions are found. These locational conditions are not specific for IC production but are shared by inland location-type manufacturing industry in general. Looking at industrial water in the production process of silicon wafer, large quantities of water are used for washing. In the case of silicon wafer production for LSI, the water has to be ultra pure so that the impure elements such as minute particles, micro-organisms, melting organic matters have to be a minimum value measured by ppb (parts per billion).

There is no natural water with such high purity. But because every IC factory is equipped with ultra pure water production apparatus, it is sufficient for ordinary soft water to be available for wafer washing and such quality water can be easily obtained in many areas. Thus many peripheral areas have the conditions for IC factory location, though, of course, metropolitan areas may "repel" the industry because of polluted water.

In local areas other than main metropolitan areas, there are some small centres of microelectronics-based industry with high level technology which have a national and overseas market. In these regions the machinery industry developed in 1950s and 1960s taking over from the former growth industries such as textiles, woodworking and mining. The transfer was the result of the effort to meet the needs of the times and change industrial structures. Suwa region, located in mountainous central Japan, has been associated with precision machine industries such as watches (Seiko), cameras, music boxes and microscopes. Since the early 1970s, a transfer to microelectronics-based industries began. There are now 5 IC factories, 3 computer factories and 2 industrial-robots factories in the Suwa region. Hamamatsu region, located between Tokyo and Nagoya, was well-known as the centre of musical instruments (Yamaha and Kawai), motor-cars and motorcycles (Honda, Suzuki and Yamaha) and machine tools. The necessity to adopt ICs and other microelectronics-based apparatus and the technology cultivated in the existing machinery industry promoted the development of new industries in Hamamatsu: there are an IC factory, 4 computer factories and 3 industrial robots factories.

As the development of these local centres was mainly based on local entrepreneurship in the development of existing industries, the growth and formation of new centres of the microelectronics based industries in other areas cannot be easily expected. To induce such high-technology industries as electronics, electromechanical engineering, biotechnology and new ceramics, the government's "technopolis" programme has got underway in 14 areas throughout the nation. At the same time, the programme bolsters academic and cultural facilities like universities, R & D laboratories and civic centres for people who work in new industries and academic institutions. The technopolis concept is a new type of industrial city. Of the variety of financial assistance available from the government for technopolis, the most important is the tax break aimed at industrial promotion in the technopolis. Under the system, an enterprise in a designated field of industry will be allowed a specific depreciation - 30 per cent on machinery and 15 per cent on structures, both in the first year - when it has made an investment in machinery, equipment or building. For promotion of R & D, the existing subsidy system will be utilised: one-third of the outlay for facilities and equipment will be subsidised by the state when prefectural industrial R & D laboratories and smaller enterprises jointly set up an R & D laboratory.

The "new industrial city" programme was strongly promoted by government investment in industrial infrastructure in the rapid economic growth of the 1960s, but now in a period of low economic growth, localities have to play the central role in the technopolis programme. In part, this will make the realisation of the technopolis policy difficult. The basic character of a technopolis is close cooperation between research and production but, as noted above, the R & D functions including universities in local areas are considerably inferior to the main metropolitan areas. Owing to existing structures such as the education system, life-time employment system, the seniority wage system, it will be difficult to develop research ability in the local universities in the short term. Parts supplies and related subcontractors are extremely limited in many local areas. Moreover, the R & D laboratories of local governments usually find it hard to lead in high technology for the existing smaller enterprises because of the antiquated facilities and a shortage of information and talents. Regarding finished goods, products like desk-top calculators and small size personal computers will gradually be transferred to local factories. When a nationwide information network by new media is consolidated, the R & D functions for application will be decentralised to meet the demand of the production sites in local areas. However, such a change in regional structure belongs to the future. For the time being, any marked change in the regional division of labour in Japan cannot be expected.

Chapter Fourteen

TECHNOLOGY TRANSFER TO THE EEC PERIPHERY:
THE CASE OF GREECE

Evangelia Dokopoulou

The role of multinational enterprises (MNEs) in technology diffusion between North and South is very important, indeed often critically decisive, even when taking into account East-West-South or East-South investments (Gutman and Arkwright, 1981; Gulcz and Gruchman, 1981). However, such directions of technology diffusion appear today to be a less marked phenomenon than a decade ago, with more transfer now being confined within the North. The industrial development of the latter global area, associated with the growth of high research intensity industry, the information sector and the rapid adoption of innovations, follows a different socio-economic model from that of developing countries which are dislocated in the international division of labour by the time lag in technological advance (Vernon, 1966). The advantage of the North in localising high research intensity industries lies in their greater profitability relative to low technology sectors. Dunning and Pearce (1980) studying a sample of 866 major industrial enterprises in the world found that from 1962 to 1977 high research intensive sectors (except aerospace, electrical and electronics industries) had higher returns on sales compared with the medium and low research intensity sectors. Dunning and Stopford (1983) observed that MNEs have increased their importance as suppliers of proprietary technology (c.f., suppliers of direct investment), so displacing the technological capabilities of developing countries, for the following four reasons:

receipts of royalty fees by the leading home countries of MNEs annually exceed the stock of direct investment from these countries;

intra-group technology trade is more developed than trade between MNEs and third parties;

technology trade is increasingly managed within the system of MNEs and forms part of its coordinated international strategy;

240

MNEs apply different technology strategies for developing countries relative to those for advanced countries. More competitive technologies are not readily transferred to the developing world whereas the attention of MNE focuses on the advanced countries.

These arguments are further expanded by other authorities, like Casson (1979) who concludes that the major barrier to technology transfer to LDCs is the unwillingness of the source-country firms to license or invest in LDCs because of the difficulty of appropriating reasonable shares of the wealth created by technology. Rugman (1981) suggests that MNEs prefer to control proprietary technology and not to license it because of the risk of dissipating their unique advantages. Developing the argument of Teece (1983), the more complex are the technologies now being introduced, the higher are the transfer costs, so inhibiting their wider international diffusion to what are at present apparently "inappropriate" environments.

The technology gaps between North and South are exacerbated by several factors:

First, emphasis of foreign direct investment (fdi) in technology intensive sectors towards developed countries.

Second, intra-group trade increases both in more technologically advanced sectors as the degree of multinationalisation of production rises (Leroy, 1978); more limited intra-group trade occurs in low technology sectors (Dunning and Pearce, 1980); Hood and Young (UK Department of Trade and Industry, 1983) found that in 1980 70 per cent of the sample of plants (140) of MNEs operating in the UK purchased inputs from other affiliates principally located in the USA and 3 advanced European countries (p. 131). Around 36 per cent of inputs purchased from abroad were imported from the USA (p. 156). And there were obvious ties of subsidiaries with their parent's home countries. One can deduce from Dunning et al. (1980) that, at the present time, intra-group trade in high technology confines the expansion of high technology industries within the organisational framework of a few major MNEs. These are exclusive suppliers in the western world of office, telecommunications, banking, laboratory and defence equipment and in control systems. Moreover, being the single source of supply to governments, they can control strategic national activities.

Third, MNEs in high technology sectors do not choose developing countries as production centres (see Bakis' Chapter in this volume).

Finally, according to Dunning and Stopford (1983) the industrially-advanced home countries of MNEs facilitate investments in low technology and labour-intensive processes in developing countries by reducing or even abolishing tariffs on goods manufactured by the foreign affiliates of their own firms. It can be hypothesised that MNEs engaging in such practices will alter the mix or the specification or the spatial allocation of production abroad to obviate any of the protectionist measures against selected newly-industrialising countries currently being threatened in the USA or the EEC.

CHARACTERISTICS OF MNE TECHNOLOGY TRANSFER TO GREECE

By themselves, policies of governments for protection, like tariffs and various forms of economic nationalism, are generally unsuccessful in sustaining domestic technological advancement. Besides, such measures have often created a permissive environment for the transfer by MNEs of outmoded processes and of bad quality products through the absence of regulations and codes found in more advanced countries. Some countries, like Greece, establish export platforms in low technology products whose markets are those countries accepting low standards as well. Policies suffer also from mismatches between the demand for, and supply of, skills developed in educational and training facilities.

This briefly sets the framework within which MNEs have been operating in Greece. Their development and dynamics, effects on competition and market structure, role in manufactured exports from Greece within the enlarged EEC, urban and regional impacts in the country are detailed elsewhere (Dokopoulou, 1985; 1986b; 1986c). Although the OECD, World Bank and United Nations now classify Greece as a developed country according to its GDP per capita, manufacturing still contributes a small proportion and is typified by small firms (Dokopoulou, 1986a). Nevertheless, the development of MNE subsidiaries did raise the level of industrialisation in the country in the 1960s and early 1970s, though for some of the reasons clearly set out below, their behaviour also explains substantial stagnation during the last decade.

The chapter examines the salient features of the technology transferred to Greece by a sample of 120 manufacturing subsidiaries of foreign-owned MNEs, representing 46 per cent of the 260 MNEs operating in the country during the survey period (1982-3). The sample was collected from information in the CAP financial directory of Greek companies, 1981. It then represented 65.5 per cent of the assets and 62.0 per cent of employment in all foreign-owned manufacturing firms. The research was based on in-depth interviews of the 120 firms. The chapter also focuses on the major constraints on the policy options of a small peripheral EEC country in dealing with the MNEs. It begins by discussing the importance of the size of assets and scale of production and then analyses in turn the subsidiaries' R & D in Greece, the equipment they use in production, their organisation, relationships with the Greek public and private sectors and the policy options open to the government.

Size of Assets and Scale of Production

The Economic and Social Development Plans of Greece since the late 1950s opted for both export orientated and import substituting, modern, large, capital intensive plants built partly or wholly by foreign as well as by national firms, viewing them also as an index of high technology transfer. This view is supported by the research of Nikolaou (1980), who found an association between the large size of plants in Greece and labour substitution. Yet, as Table 14.1 suggests, the majority of 74 subsidiaries' respondents said that the company's plant was not only small by European standards, but they were the smallest within their groups. Even major Greek subsidiary companies in vehicle assembly (Biamax and Steyer), vegetable fats (Elais [Unilever]), petrochemicals (Ethyl Hellas, Thessaloniki Refining [formerly owned by Exxon]), steel products (Hellenic Steel [formerly owned by Nippon Steel]), cables production (Manuli), machinery work-shops (Kouppas) and tyres (Goodyear) were all small. This finding indicates that protectionism is crucial in economically supporting (subsidising) small-scale output and in determining subsidiaries' profitability. Indeed, only in two cases were Greek subsidiaries found to be about the European average in scale: one manufacturing tiles, the other preserving fruits and tomatoes. It appears, then, that the role of small economies like Greece is to scale down efficiently production from that of the intermediate products made on a large scale in advanced economies to that of short runs of final and custom-made products.

Comparisons of output size between subsidiaries operating in Greece and in advanced countries must take account of the following points:

1. The revision of optimum scale of output upwards or downwards because of changes in the technology and the organisation of production. Some processes may be subcontracted out as, for example, packing in food processing.
2. There is a different mix, and range of products and the degree of vertical integration, specialisation and automation. An example is the subsidiary of a British chemical firm which makes 57 products for cleaning

243

TECHNOLOGY TRANSFER TO THE EEC PERIPHERY

Table 14.1: Size of Plants of Foreign Subsidiaries in Greece
in 1981, by Comparison to European Standards.

Size	No of Subsidiaries	(%)
Small; smallest in the group of affiliated	64	86.5
Average size; average in the group	8	10.8
Large in Europe and in the group	2	2.7
Total	74	100.0

Source: Interviews.

and maintenance in houses and ships; employs 27 works and only segments of processes of the Greek plant can be compared to those of the parent in England. In small markets there is a wide range of parameters, consumers, and numerous inputs, all requiring small outputs which prevent specialisation, automation and large scale of production. However, some automation may be introduced in smaller parts of processes such as materials handling, storage and packing. Also one-third of the 120 foreign subsidiaries undertake custom-made orders as part of their production. For instance, in 1980-1, 1 firm assembling transport equipment produced 5 types of buses in a run of only 1200; a second firm 3 different types of buses in a production run of only 300.

Lack of standardisation and specialisation characterises also the major firms in the electrical engineering and machinery sectors. The manager of the largest firm in the non-electrical engineering sector described the 2 branch plants of the firm as "workshops with old methods of production where most work is done by hand and there is little use of numerically-controlled tools". Each year the firm undertakes an export order for, or wins a tender from the Public Electricity Corporation for different types of equipment. An example of low levels of specialisation as due to the segmentation of the market is the pharmaceutical sector: a large number of preparations apply to the same prescription; the number of MNEs represented by sales subsidiaries of pharmaceuticals is 450 and some 100 MNEs have licensed local manufacturers to produce drugs.

3. Many of the large plants are suffering overcapacity. The major firm in vehicle assembly - in terms of

244

sales, assets and jobs - had in 1983 50 per cent surplus capacity. A steel products subsidiary, with 800 employees, amongst the top 10 of all manufacturers in Greece by sales and exports, had 15 per cent surplus capacity between 1980 and 1983.

4. Labour intensity varies considerably between plants of different, or of the same subsidiaries and also within several parts of the plant, forming something of a dualistic structure, a point explained in the section on the use of secondhand equipment.

Research and Development

Table 14.2 shows that amongst 108 respondents only 9, 12.5 per cent, had carried out original research and development in Greece. This was done either on a temporary or on a permanent basis, while, in parallel, the subsidiary used licences and patents from the parent plant. R & D involved development and adaptation of standardised processes and products with the use of imported components: design of knitted garments; shapes for PVC irrigation pipes; design of a disposable razor; improvement and development of miniature circuit breakers using the parent's high technology imported components; design of a lamp; adaptation and development of freezer trailers and buses; design and improvement of machinery for asbestos cement products; exploration of local clays for the production of ceramic tiles.

From the 9 subsidiaries which had carried out original R & D, only 3 had permanent technical personnel totalling 26 working on research projects. As Table 14.3 shows from the sample of 108 subsidiaries, 15 employed 86 persons on research projects; this represented 0.012 per cent of their office employment. Six of the 15 subsidiaries with the R & D activities employed 36 on a full-time basis. In 10 subsidiaries, the administrative personnel, including directors, were employed occasionally or part-time on research projects, the context of which is detailed in Table 14.2. Some 89 subsidiaries revealed the source of their technology supply. Most frequently this is a single country and most often an EEC one: 56 (63 per cent) of subsidiaries are dependent on 3 countries for technology, first on West Germany, second on UK, and third on USA.

Product Cycle

The production of foreign subsidiaries operating in Greece involves mature products and emphasis is on assembly operations. Table 14.4 summarises the information given by 68 foreign subsidiaries on the standards of the technology of their principal product in 1982. The sample, which does not include pharmaceuticals firms, reveals the backward product

Table 14.2: Research and Development Activity in 108 Foreign Subsidiaries in Greece, 1981.

Research and Development (R&D)	Subsidiaries	(%)
Original R&D	9	8.3
Employ personnel on R&D	15	13.8
of which: full-time	6	5.5
part-time	10	9.2
Total	108	100.0

Source: Interviews.

Table 14.3: Personnel Employed in 16 Subsidiaries in Greece in Research and Development, 1981.

Subsidiaries	Projects	Employees	Status
6	Adaptation of cosmetics; development and packing of vegetable oils; cereals; exploration of minerals; improvements and adaptation of freezer trucks; and buses	36	Full-time
10	Adaptation and scaling down of pharmaceuticals and cosmetics; final uses in fertilisers; design of lamps, furniture and equipment for asbestos-cement products; applications of boilers; adaptation, design and improvements on circuit breakers; adaptation of farm tractors	50	Part-time
Total 16		86	

Source: Interviews.

technology of the overwhelming majority of respondents. Few foreign firms use relatively modern technology. Most often they transfer either a standard traditional product or a low and older technology product of the "modern sector". In all these cases the product is made with the same technology and has undergone minor adaptations and adjustments to the physical conditions and to consumers tastes. The major

Table 14.4: Product Technology of 68 Foreign Subsidiaries in Greece, in 1982.*

Product Technology	Subsidiaries	(%)
Old technology but in use and of comparable standard to those in Europe	59	86.7
Old technology, satisfactory standard but not in use in Europe	34	50.0
Old technology, in use in Europe but inferior standards in Greece	7	10.2
Modern technology developed during the last 1-4 years in Europe	7	10.2
Total	68	100.0

Source: Interviews.
* The samples excludes pharmaceutical firms.

Table 14.5: Age of Product and Process Technology Upon Introduction into Greece in Major Innovation Processes Completed between 1977 and 1983, and Planned for 1984, by 12 Foreign Subsidiaries.*

Product Innovation	Age of product when introduced (years)	Date of process technology
Roller dried cereals	traditional	outdated
Plastic distribution panels	10	"
Military transport equipment	10	1972
" " "	9	1975
Professional materials for baking and confectionery	6	1977
Fiber optics	5	1977
Welded beer cans	3	1977
Tub margarines	3	1977
Radial tyres	4	1979
Welded open top tins	4	1979
Miniature circuit breakers	own design	1982/83
Electrical switches	5	1982
Melaminated chipboards	10	1983
Flexes	standard	1970
Total projects 14		

Source: Interviews.
* Clothing and pharmaceutical firms are excluded.

investments by foreign capital in the 1960s in the basic industries of Greece involved processes for intermediate standardised products such as aluminium, steel products, fertilisers and refined oil. Technological changes in these industries occurred as small improvements and as new uses in final products, energy savings, environmental protection and processing equipment. In mature industries and traditional products it is the processing equipment that undergoes important change rather than the product itself. Examples of backward technology transferred by MNEs subsidiaries in Greece in mature products include: roller-dried breakfast cereals (see Table 14.5); hand operated fruit sorting, cutting, peeling and stemming; hand-operated metal-welding, steel rolling, galvanising and metal-working.

Less frequently, the outmoded products are of inferior standards to those accepted in Europe. A smaller percentage of subsidiaries produced goods that had been largely displaced in other West European markets. This displacement was largely due to the need to provide after-sales services for the new products in those markets. For example, sack packing in Europe has been replaced by containers and silo-lorries. The subsidiaries in Greece producing outmoded goods sell imported latest technology goods, i.e., insulating materials, electric distribution panels, baby slips, chipboards, TV sets and telecommunications equipment. Only a small proportion of the respondents in 1981 had a new product in their line, which was less than two years old, and these firms had created some product and equipment innovation.

Table 14.5 shows information from 12 foreign subsidiaries regarding the age of their products and of the production technology used in 14 projects (excluding pharmaceuticals and clothing firms) completed between 1977 and 1983 or planned for 1984. Only one product amongst the 12, miniature circuit breakers, when introduced in Greece was less than a year old. In 11 products, technology at the time of introduction was traditional, standard and or between 3 and 10 years old. In 3 projects, methods of production were introduced after 1980; in 6 projects, process technology dated after 1980; in 6, process technology dated from between 1975 and 1979; and in 3 was outmoded. The majority of the 14 projects of the 12 subsidiaries involved either mature or low technology products, the largest subsidiaries investing in textiles, drinks, bus assembly, steel products, detergents, fertilisers and petrochemicals.

Equipment

The difficulties of comparing plants in Greece with those in other advanced countries were explained earlier. The gaps in technology standards between plants of subsidiaries in Greece and their affiliates in advanced countries in 1981 are shown in

Table 14.6. Around half of respondents, including very large ones, admitted that their equipment was much inferior in technological status compared with that in their European counterparts. Large segments of production were hand-operated with low automation, especially in the largest subsidiaries in clothing, plastics, detergents, mechanical and electrical engineering and metal goods.

Only 12 respondents in 67 considered their production installations to be comparable in large measure to European standards and in 11 subsidiaries only sections of equipment were as advanced as those in affiliated plants. Modernisation of the latter included:

1. Extension of capacity, without replacement of outmoded equipment. For instance, new capacity in 1980-83 of subsidiary in cold steel rolling and galvanising mills raised the existing output steel products threefold. The older secondhand purchased mills of 1966 were retained to facilitate the undertaking of small scale specialised orders. But the old galvanising baths were replaced by modern ones, though galvanised plates represented less than 10 per cent of the firm's sales after the investment. In the older galvanising method, black metal was cut into shapes before being placed in the electrolytic bath.

2. Replacement of only part of the outmoded equipment because of product change. This was most characteristic in cotton spinning and food processing. A subsidiary employing 1100 workers had 3 units for spinning carded cotton yarn; the first, established in 1963, contained 23 per cent of the spindles; the second since 1975 had 40 per cent of the spindles; and the third in 1979 had 37 per cent. In 1982 the firm innovated the older mills built in 1963 and converted their output to higher-technology cotton combed yarns to meet competition from low-cost countries in carded yarns.

3. Replacement of some machinery used in oil refining, petrochemicals and fertiliser production. The reasons given by the firms for their backward installations were the small scale of output and the lack of stimulus to local plant modernisation. For example, the formulation of insecticides at a small plant of 40 employees was basically hand-mixing of active ingredients in a workshop where office personnel are also involved in manual occupations from time to time. Hand bottling of Liquified Petroleum Gas (LPG) is carried out at the installations of 2 subsidiaries, the management of which admitted that the standards are the worst in safety and technology in the whole

TECHNOLOGY TRANSFER TO THE EEC PERIPHERY

Table 14.6: Comparison of Plant Equipment Technology in 67 Foreign Subsidiaries Operating in Greece, Relative to their European Counterparts, 1981.

Technology of plant equipment	Subsidiaries	(%)	Sectors
Inferior, small scale automation and innovation	34	51	food processing, knitting, clothing, packing, chipboards, plastics, detergents, paints, drugs, LPG, bricks, non-electrical machines, telecommunication equipment, car batteries, tins
Comparable in large measure	12	18	drugs, cosmetics, paper, plastics, pipes, asbestos, cables, porcelain goods, microprocessors, electrical goods
Comparable only in sections	11	16	margarines, cotton spinning tiles, petrochemicals, fertilizers, asbestos products, cold rolled steel, electrical goods, transport equipment
Incomparable	10	15	
Total	67	100	

Source: Interviews.

of the Mediterranean region: in most western European countries LPG is supplied by pipe. Specialised insulating paints and materials are prepared by mixing additives in quite elementary installations of a subsidiary employing 7 workers. The Greek partner of a West German manufacturer of tubular heating elements employing 40 employees, pointed out that whilst their equipment was inferior to West German affiliated plants, it was much better than their Greek competitors' plants of larger size. The technical manager of an Italian - formerly West German - subsidiary assemblying 300 buses and employing 152 workers, argued that: "the plant has an elementary workshop organisation, connected with its backward equipment".

250

Outmoded equipment is the cause of substantial productivity differentials between the Greek subsidiaries of MNEs and their affiliates abroad. The director of a plant making chipboards explained that affiliated plants in Belgium with the same number of workers have a five-fold larger output per worker. A Swedish subsidiary's manager explained that productivity differences in time per car battery per worker in the sector in 1982, were approximately 45 minutes in Greece, 23-24 minutes in Sweden and 12 in Japan. The production of one bus involves the employment of 2 workers per year in the plant of an Italian subsidiary and there is little motive to raise productivity because of protection against cheaper imports.

The lack of stimulus to plant modernisation is due to several factors:

1. High costs of investment, linked with the economic recession.
2. Unsuitability of local skills. The respondent from a clothing firm, a subsidiary of a West German one, said: "The clothing subsidiaries, especially those on subcontracting, utilise inferior equipment compared to that in plants in West Germany. Modernisation is constrained by unsuitable educational standards in Greece and the lack of appropriate people for maintenance of equipment. None of our employees had any vocational qualification; as a result they were trained in the plant".
Representatives from a steel plant and from a ceramic-tiles unit said that the low skills level and the lack of industrial tradition in their respective sectors in Greece attract less technically sophisticated equipment. Most automated machines wear out quickly because of improper use by workers.
3. Dependence on parent plant decisions for larger investment. Respondents from 6 subsidiaries in electrical engineering, plastic, chipboards, cosmetics and tractors said that modernisation of their Greek subsidiary is decided in relation to the interests of the whole group. For example, the liability position of the corporation rather than that of the subsidiary is important. The parent may also decide to cease production of its Greek subsidiary when it has inventories to sell from more strategic production centres.
4. Although gross hourly earnings by manual workers in Greece increased by 450 per cent between 1975 and 1982, the largest rate in the EEC 'ten'

251

(Dokopoulou, 1985, p. 64), wages are still well below the EEC average and thus may not have increased sufficiently to justify automation of some production processes, like hand sorting and packing.

5. Modernisation can be constrained by differences in the rates of equipment depreciation between Greece and other countries where competitors operate. The link between variations in profitability and depreciation rates amongst EEC countries was demonstrated by Snoy (1975). The executive of a plant spinning cotton explained that the firm had purchased equipment in 1983 for combing yarns and depreciation was expected to take place in 8 years and 4 months. Competitors in West Germany, however, were permitted to depreciate their equipment in only 4 years, which is about the time lag between innovations in this field. The discrepancy between the frequency of innovations and the time allowed for depreciation was often stated as an important reason for the lag in plant modernisation in Greece. Similar comment was made in cable manufacturing.

The Use of Secondhand Equipment

A sample of 28 subsidiaries were asked if they made use of secondhand equipment. Nine of them utilised secondhand equipment – 7 of these were amongst the larger in the sales in their sectors. One rented all its equipment for fruit preserving, which was secondhand, from a US subsidiary which specialises in hiring machinery to plants in less developed countries; a Swiss subsidiary, which started with secondhand equipment purchased in 1963 for knitting and sewing underwear, was still using it in 1983. A top maker of PVC sheets, a West German firm, utilises partly secondhand machinery bought in 1963! Another West German firm, assembling components for comparatively outmoded telephone switchboards, also employs secondhand equipment. Similarly the machinery used in transformer assembly had been delivered to the Greek plant from another company affiliate abroad which had been closed and, in 1983, this represented the largest proportion of the value of the assets of the Greek subsidiary. Secondhand equipment makes up more than 10 per cent of the productive installations of the largest foreign-owned cable-making plant. In one steel plant, the old cold rolling mills were retained to cater for small-scale custom-made orders. Finally, from 1975 until 1983 a Swiss-owned electrical engineering subsidiary used processes which were largely outmoded in Europe; only in 1983 did the firm install new machinery, but this still represents only 5 per cent of the subsidiary's total assets.

TECHNOLOGY TRANSFER TO THE EEC PERIPHERY

This situation shows <u>dualism within</u> plants of MNE subsidiaries in Greece, a phenomenon which seems to have attracted little or no research attention: part of the plant equipment is secondhand and is not scrapped when newer machinery is installed. That shows the <u>coexistence on one site</u> of different production processes apparently of different performance, yielding different product designs and standards, and possibly serving distinct market segments. This situation contrasts with more advanced countries and their major companies, often multinationals, which retool entire production units, as is outlined in the case of Volvo AB in Chapter 3 by Ellegard and Alvstam.

Technology Transfer in Production Organisation

The 1983-87 Draft Plan for Economic Development (Greek Parliament, 1983) favours the transfer of experience and management by the MNEs into Greek manufacturing as it is anticipated that this would upgrade the initial industrial structure and improve the productivity, efficiency and decision-making of local firms. Similar views, expressed by the managements of MNE respondents, were summed up as follows by the manager of a tractor-assembly subsidiary:

> "Production of technologically-advanced products cannot be transferred into Greece only by the purchase of licences and know-how by the local capitalists. Direct involvement by foreign management is essential to give the local labour experience in engineering and highly skilled jobs and in the management of production".

One important aspect of the transfer of organisational skill is the expected productivity gain. But gains from improvements in the organisation of production occur with parallel investment in modernisation. This is true for the clothing and knitwear industries in which the increase in the speed of machines in sewing and knitting is more important for the replacement of work. Reorganisation of work without investments may not achieve cost reductions to compensate for wage increases. Some assembly processes may undergo improvements in productivity from reorganisation of positions of work as, for example, the assembly of buses or of electrical devices, restructuring and replacing old routine tasks by jobs of a more composite nature (see Chapter 3 in this volume). The most significant effect on raising productivity without investment was mentioned by the manager of a firm making baby slips:

> "A French technical director, who was sent from the parent plant, increased output per day from 100,000 pieces to 250,000 simply by better work organisation".

The size of output may limit the effect of organisational improvements. For instance, assembly workshops of foreign subsidiaries often lack proper organisation, a problem also common to small Greek family-run firms. According to the technical director of a bus assembly workshop:

"Employees work as individuals in non-supervised tasks trying to self-adjust in their group. Organisation is elementary, jobs are manual, the floor space is small and its shape most inappropriate for an efficient arrangement of tasks. The development controls prohibit in situ expansion within Athens and the firm cannot solve this problem by buying a plot next to it. The present organisation is also influenced by the values and attitudes of its previous management, a foreign firm also; its aim was to reduce spending on equipment and supervision and opted for empiricism in a workshop".

Major organisational changes may come because of structural changes in equipment, the motive for which is the reduction of working time. These changes may or may not shift the occupational structure of the plants to one with a less skilled content, but may create a new model of work and demand for different traits in labour. According to executives from Aluminium de Grèce:

"The old type of skilled manual worker had to intervene directly in the materials with his mastery and dexterity; the new type of work demands by contrast specialisation, less hand work and more responsibility, attention, discipline and higher education. For example, the firm has converted the older side-fed electrolytic basins into centrally-fed ones. The effect is a reduced number of workers moving in the same floorspace and more workers supervising".

In other instances the increase in the speed of machines has increased the output per worker and the repetitive nature of tasks as, for example, in rolling mills and can manufacture. If the project is of a strategic nature to its parent, labour may not be reduced because good industrial relations are important.

Organisational innovations need an appropriate infrastructure for vocational training, modernisation of the labour institutions and policies, and a change in attitudes of policy makers. National policies have the task to encourage qualitative changes in occupational structure brought about by the new technology requiring the demise of the traditional model of work and workers. In this context, policymakers and managements of firms collaborate to dismantle the system of benefits of the working class acquired over a long period of time. Their argument in doing so is that the existing system of labour remuneration is a disincentive to introduce innovations. The onus of defending a welfare system for the working class, whilst maintaining or improving national competitiveness in world markets and of encouraging innovation, thus falls entirely on the workers. In this context, then, the issue least understood by policymakers is the link between the need for provision of social capital - generally considered by policymakers as unproductive - and the technological innovations embodying a new model of worker and work. This point was best illustrated by the manager of a steelmaking plant:

> "The qualitative background of and the need for higher living standards of workers required by the modern technology has not been understood by the policymakers in the post-war years who envisaged the transformation of peasants into industrial workers. The qualitative improvement of labour in peripheral areas is constrained by the poor environmental conditions as bad housing and deprivation of social facilities essential to maintain a level of labour productivity in an advanced technology plant".

TRANSFER OF TECHNOLOGY TO GREEK PUBLIC AND PRIVATE SECTORS

Policies in Greece on technology transfer consider MNEs as a principle supplier of proprietary technology. The potential of attracting MNEs in high technology industries in Greece contrasts with the policies of advanced countries to develop and retain high technology industry within their territory (Hills, 1984); it has also been confronted with the adjustment and reorganisation of the production by the parents of the foreign-owned subsidiaries operating there; some of these subsidiaries changed products and some ceased production.

The transfer of proprietary technology involves a substantial transactional cost for the MNE in engineering, adaptation, learning of skills during the start-up phase, and in communications and documentation due to the local and national bureaucracy (Teece, 1977). Moreover, costs of technology transfer are high: some knowledge cannot be transferred in codified form and without the transfer of people who possess skills because intimate personal contacts, demonstration and involvement are required (Teece, 1983).

Unfavourable factors which discourage investment from MNEs in high technology industries in Greece are: the limited market potential for high technology industries; the state purchasing of high technology equipment from a particular source; the uncertainty about governmental support for an important foreign investment; and the lack of appropriate local skills. An effective technology transfer to public or private sector firms should be seen in connection with the potential of marketing the new products and technology. The public sector has limited competence to do so, while the private sector's incentive for marketing the licensed advantages can be motivated or constrained by the government's protectionist measures.

The public sector could become an important driving force in the transfer of high technology industry to Greece. It has the potential of spending on R & D and on minerals exploration and exploitation, on agriculture, health, education, transport and telecommunications - all sectors controlled by the state in Greece. Yet spending on R & D in both public and private sectors has been very low since 1960, representing less than 0.02 per cent of the GNP annually. Persons employed on R & D were fewer than 2500 in 1981 (Centre for Planning & Economic Research, 1982; and Greek Parliament, 1983).

Governments may intervene in the tenders of public corporations by setting low standards. This may have the effect of displacing higher-cost, higher-quality bidders such as MNE subsidiaries and favour locally-owned low-cost bidders, some of whom in a country like Greece may effectively belong to the informal sector. Such governmental behaviour can be explained as efforts to reduce public expenditure during economic recession or to maintain trading arrangements with socialist countries which can supply "mature" industrial equipment more cheaply. Greek public corporations have purchased capital goods such as telecommunications equipment, power plants, transformers, railway vehicles, trolleybuses and buses from Eastern Europe and the USSR under barter trade agreements arising out of the demand in these countries for surplus Greek primary produce, particularly fruits, vegetables and bauxite. Indeed, the sale of part of the surplus farm produce to CMEA countries through the barter trade helps to dampen the persistent economic and social problems of the rural population. It must be emphasised that agriculture still employs 30 per cent of the Greek workforce, while 30 per cent of the entire population live in rural communes with fewer than 10,000 inhabitants. So the scale of the problem is relatively great, especially bearing in mind that agriculture contributes less than 13 per cent of GDP. So, in fact, sales to the CMEA acts as a safety valve to reduce the incidence of demonstrations in which Greek farmers block major roads with their State-subsidised "Datsun" pick-up trucks.

There are also other vital sectors of the economy depending on State spending for the quality of their inputs: hospitals, farming and education, and in which MNE proprietary technology is important. Economic recession and reductions in State spending led policymakers to attempt to limit the profit margins of companies supplying goods to the State, amongst which are fertilisers, animal feedstuffs and pharmaceuticals. Such controls may thus discourage MNEs from investing in higher standard products and hence in introducing more advanced technologies. The transfer of technology by the public sector in Greece requires flexibility and speed in the structure of public administration, de-centralisation in decision-making on development issues, and fundamental changes in the attitudes and capabilities of the civil servants. It also requires modernisation of the capital-financing structures that are controlled by the State.

In the private sector the transfer of high technology by MNEs has been associated with, first, the strengthening of the competitive position of the firm as technology lowers costs per unit. Pigagniol (1972) distinguishes three types of improvements designed to lower production costs: product improvements concerned with higher quality at the same or lower prices; substitution which involves changing techniques to reduce output costs and transform materials; and innovations which mean capturing a market niche not occupied by competitors.

Second, mass production of consumers' goods during the mature stage is associated also with technology transfer (Vernon, 1966). There is evidence that MNEs participated with local capitalists in joint ventures and that most often MNEs set up their operations in Greece with a financial con-tribution from Greek investors rather than through the take-over of a local firm (Dokopoulou, 1985). The response of the Greek capitalists to the opportunities offered by MNEs to cooperate was significant, the motive often being to innovate and modernise existing plants. It is suggested, therefore, that a policy for joint projects between MNEs subsidiaries and local entrepreneurs is one field for high technology promotion. Moreover, export-orientated firms tend to invest more readily in innovations because of their need to retain international competitiveness. By contrast protectionist policies reduce the incentives for the private sector to innovate.

POLICY OPTIONS FOR TECHNOLOGY TRANSFER TO GREECE

The policy to attract technology to Greece, incorporated in the 1983-87 Draft Plan, mainly points to the need to upgrade Greek industrial structure which has experienced increasing technological obsolescence throughout the 1970s and early 1980s. Little innovation and modernisation occurred after 1971 to replace labour, the cost of which was rising relatively. The investment rate fell considerably, becoming negative by 1982. Policy favours a restructuring of Greek manufacturing towards advanced technologies and information industries rather than the expansion of labour-intensive ones. This aim is in conflict, however, with the broader strategy of the Draft Plan which is to transform the rural labour force to the greatest extent, a change which is envisaged to take place through the development of manufacturing and services to absorb population from less productive agricultural occupations. The achievement of this goal has been set precisely when inter-firm technological competition and restructuring worldwide has shed millions of workers from manufacturing in the developed countries.

The strategy to promote high technology industries, and in particular the information sector, and ways to achieve it need to be elaborated in greater detail. At present they are stated too broadly by the government. For example, Hills (1984) defines 6 strategic choices which are designed to eliminate technological gaps: (1) to allow a free market in technology and hand over the product market to MNEs (a strategy adopted by Belgium, Italy, Spain, Portugal and Norway); (2) to borrow foreign technology for domestic manufacture and allow free product market (UK); (3) to borrow foreign technology for domestic manufacture and exclude foreign investment and imports (Japan); (4) to develop domestic technology whilst excluding foreign investment and imports (Japan): and (5) to develop domestic technology whilst allowing foreign investment and imports (UK, France, West Germany and Sweden).

MNEs in Greece account for major modern product markets (chemicals, metals, engineering, electrical goods and transport equipment). This is to a large extent the result of State monopoly power over sectors where high technology can be sold. The "borrowing" of technology from MNEs is more economic than developing an indigenous one because of the lack of resources and local infrastructure. The cost of adapting technology to local conditions in Greece is a major field for research. In this case, investment from MNEs should be encouraged in cooperation with local entrepreneurs, shareholders and cooperatives but away from the central bureaucratic State. MNEs will provide process engineering design of production and planning of process knowledge which small and medium sized local entrepreneurs and cooperatives lack. The purchasing of technology from leaders is prohibitively costly, and in Greece this is constrained by two factors. First, local capitalists are not allowed to export currency for such purchases - there has been only one exception so far, the take over by Piraiki, a German textile firm. Second, parents get rid of subsidiaries with rather obsolete equipment; this was the case with the oil refining and petrochemical installations of Exxon taken over by the Greek government in 1983. But even if the State would purchase a plant with relatively modern equipment working at full capacity, it would be faced with an inefficient civil service apparatus to run it.

TECHNOLOGY TRANSFER TO THE EEC PERIPHERY

A major constraint in technology transfer choice in Greece has been the non-existent or weak linkages between the government, industry and the educational community, the so-called research triangle (Behrman, 1980). Governments in Greece have not undertaken yet the catalytic role of supplying funds for developments of products and research in manufacturing; this is because their function has been confined to control demand for high technology services and products; and because their objectives and priorities have been conflicting with those in industry and in the Universities. Policies for regional development in Greece need to adopt flexible classification of manufacturing investment regarding sectors which are of low, medium and high technology; and of subsidies given to firms to locate in problem regions, for instance. A more appropriate classification according to the technology content of the project should take into account changes in the product itself; in material inputs; in processing equipment; and in office-related services.

REFERENCES

Behrman, J.N. (1980) Industry Ties with Science and Technology Policies in Developing Countries, Oelgeschlager, Gunn and Hain, Cambridge, Mass.
Casson, M. (1979) Alternatives to the Multinational Enterprise, Macmillan, London
Dokopoulou, E. (1985) Foreign Investment in Manufacturing in Greece: Linkages and Spatial Impacts, unpublished Ph.D. Thesis, University of London
Dokopoulou, E. (1986a) 'Small Manufacturing Firms and Regional Development in Greece: Patterns and Changes' in David Keeble and Egbert Wever (eds.), New Firms and Regional Development in Europe, Croom Helm, London, pp. 299-317
Dokopoulou, E. (1986b) 'Foreign Manufacturing Investment in Greece: Competition and Market Structure' in F.E.I. Hamilton (ed.), Industrialisation in Developing and Peripheral Regions, Croom Helm, London, pp. 186-202
Dokopoulou, E. (1986c) 'Multinationals and Manufactured Exports from the Enlarged EEC Periphery' in F.E.I. Hamilton (ed.), op cit., pp. 203-229
Dunning, J.H. and Pearce, R.D. (1980) The World's Largest Industrial Enterprises
Dunning, J.H., Haberich, K.O. and Stopford, J.M. (1980) The World Directory of Multinational Enterprises, Macmillan, London
Dunning, J.H. and Stopford, J.M. (1983) Multinationals, Company Performance and Global Trends, Macmillan, Basingstoke

Greece, Centre for Planning and Economic Research (1972) Technology: The Plan for the Long-Term Development of Greece, 1973-1978, Centre for Planning and Economic Research, Athens, in Greek

Greek Parliament (1983) Five Year Plan for Economic and Social Development 1983-1987, Greek Government, Athens, in Greek

Gulcz, M. and Gruchman, B. (1981) 'Industrial Investment Assistance: the Socialist Countries' Approach to the Third World' in F.E.I. Hamilton and G.J.R. Linge (eds.), Spatial Analysis, Industry and the Industrial Environment, Vol. 2, International Industrial Systems, Wiley, Chichester/New York, pp. 215-224

Gutman, P. and Arkwright, F. (1981) 'Tripartite Industrial Cooperation between East, West and South' in F.E.I. Hamilton and G.J.R. Linge (eds.), op cit., pp. 185-214

Hills, J. (1984) Information Technology and Industrial Policy, Croom Helm, London

Leroy, G. (1978) 'Technology Transfer within the Multinational Enterprise' in M. Ghertman and J. Leoniades (eds.), European Research in International Business, North Holland, Amsterdam

Nikolaou, K. (1980) Economies of Scale in Greek Manufacturing Industry, Centre for Planning and Economic Research, Athens, in Greek

Pigagniol, P. 'Industrial Competition and R & D' in A. Kapoor and P.D. Grub (eds.), The Multinational Enterprise in Transition, Darwin Press, Princeton, N.J.

Rugman, A.M. (1981) Inside the Multinationals, Croom Helm, London

Snoy, B. (1975) Taxes on Direct Investment Income in the EEC: A Legal and Economic Analaysis, Prager, New York

Teece, D.J. (June 1977) 'Technology Transfer by Multinational Firms: The Resource Cost of Transferring Technological Know-How', The Economic Journal, 87, 242-61

Teece, D.J. (1983) 'Technological and Organisational Factors in the Theory of the Multinational Enterprise' in M. Casson (ed.), The Growth of International Business, Allen and Unwin, London

UK Department of Trade and Industry (1983) Multinational Investment Strategies in the British Isles: A Study of MNEs in the UK Assisted Areas and the Republic of Ireland, HMSO, London

Vernon, R. (May 1966) 'International Investment and International Trade in the Product Cycle', Quarterly Journal of Economics, 80, 190-207

Chapter Fifteen

POLICY AND HIGH TECHNOLOGY COMPLEXES:
OTTAWA'S "SILICON VALLEY NORTH"

Guy P. F. Steed

FORLORN HOPES? POLICYMAKERS UNDER PRESSURE

Many communities across North America and Europe have been
beset for several years with a host of economic ills. Their
local and state or provincial policymakers have been subject
to great pressures to act. Many have sought a panacea in
programmes to make them 'high technology' communities. What
constitutes high technology has proved difficult to define
(Tomaskovic-Devey and Miller, 1983). A Canadian community
aiming to become Silicon Flats and American communities follow
a similar path (see Task Force on High Technology, Province
of Saskatchewan, 1983; Denny, 1983).
     The common prescription? Attract and enhance the
performance of R & D and introduce new technology to transform traditional manufacturing; nurture new technology-based
firms and support the emergence of new industries. To fulfil
that prescription, policymakers have sought to learn from the
experience of those who set the pace. Early approaches have
revealed some naive understanding and emulation of two high
profile success stories - Silicon Valley and Route 128 around
Boston (MacDonald, 1983). Many have assumed a close relation
exists between R & D and regional development and that a
university can provide the nucleus for success (Buswell,
1983). But is that a necessary or sufficient recipe? What
other models are there to emulate?

WHAT'S YOUR EXPERIENCE? CONFLICTING ADVICE

The pressure of quick action and speedy solutions is intense.
Policymakers have not had the good fortune to await the
results of researchers. Policymakers and researchers, of
course, live and operate in quite different worlds. Moreover,
ideas produced by ostensibly 'dispassionate' researchers need
to be adapted and changed to meet the political, institutional
and financial constraints of the real world. Early action has

261

preceded understanding, often leading to preposterous expectations.

Policymakers now have access to some research results, and there is better understanding of some mechanisms at work. Among those mechanisms, a key one has been the formation of new firms. What combination of conditions stimulates the concentration of people well versed in the commercial aspects of science and technology and contributes to the formation of new firms? A correspondent for The Economist Newspaper July 23 1983, p. 6, in reviewing the American experience, argued that new high technology companies seem to germinate best where: (1) skilled people in big firms are footloose and ready to leave; (2) people who know how to get businesses going and enjoy it can be drafted in to help; (3) universities are brimming over not only with ideas but also with academics who want to make them commercial; (4) well-known entrepreneurs have already shown that there are fortunes to be made and spurred others into imitating them; and (5) investors are ready to take risks with their own or their clients' money. These findings are supported by Bollinger, Hope and Utterbeck (1983) and Malecki (1983).

Two general types of studies provide insight into the geographic development of high technology communities: (a) macro-industry and (b) micro-community studies. The results of these studies tend to identify rather different factors or mixes of factors as keys to success. Consider for instance, three macro-studies. A 1983 Brookings Institution Report made a regional assessment for the United States and concluded that the one factor especially important to high technology development was the proportion of employment in scientific, engineering and technical occupations: "The importance of this variable must be underlined since it is somewhat amenable to public policy. Quality education from the primary to the post-graduate level can be an important factor in attracting prospective entrepreneurs, firms and employees in high technology fields" (Armington, Harris and Odle, 1983). The point is of particular pertinence for a city such as Montreal. The Fantus Corporation, for instance, reportedly has revealed that operating a high-technology plant in Montreal in the early 1980s costs significantly less than it does in leading American cities. However, those leading US cities are not Montreal's primary competition. Moreover, qualified engineers, scientists and technicians have been unwilling to relocate to Montreal compared to other cities because of language legislation affecting education, as well as other factors such as high personal income taxes and political uncertainties (The (Montreal) Gazette, February 4, 1984).

Relate that to Markusens's (1984) results. The key factor, albeit with a low explanatory level, in her model of high-tech dependence by county for the United States was defence spending. Defence spending, she argues, helped create amenity communities and attract science and technology personnel (United States Office of Technical Assessment, 1984). And contrast these results with the findings of a survey of American high technology companies by the Joint Economic Committee of Congress (1982). The survey listed a region's skilled labour, taxes, and academic institutions to be its most important attractions to high technology companies.

Turn now to the studies of successful high-tech communities. What conclusions and advice do researchers offer policymakers this time?

Four factors (Malecki, 1984) usually receive emphasis as the bases leading to successful high-tech regional development, namely the roles of: local universities; state or provincial and local government policies; federal government institutions and programmes; and private sector high-tech activity - spin-offs and venture capital.

But these factors play different roles in different communities. And even within the same community, agreement on the factors does not necessarily mean agreement on their role. For instance, a common assumption in the Silicon Valley model, one that has driven policy advice in communities from Adelaide, Australia to Vancouver, Canada, is that high technology of the original Silicon Valley has been derived from the universities. This is based, however, on what some argue is an inappropriate adherence to the linear model of technological change (Braun and MacDonald, 1982). While there was certainly significant information flow between the universities and industry in the Silicon Valley, key flows were reputedly as much from industry to university as vice versa.

Universities clearly played a significant role in the formation of the Silicon Valley and Route 128 complexes, but that does not mean high technology complexes necessarily can only germinate in proximity to universities. It may also be questioned whether academic institutions less steeped in a tradition of research at the frontier of developments in science and technology can provide the same stimulus to regional innovation (see Dorfman, 1983).

A simplistic summation of the available literature on the role of these four factors in the emergence of four American high technology communities is provided in Table 15.1. It is interesting that in the case of the two less high-profile success stories, state and local government policies have had a large role. Does this augur well for other communities? Hardly so. Certainly it does not necessarily mean there is hope for any and all state and local governments to get in on the high tech action. But frequent reference to the footloose-ness of such industries only contributes to feverish expectations of being able to dig Silicon Valleys, Cities, Glens, Corridors, or Flats at will. Is the end product likely to be a negative, zero, or positive sum game?

Table 15.1: Key Factors in Development of Five High Technology Communities.

Factors	Silicon Valley	Boston Route 128	N.Carolina Triangle	Austin	Ottawa
1. Local Universities	3	3	2	1	
2. State/provincial and local government policies			3	3	
3. Federal government institutions and programs	3	3	2		3
4. Private sector activity - spin-offs, venture-capital	3	3		1	1

3 - critical; 2 - very important; 1 - important

Source: Based on Malecki, op.cit. footnote 8, and Steed and DeGenova.

Again, policymakers are subject to widely diverse advice. Many economists, in particular, are antagonistic to intergovernmental competition for high technology development - at the state or provincial and local government levels. They argue, as does Kitchen (1983) for example, that there is little, if any, role for local government policies designed to attract new capital and new business. Of course, local politicians and administrators tend adamantly to disagree. And so does the staff study for the Joint Economic Committee of Congress (1982). It judges state and local government efforts to promote high technology development as likely to be a positive sum game.

A more recent evaluation of the growing community competition for high technology industry in the United States noted a proliferation of initiatives and programmes. It found that most of the programmes are designed to encourage technological innovation and local business development by mobilising resources or removing barriers in six general areas: research, development and technology transfer; human capital, including education and training; entrepreneurship training and assistance; financial capital; physical capital, such as incubation facilities; and information gathering and dissemination (United States Office of Technology Assessment, 1984). It is still too early to evaluate the effectiveness of these highly varied initiatives.

OTTAWA'S EXPERIENCE AS SILICON VALLEY NORTH

The author's own research indicates yet another path toward formation of a high technology community. Its focus is Ottawa, Canada's high technology success. It is based mainly on three studies: Threshold Firms (Steed, 1982), which notes the varied role of federal grants or contracts in aiding development of several local medium-sized firms formed in the past twenty years; and research with two graduate students on locational determinants (Steed and De Genova, 1983), spin-offs and the new firm formation process (Steed and Nichol, 1985). What are our conclusions?

First, returning to the four factors mentioned earlier (Table 15.1): for Ottawa 1 (local universities) and 2 (provincial and local government policies) were largely insignificant, 3 (federal government) was crucial, and 4 (in the form of spin-offs and more recently venture capital) has become of growing relevance. So in this sense, the Ottawa model certainly differs from the other four communities.

Second, as others have found, the building of a large pool of scientists, engineers and technicians is important. However, in the case of Ottawa that pool did not derive from the formation of major universities. Ottawa is a centre of both government R & D and industrial R & D in Canada. The government R & D is of long-standing and in many respects attracted some of the key performers of industrial R & D - such as the Bell Northern Research Labs, which rank in size among the top one per cent in North America. The pool of scientists and technologists located there is only the fifth largest concentration in Canada (ranking close to Calgary and Vancouver and a long way behind Toronto and Montreal), but is greater than might be expected from population size. Its location quotient of 2.0 is exceeded by only one other Canadian metropolitan area - Calgary (see Science Council of Canada, 1984, p. 56).

Third, the growth of what is here called Ottawa's technology-orientated complex was a long time in germination. It has evolved in four stages: from an early stage as a research-orientated complex, to a second stage when emphasis shifted towards large expenditures of government funds for development work, particularly at the National Research Council, and to a third stage involving addition of private sector research labs and manufacturing facilities, including attraction of large outside firms (Northern Electric, Digital Equipment), as well as expansion of the government's own science and technology capabilities. The most recent stage of

OTTAWA'S "SILICON VALLEY NORTH"

Table 15.2: Ottawa's Technology Orientated Complex: Importance to Firm of Federal Government Proximity, by Ownership, Size, and Age of Firm, 1981.

	Very Significant 1		2		3	4	Very Insignificant 5	Total	
	No.	%	No.	%	No.	No.	No.	No.	%
Ownership									
Domestic	9	23.1	13	33.3	5	5	7	39	100
Foreign	2	33.1	2	33.3	1	–	1	6	100
Size (employees)									
1–24	3	20.0	4	26.4	2	3	3	15	100
25–49	3	33.3	2	22.2	2	1	1	9	100
50–99	1	11.1	5	55.6	–	1	2	9	100
100–450	3	37.5	2	25.0	1	–	2	8	100
451 and over	1	25.0	2	50.0	1	–	–	4	100
Age (years)									
1–5	3	21.4	4	28.6	3	1	3	14	100
6–10	3	23.1	3	23.1	1	4	2	13	100
11–15	2	22.2	3	33.3	1	–	3	9	100
16–25	1	25.0	2	50.0	1	–	–	4	100
26 or more	2	40.0	3	60.0	–	–	–	5	100

Source: Steed and DeGenova.

266

Table 15.3: Ottawa's Technology-Orientated Complex: Factors Stimulating Firm's Initial Development in Ottawa*

Factors	Firm Ownership		Firm Age (years in Ottawa area)				
	Domestic	Foreign	1-5	6-10	11-15	16-25	26 or more
Potential of the local market	7	1	3	–	3	2	–
Access to the national market	4	1	2	2	–	–	1
Availability of highly skilled labour	7	2	4	3	–	–	2
Universities	2	–	2	1	–	–	1
Research facilities	5	1	1	–	–	1	1
Land prices and rents	4	1	3	1	–	1	1
Availability of capital	4	1	2	1	–	1	–
High-tech agglomeration	12	–	4	6	2	–	–
Presence of federal government	17	4	5	4	5	3	4
Technical services	1	–	–	–	1	–	–
Professional services	1	–	–	1	1	–	–
Supplies from local manufacturers	3	–	–	2	1	–	–
Resident of area	14	1	6	6	3	–	–
Residential attraction	5	–	3	2	–	–	–

* Entries refer to number of respondents indicating that this factor was at least one of the three most significant stimulating their firm's initial development in Ottawa.

Source: Steed and Degenova.

267

development has been accompanied, if not led, by the rapid emergence and growth of locally-initiated firms and spin-offs, assisted by local venture capital, a good sign of regeneration capabilities.

And fourth, the federal role appears to have differed at each stage. In the earlier stages the government created and funded a growing pool of scientists and technologists, oriented initially to research and later with a growing development focus. Later, it also contributed to attracting some key larger firms. Their interest lay primarily in its defence contracting and information gathering roles. And, most recently, it has played a more complex and varied range of roles. As indicated in a survey of 45 high-tech manufacturing firms, it has offered, in particular, proximity advantages to many firms entering the complex (Tables 15.1 and 15.3). Interestingly, it is the most recent entrants who argue that federal government proximity is of little importance to them.

Among its roles, the federal government in Ottawa has also acted as an incubator organisation. Indeed in a survey of 88 new high-tech manufacturing and computer service firms, one-third were spin-offs from local organisations, including 10 from federal agencies. None was from the major National Research Council labs or the universities (Steed and Nichol, 1986). The federal government also had a significant role as a customer in the formation of 16 per cent of those new firms. By contrast, the provincial role has been very small. Only 10 per cent of these 88 new firms felt that the provincial government had much role in their formation, and that was mainly through loans and contracts.

A UNIQUE MODEL?

In sum, the Ottawa model, therefore, bears only a minor resemblance to the better known American models. Ottawa's high-tech development has arisen despite the absence of a strong research university and lack, until recently, of significant venture capital support. Its experience in the linkage of R & D with regional development is not likely to be easy to replicate by other communities. That is hardly a popular view among those who feel the federal government could create many equivalent high-tech communities in Canada simply by spreading industrial and innovation grants and decentralising government labs.

REFERENCES

Armington, C., Harris, C. and Odle, M. (1983) Formation and Growth in High Technology Businesses: A Regional Assessment, Brookings Institution, Washington D.C.

Bollinger, L., Hope, K. and Utterbeck, J.M. (1983) 'A Review of Literature and Hypotheses on New Technology-Based Firms', Research Policy, 12, 1-14

Braun, E. and MacDonald, S. (1982) Revolution in Miniature, Cambridge University Press, Cambridge

Buswell, R.J. (1983) 'Research and Development and Regional Development: A Review' in A. Gillespie (ed.), Technological Change and Regional Development, Pion, London, pp. 9-22

Denny, B.C. (27 August 1983) 'The High-Technology Fix', Science, 217, 791

Dorfman, N.S. (1983) 'Route 128: The Development of a Regional High Technology Economy', Research Policy, 12, 299-316

Joint Economic Committee (1982) Location of High Technology Firms and Regional Economic Development, US Government Printing Office, Washington D.C.

Kitchen, H. (1983) 'Is There a Role for Local Governments in Attracting New Capital and New Business?', Background Paper, Economic Futures Conference, Western Lake Ontario Growth Corridor, Hamilton, Ontario

MacDonald, S. (1983) 'High Technology Policy and the Silicon Valley Model', Prometheus, 1(2), 330-349

McCallum, J. (16 October 1982) 'Why it Really Matters where High-Tech Grants Go', The Financial Post, p. 8

Malecki, E. (1983) 'Technology and Regional Development: A Survey', International Regional Science Review, 8(2), 89-125

Malecki, E. (1984) 'R & D and Regional Development', Symposium on Technology & Regional Development: The Policy Issues, Syracuse University

Science Council of Canada (1984) Canadian Industrial Development: Some Policy Directions, Supply and Services Canada, Ottawa, p. 56

Steed, G.P.F. (1982) Threshold Firms, Science Council of Canada, Ottawa Background Study No. 48

Steed, G.P.F. and De Genova, D. (1983) 'Ottawa's Technology-Oriented Complex', Canadian Geographer, 27(3), 263-78

Steed, G.P.F. and Nichol, L. (forthcoming) 'Spin-offs and New Firm Formation in Ottawa'

Task Force on High Technology, Province of Saskatchewan (1983) Partners in Economic Growth

Tomaskovic-Devey, D. and Miller, S.M. (May-June 1983) 'Can High-tech Provide the Jobs?' Challenge, 57-63

United States Congress Office of Technology Assessment (1984) Technology, Innovation and Regional Economic Development, US Government Printing Office, Washington D.C.

Chapter Sixteen

BUSINESS SERVICES FOR MANUFACTURERS: DEMAND
BEHAVIOUR BY ENTERPRISES IN LOWER SAXONY

Eike W. Schamp

For more than 10 years the behavioural perspective has been
applied in industrial geography, examining individual enterprise from the micro-economic perspective. As such, decision-
making and the actions of an enterprise's management are
analysed within its spatial economic environment. According to
the fundamental conception of economic geography, that
environment consists of spatial and temporal dimensions, both
shaping manufacturers' behaviour. The methodology used is
the systems approach which has proved successful in laying
open the relationships between enterprise and environment
(Hamilton and Linge, 1979). In this approach a plant may be
defined as an element of the 'enterprise-system', the enterprise an element of the regional, national and international
system. The elements and sub-systems are interrelated and
have always been the object of analysis in industrial geography. They were introduced by A. Weber to explain the
location of an enterprise, using its relation to raw material
deposits, the market, and the labour market. In time,
changes took place in both, enterprise and environment, thus
modifying their interrelationship. This forms the context for
the following analysis of service demand by manufacturers.

THE ROLE OF BUSINESS SERVICES IN INDUSTRIAL
GEOGRAPHY

Among all enterprise linkages with the environment it is
mainly the material linkages which have been studied so far.
The findings in the industrialised nations were that linkages
between plants or enterprises are hardly determined by costs
of transport so that it is not necessary for those tied
together by material linkages to be neighbours. Consequently,
analysis of material linkages is little help in explaining the
economic structure of a region. Moreover, decreasing relative
costs of transport permit an increasing division of labour and
specialisation in industry. Recent studies reveal an increasing

270

portion of non-production employees in manufacturing enterprise and in manufacturing as a whole (Crum and Gudgin,
1977; Geilinger, 1983). The auxiliary activities for production
are obviously becoming more extensive and differentiated,
especially in multi-plant enterprises which exhibit a certain
functional and spatial division of labour among different
plants. This expresses well the long-term structural change
from secondary to tertiary sectors in national economies,
structural changes occurring both between different enterprises and inside them as well.

Thus it is not by chance that industrial geography
studies tend to deal more with service linkages between the
enterprise and its economic environment (see: Britton, 1974,
Bater and Walker, 1977, in Canada; Marshall, 1979, 1982, in
Great Britain; O'Farrell and O'Loughlin, 1981, in Ireland;
Dézert, 1976, Rousset-Deschamps, 1984, in France; Grotz,
1980, Schickhoff, 1983, in the German Federal Republic). In
classical location theory externalised services are factors
which determine the urbanisation economy. The availability of
short-distance services ('low order services', according to
Britton) indicates a promising environment for industrial
enterprise (Britton, 1974, p. 378; Norcliffe, 1975, p. 48;
O'Farrell and O'Loughlin, 1981, p. 440). As services are
concentrated in towns, the type of regional urban system is
an important determinant for the quality of the regional
environment for industrial enterprise. Hence discussion in
West Germany to work out urbanisation policy for 'depressed
areas' in rural regions to create the basic requirements for
establishing industry in those parts (e.g., Fester, 1976).
This recommendation, however, seems not to solve the
problems of today as there are scarcely any industrial enterprises willing to locate in these areas. Efforts are rather
concentrated on maintaining at least the established industry
in the depressed areas. A dense urban network, however, is
also important for a policy which aims at safeguarding the
survival of old enterprises as well as securing their chances
of growth.

Nevertheless, most studies still concentrate on the
plant-level spatial pattern of business service linkages and
follow Britton (1974) who identified two basic determinants of
the decision on service inputs: the spatial environment and
the organisational structure of the plant. Though Britton and
others do not neglect the fact that some services can be
internalised, they concentrate solely on services rendered
from outside the industrial plant, so relating the range of
service demand to the regional and national urban system.
Accordingly, plants of single-site enterprises show a different
pattern of behaviour from plants in multi-site enterprises.
Several possibilities arise for branch plants to obtain the
services needed: they can be provided externally, and
rendered either internally or externally by the head office in

the metropolis. A single-plant enterprise, however, is largely dependent on external services available locally, a fact verified by several studies in industrialised countries (Britton, 1974; Marshall, 1975, 1982; Schickhoff, 1983). By contrast, certain services are not subject to distance constraints - at least if provided by the enterprise itself.

Most research has examined a limited number of services, ranging from six (O'Farrell and O'Loughlin, 1981) to fourteen (Marshall, 1982), and preferred services for the administration and management of a plant or enterprise. Yet, clearly, there is a ranking of internalised services in a multi-plant enterprise. Low-order services, like bookkeeping, are carried out in the branch plant while high-order legal or banking services are ordered from head office. The ranking and distance of services thus depend on the enterprise's organisational structure which, being defined as the difference between one- and multi-plant enterprises, is a major factor explaining service demands (e.g., Marshall, 1979, p. 48).

THE DECISION TO MAKE OR BUY SERVICES

As most studies are restricted to the problem of buying service from within or outside a region the possibility of deciding whether to make or buy services has been neglected. This is striking as the increasing proportion of non-production employees in an enterprise clearly shows that there is a margin of decision as to whether to make or to buy certain services. Before deciding where to buy services it is necessary to consider whether the service should be internalised or not. This decision process may be complex and thus one cannot agree that it may be reduced to 'the nature of the service activity carried out' alone (Marshall, 1982, p. 1528). Certainly the regional scientist is ultimately interested in the spatial linkages between industry and service business, but is constrained to examining a residuum by excluding the decision to make or buy from the analysis. This decision has not been considered so far in any study in industrial geography. Rousset-Deschamps (1984) pointed out the necessity of such analysis when laying open the strategic reasons of an enterprise to internalise services. It is even more astonishing that while there is indeed a theoretical discussion of this problem in economics, empirical study in the German language is still missing. Moreover, studies on the decision to make or buy are still restricted to production (e.g., Weilenmann, 1984).

This chapter first concentrates on the decision to make or buy services before examining the range of externalised services. Two basic hypotheses are proposed to explain the spatial behaviour of industrial enterprises.

First, the decision to make or buy services is mainly defined by the structure of the industrial enterprise concerned. As the enterprise grows in size and complexity one may suppose it requires both more services and a structural shift in the kind of services. At least there may be a change in the balance of internalising or externalising services. This means that the amount and range of externalised service activities within a region are determined by the industrial structure in that region. Second, as the decision to make or buy services can be treated as a reaction to the local environment, the location of the enterprise 'explains' the amount and range of externalised services. Thus enterprises located in poorly urbanised regions may internalise more services than is normally the case in regions with a good network of towns.

THE RESEARCH

Study Design

These basic hypotheses indicate a structural approach. The decision to make or buy services is subject to all factors determining a dynamic economy, i.e., the growth strategy of the individual enterprise, market conditions, and the long-term changes of the world economy. There is at present a strong tendency in German industry to externalise services such as transport or cleaning. These tendencies, however, can only be analysed for individual industrial sectors and services. It has been necessary to omit a time series study of the regional aspects even though it would have been very instructive. A cross-sectional study is made instead in 1980-81.

This chapter complements former research in several ways:

(a) If a study centres on the decision to make or buy, the only sensible object is the management who makes the decision. Thus, only independent enterprises are examined: single-plant enterprises and the parent plants of multi-plant enterprises, so differing from previous studies.

(b) Decisions to make or buy the services needed by enterprises should be analysed in a disaggregated manner. Thus it is important to distinguish services for manufacturing from those for administration and management. Altogether, 43 kinds of service are analysed, 19 for production, 24 for administration and management. Figure 16.1 shows that some services are highly internalised: product styling, quality control, production preparing, maintenance of machinery, and production stock-taking, book-keeping, salary accounts, and typing. Thus routine activities form the greatest part of services

demanded by an enterprise. Yet, these services are
not always provided intra-firm, but extra-firm, too.
Other activities show a high degree of externalisation, e.g., tax consultancy, auditing, and
management consultancy. Figure 16.1 also indicates
that individual services are required in completely
different ways. Thus basic needs must be dis-
tinguished from supplementary ones.

(c) Before studying the range of externalised services,
it is necessary to analyse the decision to make or
buy services.

(d) To clarify the influence of locational factors on the
decision to make or buy, it is essential to distinguish four different types of regions for
research.

This framework of research was carried out in the state
(Bundesland) of Lower Saxony which is relatively little industrialised compared with other federal states. Lower Saxony is
divided into four research zones, each with about 500,000
inhabitants (cp. Schöller et al., 1980, pp. 24, 29, 31).
These, set out in Figure 16.2, are:

1. The fringe of a metropolitan area, i.e., the district
(Landkreis) of Hannover where the important industries are foods, electrical and mechanical engineering.

2. Hilly regions with a dense net of towns where the
industrial structure ranges widely between mechanical and electrical engineering, wood processing,
and automotive industries.

3. A region with few urban centres lying between the
metropolitan areas of Hamburg and Hannover where
the food industry is significant.

4. A peripheral region with few towns on the coast
where, apart from some large-scale vehicle and ship
building enterprises, small and medium sized firms of
food, electrical engineering, and automotive industries prevail.

Data

As the four regions are comparatively poorly industrialised
for West Germany, it proved necessary to include all industrial enterprises in the survey. Thus, this is a cross-
sectional analysis in which all manufacturing enterprises with
more than 20 employees have been considered, except those in
energy supply and construction. Lists of the Chambers of
Industry and Commerce were used but these proved to
contain many errors which had to be corrected. Some 278 of
the 1,236 plants in the study area answered the postal survey

274

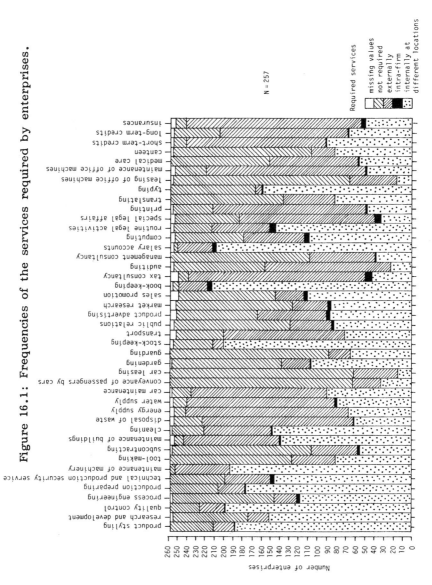

Figure 16.1: Frequencies of the services required by enterprises.

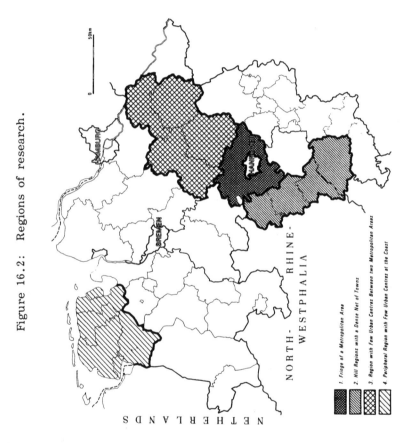

Figure 16.2: Regions of research.

BUSINESS SERVICES FOR MANUFACTURERS

Table 16.1: Characteristics of the Research Region (Lower Saxony)

Region	Inhabitants	Industrial employees per 1,000 inhabitants (1979)	No. of -lower order towns	Inhabitants of region per lower-order towns
Region 1	541,568	60.0	10	54,157
Region 2	554,328	106.4	11	50,397
Region 3	518,743	70.7	5	103,749
Region 4	565,345	67.9	7	80,764
Lower Saxony	7,234,000	98.6	-	-

in a way that the questionnaires could be analysed. The 22.5 per cent response rate is nearly the same as in Marshall's study (1982) on the city regions of Birmingham, Leeds, and Manchester. Another problem was that for well-known organisational reasons only 21 branch plants answered the questionnaire; these were excluded from the analysis. Among the remaining 257 enterprises there are more multi-plant enterprises than were given in the official lists, but the distortion cannot be calculated exactly because of the different regional delimitations used in the lists and in the present study.

There are comparatively few large-sized enterprises in Lower Saxony. That is why the study is mainly focused on small and medium-sized industrial firms. Enterprises with 50 to 500 employees and those in the consumer-goods industry are slightly over-represented. In former studies the demand for services by enterprises has been measured in very different ways. O'Farrell and O'Loughlin (1981) and Marshall (1982) made out the costs connected with the purchase of a service. Polese (1982) has extensively discussed the problem of calculating the costs of intra-firm services. There are two reasons not to ask for detailed information on this matter in the questionnaire: first, there would be a large number of missing values; second, the costs of services are often linked up with the costs of performances in kind so that it is difficult to conclude the real position of the service from its costs. So all transport costs connected with materials will be higher than, for instance, the costs of market research (cp. e.g., Bater and Walker, 1977, p. 15; Polese, 1982, p. 161). Anyway, the study was not intended to reveal regional multiplier effects but is confined to the location and range of the required services. Thus, only binary data are used as in several earlier studies. This leads to a problem which could not be solved and which limits the results of this study: as it was only possible to answer the question on service demand by 'yes' or 'no', two important pieces of information could not be obtained.

First, it was impossible to detect if a service is provided internally and, at the same time, bought externally. The informants could only give evidence on what was mostly done. There is one thing, however, we learn from economic studies: it is not only a rise in the amount of services that accompanies the growth of an enterprise, but also in the requirements for the quality of service. That is why, especially in the medium-sized enterprises in this study, the routine services are internalised while non-routine activities within the same service are bought. This distinction in demand behaviour could only be proved in a few cases, as in banking and legal matters.

Second, the 43 service activities could be related to the hierarchy of decision level in an enterprise only by reflections of plausibility. Consequently, it was difficult to distinguish between services with a routine character which are essential for the working of an enterprise, and non-routine services which are required in important decision situations only. In this respect, it was not possible to go beyond Britton's differentiation (1974) between low-order and high-order services.

Enterprise Structure and Decision
The average rate of internalisation amounts to 58.4 per cent which is rather high. In the attempt, however, to prove the first basic hypothesis it is more important to find out the circumstances under which the enterprises differ from this average. Certainly, structural characteristics of industrial enterprises have an impact on the demand for business services: Britton (1974) studied both the status of property and the size of plants; while Marshall (1979, 1982) tried to measure the influence of the size of organisation, its degree of complexity, spatial dispersion, and the technology of production on the service demand. The results, however, are in most cases limited to few services. This study, on the other hand, is an attempt at disaggregation so that results are expected to reveal the significance of the structural factors for the decision to internalise or externalise each individual service. As Figure 16.3 shows, 5 factors are differentiated first: the demand of the organisation, size, production technique, degree of complexity, and performance. The measuring criteria are given in parentheses. Relations between two variables have been tested by chi-square analysis and Cramer's V. The question marks signify the assumption of multiple relationships. This, however, could not be checked because of the various scales of data.

Table 16.2: Frequency of Use and the Decision to Make or Buy Services.

	Part of enterprises in which the required service is externalised		Intensity of relationship	Correlation to the size of enterprise
	Required one a month or more frequently	Required less frequently than once a month	phi/corr.	chi-square
Production				
Product styling	4.1	23.3	0.7000	
Research and development	5.3	25.4	0.6736	xxx
Quality control	7.4	50.0	0.4969	
Process engineering	2.1	38.2	0.9346	xxx
Production preparing	7.9	40.4	0.5658	x
Technical and production security service	10.7	50.7	0.6460	xxx
Maintenance of machinery	12.6	62.1	0.5518	xx
Toolmaking	24.0	71.8	0.4887	xx
Maintenance of buildings	18.2	59.8	0.6152	xxx
Cleaning	31.7	51.2	0.2286	
Car maintenance	57.0	81.4	0.4488	
Administration and Management				
Public relations	33.1	59.1	0.2764	
Management consultancy	18.2	76.5	0.7340	
Routine legal activities	16.3	44.3	0.5442	xx
Printing	67.8	88.3	0.4032	xxx
Translating	18.9	65.5	0.5952	xxx
Maintenance of office machines	67.6	85.4	0.1947	
Medical care	43.2	82.1	0.4355	xxx
Conveyance of passengers by car	30.8	72.0	0.4288	xx
Gardening	13.5	38.0	0.4719	xx

Significant levels: 0.1%, 1%, 5%.

First, the demand of an organisation for a service is defined by frequency of use. It may be assumed, then, that frequently-required services are internalised, whereas services required less often are externalised. In micro-economic terms this may be explained by the goal of an enterprise to raise its performance ability and by the minimum capacity threshold. Indeed, there is a significant correlation for 11 of 19 services for production. But this is true for much less services for administration and management, i.e., for 9 out of 24, among them especially translating, routine legal activities, and management consultancy.

Second, this result depends on enterprise size. Above all, small enterprises make no or only rare use of several services. To that extent enterprise size is especially important for the decision to make or buy. This study suffers from the fact that only small and medium-sized enterprises have been investigated. Yet, the number of the services required by an enterprise also rises with its size, as shown in Figure 16.4. In the transition from size order 3 to 4 the graph for all services stagnates, while the number of internalised services rises and that of externalised services falls. This size (i.e., 100-200 employees) seems to be a critical growth threshold for the service demand of an enterprise. During further enterprise growth the extent of intra-firm services seems to rise - a fact also stated by Marshall (1982, Table 8) for expenditures on business services. This bears out reflections on growth thresholds and crisis in enterprises as exemplified in industrial geography (e.g., Taylor, 1975) and micro-economics (e.g., Albach, 1976; Albach, Bock and Warnke, 1984). The thresholds concerning employment or problems of financing, however, have been fixed differently in these studies. Must one assume more than the two or three growth thresholds named by the above authors? An answer to this question might be given by the fact that there is no correlation between the charge of costs, e.g., the part of the costs for the purchase of all services, and the size of the enterprise. During enterprise growth a shift in service demand occurs. While services like book-keeping, salary accounts, computing, printing, and medical care are significantly internalised when the enterprise grows in size, services like cleaning, transport, and maintenance of office machines are substantially externalised. Of course, there are a number of services which are not dependent on enterprise size such as the decision to make or buy them.

Third, little can be said about the significance of the production technique for the supply of services. The data yielded a high aggregation level of production techniques. If one takes the four industrial groups (basic and intermediate goods, capital goods, consumer goods, and food industry) to describe different production techniques, there are only a few correlations in foods. In that kind of industry a greater

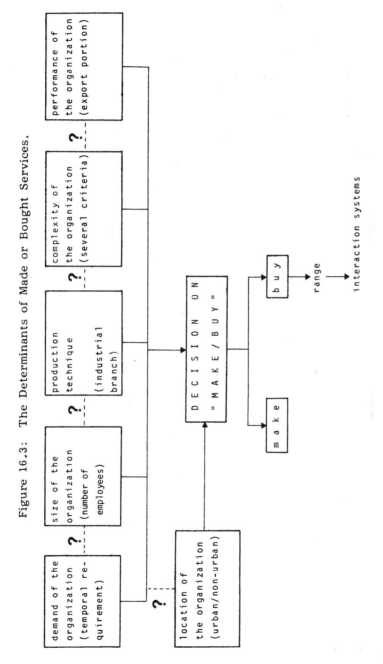

Figure 16.3: The Determinants of Made or Bought Services.

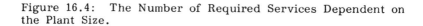

Figure 16.4: The Number of Required Services Dependent on the Plant Size.

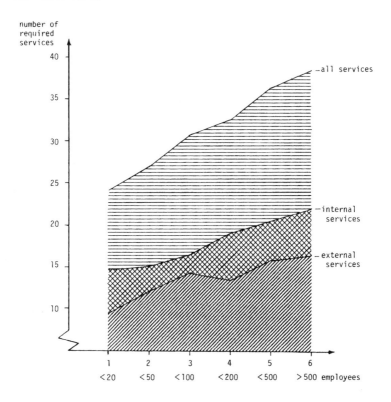

number of production services are bought (e.g., product styling, quality control, process engineering, toolmaking) while transport services are largely internalised.

Fourth, all criteria for measuring the functional complexity of an enterprise, such as the percentage of non-production employees, single- and multi-plant enterprises, and the proportion of female employees, lead to unsatisfactory results. However, this may result from insufficient consideration of complexity in our postal survey. By contrast, it was found that the performance measured by the export share if turnover is a significant determinant if the number of required services: the growth of services needed in an exporting enterprise is mostly internalised.

This study examines, by steps, the influence of structural variables on the decision to make or buy services. On the one hand, the composition of structural variables is very complex because the decision regarding each individual service is obviously not determined at all by structural factors. This is true for services which are nearly exclusively internalised, e.g., stock-keeping, typing, sales promotion, and for services which must be mostly bought, e.g., electricity and water supply, leasing cars and office machines, tax consulting, auditing and financial services. On the other hand, several services are positively determined by structural variables; so, printing is internalised when the enterprise grows or belongs to the basic, intermediate and consumer goods industries.

Finally, there are services for which the decision to make or buy is determined by structural factors in various ways. Thus, generally speaking, transport is externalised when an enterprise grows. It is increasingly internalised, however, if the enterprise is in food or basic materials goods industry. As for our first basic hypothesis, this leads to the conclusion that structural characteristics of industrial enterprises do not offer a clear and satisfying explanation of the complete external demand for business services.

Location and Decision

If particular services are absolutely necessary for an enterprise and their supply is to a high degree dependent on short distances - as claimed in a number of theses - enterprises are forced to internalise in those regions where the services are not ubiquitous. Accordingly, the local availability of services should be expected to favourise externalisation while the lack of services should lead to internalisation.

A glance at the average rate of services internalisation in the four regions of Lower Saxony (Table 16.3) reveals the fact that the region which is best equipped with medium-sized centres has the highest average rate of internalisation while the region with the lowest number of medium-sized centres shows the lowest rate of internalisation. This is even true when calculating the rate of internalisation for homogeneous groups of enterprise size.

This appears to be a paradoxical result, the more so that various studies show that some business service enterprises, as in computing and legal advice, are made considerably more use of by private households and trades than by manufacturing (Marshall, 1982). Consequently, their location is primarily determined by the population concentration (Klemmer, 1980). Most medium-sized centres in Lower Saxony have about 15,000 to 25,000 inhabitants. The question arises whether this is already a size where essentially more business services can be externalised as there is a sufficient local supply. This is obviously not the case: significant correlations with some services can be stated only for towns with 50,000 or more inhabitants (Table 16.4).

BUSINESS SERVICES FOR MANUFACTURERS

Table 16.3: Average Rate of Internalisation in the Four Regions of Research.

	Rate of internalisation (per cent)	Number of inhabitants per medium sized centre
Fringe of metropolitan area	57.7	54,157
Region with a dense net of towns	61.3	50,397
Region between two metropolitan areas with few urban centres	51.6	103,749
Peripheral region with few urban centres	53.8	80,764

Table 16.4: The Correlation Between Urban Location and External Demand for Business Services.

Percentage of manufacturers which buy a required service manufacturers located:-		
	in a town with more than 50,000 inhabitants	in a town with less than 50,000 inhabitants
Production preparation	28.9	9.3
Maintenance of buildings	54.7	38.4
Cleaning	57.1	25.0
Water supply	81.5	60.8
Management consultancy	82.1	58.0

(Significant at the 5% level)

Two regions are equipped with towns of more than 50,000 inhabitants, namely Lüneburg and Celle in region 3, Emden and Wilhelmshaven in region 4. This is the first hint that it is not the complete system of towns in a region which influences the degree of services externalisation, but the very existence of a few larger towns. For manufacturing, however, the concentration of population in medium-sized centres does not seem to play a role because there is no difference in demand behaviour between enterprises which are

284

located in these medium-sized centres and those located outside. Of course, this may be a result of the definition of a 'medium-sized centre' as declared by the regional planners (Regional Planning Programme of Lower Saxony, 1982; cp. also Schoeller et al., 1980, p. 16). One could reflect on the question of the minimum size of a town which makes industrial enterprises increasingly purchase certain services externally. That question is answered by Schickhoff (1983) in a study of the periphery of the Rhine-Ruhr metropolitan area where business services are externalised primarily in cities with more than 250,000 inhabitants. Studies on Canada and the United Kingdom, quoted earlier, also show the importance of towns with more than 100,000 inhabitants. As there are practically no such towns in Lower Saxony, one may conclude that the second basic hypothesis on the importance of location for the decision to make or buy services cannot be confirmed.

Service Linkages in the Urban System

Till now only the decision on the supply of services has been considered. The hypothesis on the impact of distance on externally-provided services, however, aims at the interaction between the location of the industrial enterprise and a business service enterprise. In former studies the importance of a service activity for an industrial enterprise was concluded from the distances of service demand - by analogy with the theory of central places. This was done, however, without naming specific distances. Britton (1974), for example, inferred 'low-order services' from short distances and 'high-order services' from long distances. When calculating the distances between the locations of the demanding and supplying enterprises in Lower Saxony, two facts are striking.

First, with a generally high dispersion, there are considerable average distances. Thus, for example, bookkeeping is purchased externally from an average distance of 112 kilometres, advanced banking services (e.g., credits) from 62 km. Bookkeeping services, however, are bought externally by only 31 enterprises (among them possibly some subsidiary enterprises) while advanced banking services are purchased from outside by 137 firms. Service activities are less liable to transport costs than it has been assumed up to now.

Second, bookkeeping and other 'low-order services' have a wider range than the 'high-order services'. This leads to the conclusion that distances are not directly determined by the significance of a service for the enterprise. There is a ranking in the ranges of the 35 services which are externally acquired to a considerable extent. It follows that those services which are very much liable to distances are linked with performances in kind or frequency needed, and are thus regularly purchased. These are indeed 'low-order services'

285

like cleaning, car maintenance, maintenance of buildings, printing, and routine banking services. Other service activities, however, which nowadays may well belong to the 'low-order services', are mostly demanded over quite a long distance as, for example, with computing, sales promotion or bookkeeping. This kind of service is in no way linked with performances in kind.

However, the specific distances of the demand for extra-firm services depend on the regional pattern of service supply. This explains the ranges of extra-firm services when comparing the four regions of Lower Saxony: the ranges are especially low in region 1, the fringe of the metropolitan area of Hannover; they are more often around the average in region 2 whereas in regions 3 and 4 they are above average. So, the maintenance of office machines, for instance, is ordered over an average distance of 13 kilometres in the fringe of the Hannover metropolitan area, while it is 28 kilometres in the hilly region, more than 50 kilometres in the peripheral inland region, and 34 kilometres in the coastal region. There is, however, no significant difference between these regions in the rate of internalisation of this service. Even though there is a ranking as to the range of service activities in the research regions, the absolute distance seems to have only little influence on the decision to buy a service. Consequently, the liability of business services to distance can only be measured in relative, not absolute, terms.

This becomes obvious if one leaves the discussion on statistical parameters and turn to the interrelations of extra-firm services in the individual regions. To describe their respective urban systems the central place hierarchy is used as defined in regional planning in Lower Saxony, differentiating between medium-sized and major centres. The centres are designed not only to supply private households with goods and services but also with jobs, making them important for manufacturing and supplementary service business.

In region 1, the fringe of the Hannover metropolitan area, all medium-sized centres are overshadowed by Hannover. Most services not purchased locally are bought in the city's core. In the remaining regions, medium-sized centres are slightly more important, providing 15-17 per cent of the externally supplied services to manufacturers. The supply, it seems, is not dependent on the number of medium-sized centres in the respective region: about one third of the extra-firm services are ordered from the major centre. In the first instance, it is the nearby major centres which have the lion's share in the supply (see Figure 16.5). The major centres for region 2 are Hannover and Göttingen, for region 3 Hannover and Hamburg, for region 4 Oldenburg. One cannot overlook the fact, however, that the demand for services is widely distributed between the whole system of major centres in the German Federal Republic. So the metro-

BUSINESS SERVICES FOR MANUFACTURERS

Table 16.5: Pattern of Ranges of Services Bought in the Study Areas.

| | | Region | | | |
		1	2	3	4
Number of bought services		227	338	369	230
(a)	Percentage thereof bought locally	35.7	43.8	52.1	45.2
(b)	in major centres outside the region	54.6	32.8	27.1	30.0
(c)	in medium-sized centres inside the region	2.2	15.1	16.5	17.4
(d)	in other locations	7.5	8.3	4.3	7.4
		100	100	100	100

politan areas of Berlin, Bremen, Frankfurt, and Munich also have a share in the supply of services to manufacturers in Lower Saxony.

Thus it is proved that manufacturers do not necessarily make use of the services which are nearest to their own location. In Lower Saxony, for instance, there are tax consultancies in every medium-sized centre. Yet, manufacturers prefer to buy this service in major centres. Hints of this phenomenon are made by Grotz (1980, p. 41): manufacturers in a small town order a certain service from the nearest medium-sized centre while other manufacturers in the same medium-sized centre buy the same service from the major centre. A plausible explanation for this lies in the different sizes of the enterprises, by analogy, for example, with the connection between plant size and community size noticed by Norcliffe (1975, p. 40 ff.). The correlation, however, between plant size and community size is statistically insignificant in Lower Saxony. There, more complex organisations have not just an increasing demand for services which is satisfied by turning from intra-firm to extra-firm supply or vice versa: there is also a shift in the quality of the services demanded that is expressed in a rising specification of the required services. Unfortunately, the complexity of organisation as well as the specific demands could not be measured to a satisfactory extent. Moreover, this cross-sectional analysis is static in that the strategic behaviour of the manufacturers is excluded. Obviously one must assume an increased demand for highly specialised services in certain situations in the 'lifetime' of an enterprise - services which can only be bought externally and are restricted to major national centres.

287

Figure 16.5:   Demand for Business Services by Manufacturers in Four Regions of Lower Saxony.

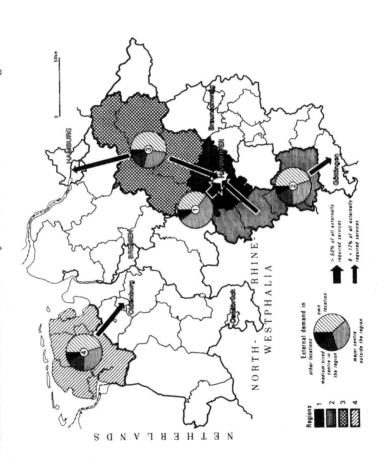

BUSINESS SERVICES FOR MANUFACTURERS

This explanation of the great spatial range from which many services are bought and examined in this study does not hold true if the position of the products in the introductory phase of a product life-cycle is an indicator of such a situation. Most manufacturers declare their products to be in the phases of maturity or saturation. Thus, the demand for business services from far away metropolitan areas like Berlin or Munich is quite usual behaviour by manufacturers in services demand.

Yet, it is the increasing competitive pressure on manufacturers producing goods in these phases of the product life-cycle that compels them to externalise certain routine services. So small and medium-sized enterprises are encouraged by Chambers of Industry and Commerce to increasingly externalise transport and cleaning services. It would be desirable to make more studies of this issue.

IMPLICATIONS FOR REGIONAL POLICY

The implications of the present study for regional policy are more difficult to judge than might be expected from former studies. The results cannot be compared directly to those of studies on other industrial countries which were often exclusively (O'Farrell and O'Loughlin, 1981) or predominantly (Britton, 1974; Bater and Walker, 1977; Polese, 1982) focused on branch plants. However, as far as independent enterprises are concerned, the results of those studies resemble those here.

There are two answers to the introductory question regarding the ultimate end of an urbanisation strategy in depressed areas. First, the demands for different services by manufacturing are differentiated to such an extent that an urbanisation policy - which would necessarily be undifferentiated - would provide no effective means to guarantee the attraction of new industrial enterprises. Second, major centres play a special role if certain services are externally acquired. Some results indicate that cities with more than 100,000 inhabitants offer particularly favourable environments to industrial enterprises in service supply. However, to suggest an urbanisation policy aimed at creating major centres in depressed areas is an illusion considering the fact that at present a process of further selection is taking place between existing major cities in the German Federal Republic (Schoeller et al., 1980, p. 25 ff.).

Additionally, the question might arise as to whether the results of this study contribute a statement on the possibility of economic development for peripheral regions. By directing a certain amount of service demand to the major centres, a centre-periphery relationship often complained about in West Germany, seems to be consolidated. Capital is withdrawn from the region when services are purchased outside it, although it was not possible to measure the amount. It is hard to judge how far this argument holds really true. In this chapter services have not been reckoned in monetary terms. Yet that alone would not suffice: multiplier effects do not arise from intra-regional purchases of services only as concluded, for instance, by O'Farrell and O'Loughlin (1981); they are also initiated by the functioning of an income multiplier stemming from the internalisation of service requirements in an industrial enterprise. Beyond this, only the nett effect of making and buying services in the region is important, but exactly this effect is hard to calculate.

One important aspect, however, recently pointed out, amongst others, by Marshall (1982, p. 1539), should not be neglected: when purchasing services the manufacturer often obtains important information which is conveyed by chance and not directly connected with the service itself. In a world, however, in which transport costs only play a minor role and regional factor costs tend to be equalised, the access to information is of increasing importance for the survival of an enterprise. Thus manufacturers have indeed access to the places with the utmost information potential if they purchase externalised services in major centres, so that such service-purchasing behaviour would help the stability and growth of the enterprise without regard to its location.

REFERENCES

Albach, H. (1976) 'Kritische Wachstumsschwellen in der Unternehmensentwicklung', Zeitschrift fur Betriebswirtschaft, 46, 683-696

Albach, H., Bock, K. and Warnke, Th. (1984) 'Wachstumskrisen von Unternehmen', ZfbF Schmalenbachs Zeitschrift fur Betriebswirtschaftliche Forschung, 36, 779-793

Bater, J.H. and Walker, D.F. (1977) 'Industrial Services: Literature and Research Prospects' in D.F. Walker (ed.), Industrial Services, Department of Geography Publication Series No. 8, Ontario, pp. 1-25

Britton, J.N.H. (1974) 'Environmental Adaption of Industrial Plants: Service Linkages, Locational Environment and Organisation' in F.E.I. Hamilton (ed.), Spatial Perspectives on Industrial Organisation and Decision-Maing, Wiley, London, pp. 363-390

Crum, R.E. and Gudgin, G. (1977) 'Non-Production Activities in UK Manufacturing Industry', Commission of the European Community Regional Policy Series, 31

Dezert, B. (1976) 'Le Tertiaire au Service des Entreprises Industrielles dans les Pays d'Economie Libérale', L'Information Géographique, 40, 64-70

Fester, F. (1976) 'Entwicklungszentren - Urbanisierung

Peripherer Regionen statt Industrialisierung des Ländlichen Raumes', Informationen zur Raumentwicklung, 135-146

Geilinger, U. (1983) 'Industrielle Mehrbetriebs-Unternehmen und die Funktionale Arbeitsteilung Zwischen Regionen, Zürich', Geogr. Institut ETH Zürich, Berichte und Skripten, 12

Grotz, R. (1980) 'Räumliche Beziehungen Industrieller Systeme' in W. Gaebe and K.H. Hottes (eds.), Methoden und Feldforschung in der Industriegeographie, Manneimer Geogr. Arbeiten, Mannheim, 7, 23-51

Hamilton, F.E.I. and Linge, G.J.R. (eds.) (1979) Spatial Analysis, Industry and the Industrial Environment: Volume 1 Industrial Systems, Wiley, Chichester

Klemmer, P. (1980) Ermittlung von Basisdienstleistungsbereichen, Beiträge d. Akademie f. Raumforschung u. Landesplanung, Hannover, 385

Marshall, J.N. (1979) 'Ownership, Organisation and Industrial Linkage: A Case Study in the Northern Region of England', Regional Studies, 13, 531-557

Marshall, J.N. (1982) 'Linkages between Manufacturing Industry and Business Services', Environment and Planning A, 14, 1523-1540

Norcliffe, G.B. (1975) 'A Theory of Manufacturing Places' in L. Collins and D.F. Walker (eds.), Locational Dynamics of Manufacturing Activity, Wiley, London, pp. 19-57

O'Farrell, P.N. and O'Loughlin, B. (1981) 'The Impact of New Industry Enterprises in Ireland: An Analysis of Service Linkages', Regional Studies, 15, 439-458

Polese, M. (1982) 'Regional Demand for Business Services and Interregional Service Flows in a Small Canadian Region', Papers of the Regional Science Association, 50, 151-163

Rousset-Deschamps, M. (1984) 'Politique d'Internalisation et d'Externalisation des Services dans les Entreprises Industrielles en France', Hommes et Terres du Nord, (1), 17-23

Schickhoff, I. (1983) 'Ausgewahlte Dienstleistungsbeziehungen von Industrieunternehmen. Eine Fallstudie am Beispiel von Industrieunternehmen am Linken Niederrhein', 43 Deutscher Geographentag Mannheim, Taguncsbericht und Wissenschaftliche Abhandlungen, Wiesbaden, 362-365

Schoeller, P. et al. (eds.) (1980) Federal Republic of Germany. Spatial Development and Problems, Bochumer Geogr. Arbeiten, Paderborn, 38

Taylor, M.J. (1975) 'Organisational Growth, Spatial Interaction and Location Decision-Making', Regional Studies, 9, 313-323

Weilenmann, P. (1984) 'Make or Buy - Kauf oder Eigenfertigung - Anspruch und Schweizerische Wirklichkeit', Die Unternehmung, Bern, 38, 207-229

Chapter Seventeen

PLANNING FOR BUSINESS DEVELOPMENT IN
THE URBAN TRANSITION ZONE

David Wadley

For over a decade advanced nations have undergone rapid
and pronounced structural change. The recession until 1983
slowed overall growth and altered intersectoral relationships.
Small towns dependent on particular industries faltered while
changing relativities have blighted sections of larger cities.
Some in Europe and North America have experienced decay
and dereliction involving emigration from inner areas, run-
down of housing and commercial stock, the shutdown and
suburbanisation of industry and some offices, erosion of the
tax base, emergence of socio-economic problems and a range
of other difficulties.

The transition zone thus became the setting for the
'inner city problem'. Still apt may be Harris and Ullman's
(1945) classical depiction of a heterogeneous and somewhat
seedy zone which, depending on urban size, extends up to
several kilometres beyond the downtown. Here light manufacturing and commercial uses bid against housing for what
space remains available. In some inner areas both large and
small business have withered, leaving severe unemployment.
Other transition zones may be more vital, though this may
have been overlooked by academics and practitioners who too
often studied more easily definable entities such as industrial
parks and shopping centres in outer areas.

The present enquiry seeks to redress this neglect by
reviewing business development strategies for inner city
areas. First is the concept of the enterprise zone as applied
in the United Kingdom and United States. It quickly emerges,
however, that this is a solution only for the most troubled
precincts. It is contrasted with a more articulated business
development planning. A case study suggests that this approach may be appropriate in transition zones which are not
excessively depressed and in which existing vitality might be
encouraged.

ENTERPRISE ZONES

Applications

The enterprise zone concept arose in recognition that, once, inner cities featured a healthy small business community which allegedly was etched away by increasing government regulation and restrictions. Such thinking was modified and effectuated after 1980 by the British Conservative government. Local authorities now submit proposals for zones which, if established, exist for ten years. Here both new and existing enterprises are exempt from local rates, development land tax, industrial training levies and reporting requirements and certain government statistical collections. One hundred per cent allowances are offered for corporate and income tax purposes for capital expenditure on industrial and commercial buildings. Planning and administrative procedures are greatly simplified and expedited. Finally, certain customs benefits may be offered.

In the United States, the Urban Jobs and Enterprise Zone Act of 1980 sought also to improve inner areas for business development by reducing tax burdens on firms locating in depressed neighbourhoods. To qualify, a potential zone required a population of around 4,000 which suffered unemployment and poverty well above the national average. Once declared, property taxes and local government levies are substantially reduced, capital gains tax concessions are offered investors, employees receive social security tax advantages and companies employing local labour gain income tax benefits (Butler, 1982: 132).

Assessment

In proposing enterprise zones, governments have had to 'back off' the private sector, a task of apparent difficulty. British commentators argue that the original concept of deregulation has been supplanted by one of concessions or assistance, and 'non-plan' has become planning in a different form (Botham and Lloyd, 1983: 27-28). Results, therefore, reflect not solely private initiative: government has a share as well. It has been maintained that the British approach leads to wholesale renovation of inner city areas, often by large-scale operations attracted by property tax benefits. In such a case, no net growth may be created: one area simply captures development from another by way of a 'deadweight' subsidy. If it is desirable to remove blight instead of developing greenfield sites, this may be achievable only at a social cost. Generally, though, the zone concept works best when genuine, new business is stimulated.

Other concerns surround the move toward an unregulated market economy in which non-wage labour benefits are substantially reduced. The demarcation of zones has also been a problem since different firms may demand to be included or excluded depending on perceived benefits or costs. The American focus on indigenous business in one or a few census tracts was roundly criticised by Jones and Manson (1982) in that to expect employees to live in so tightly prescribed areas was trying to create a nineteenth century setting amidst a modern city, unrealistic in an age of mobility.

While leftist circles have regarded enterprise zones with suspicion, they have been seen as a panacea by others. This review questions unbridled optimism following considerable operational difficulties on both sides of the Atlantic. The duality of deregulation and concession is problematic as is the establishment of equitable and efficient packages. Enterprise zones are unlikely to appear willy-nilly across nations, but will remain a specialised and restricted remedy for the most difficult socio-economic settings. The existence of such settings requires validation, since parts of the transition zone may appear ugly or blighted without necessarily being economically destitute. There is little justification for enterprise zones in more 'normal' inner areas where lesser measures may be effective. Nor should one assume that because major problems characterise some inner areas of some cities, all transition zones are economically hopeless. It is important to think of potentials since many authorities see small business, classically found in the zone, as a major generator of employment into the next century.

That said, the chapter now turns from enterprise zones to consider an alternative - spatially articulated business development planning. The focus shifts from the northern hemisphere to Brisbane, capital of Queensland, Australia (Figure 17.1). Introduction to the city and nomination of a particular suburb for intensive study point up the pitfalls in blackening all transition zones with the same brush. There follows a detailed survey of the suburb's private sector leading to recommendations tailored for each type of land use.

CITY AND SUBURB

Brisbane's Development

The latest Australian census data available for 1981 show that the population of the Brisbane Statistical Division was 1,028,600 and it had 54 per cent of the factories, and 61 and 51 per cent respectively of the manufacturing and service industry employees in Queensland. Some Brisbane industries have prospered by serving resource or mining development while other market-orientated ones are protected by distance from interstate or overseas competition and have benefited from the State's continuing population gains over the last decade. Outright growth of establishments and employment thus characterises certain industries, while others have concentrated (fewer factories, more workers) or deconcen-

Figure 17.1: Location maps: Brisbane City and its inner areas including the Bowen Hills suburb, 1983.

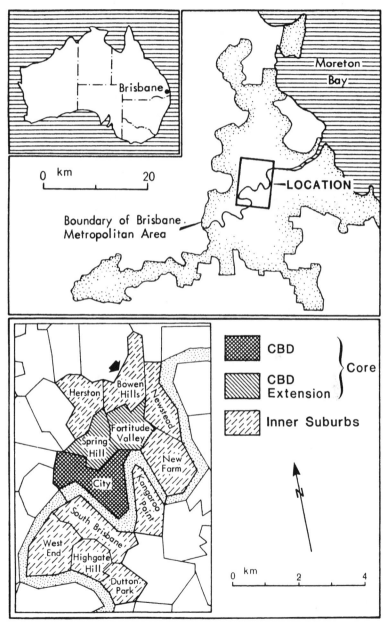

trated (vice versa), and still others have declined on both parameters.

This last trend is important for inner Brisbane. The area can be examined in two parts, the city core and the inner suburbs (Figure 17.1). Whereas in 1975-76, the parts accounted for 16.4 and 19.0 per cent of the Brisbane Statistical Division's factories and workforce, the percentages in 1982-83 were 13.8 and 16.9. Most of the decline took place not in the core but in the inner suburbs which experienced a factory loss of six per cent and an employment reduction of 18.7 per cent over the seven year period.

Despite these downturns inner Brisbane still attracts specific types of production such as clothing and footwear, printing and miscellaneous manufacturing, with metal and equipment fabricating and a wider range of functions appearing in the outer transition zone. The CBD provides important markets for many industrial and service firms and others distributing across the city also find centrality useful. Industrial and commercial zoning in Brisbane follows traditional lines and some would see it still largely a means of affording maximum protection to residential precincts. Yet efficiency as well as equity criteria are important and the benefits of zoning must often be related to the costs - unemployment or reduced job opportunities, impact on potential industrial expansion and lack of access to major transport nodes. Given the problems of Western economies in the 1980s, it is debatable whether commercial planning can 'take a back seat' (cf. Wadley and Bentley, 1981: 272). As a peripheral city in a national manufacturing economy itself described as 'semi-peripheral' (Fagan et al., 1981: 26; see also Wilde, 1986), Brisbane must counter domestic and foreign competition. Planning should recognise potentially deleterious structural adjustment and rationalisation in many key industries. To succeed, a scheme must periodically assess trends and business intentions in given sectors. Discussion with Brisbane City Council officers indicated that a relevant analysis would focus on business planning and land use policies in Bowen Hills, the northern sector of the transition zone.

Bowen Hills
Bowen Hills is an area of intensive land use and dense traffic, located on major road and rail corridors to central Brisbane (Figures 17.1, 17.2). It is also one of the city's earliest manufacturing districts, having seen soap production, motor engineering, boat-building, freezing works and railway workshops before 1914. After 1945, motor workshops proliferated, joined by motor body builders, refrigeration and ice works, and mixed businesses. In 1963, Queensland Press established a newspaper printing works which is now the largest single employer with 1,700 full and part-time workers. Yet after the 1960s, the tone of the area changed. Bowen

Figure 17.2:   Landuses, Bowen Hills, 1983.
Source: Fieldwork.

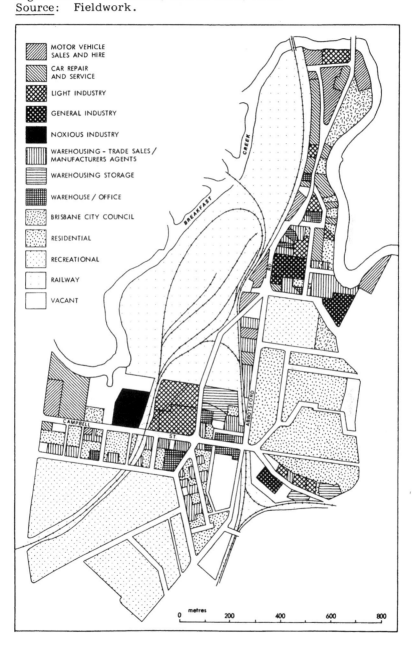

Figure 17.3: Landuse zoning, Bowen Hills, 1983.
Source: Fieldwork and Brisbane City Council zoning maps.

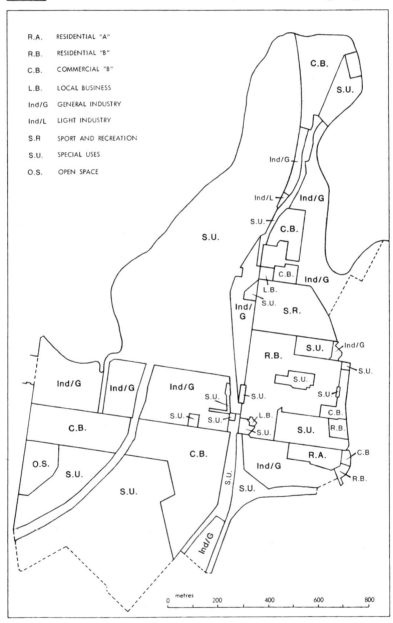

Hills has become as important for warehousing, office show-rooms and manufacturers' agencies as for manufacturing. Motor workshops remain because of proximity to the CBD and other inner areas. The railway workshops which in mid-1983 employed 1,600 are the most extensive complex in Brisbane (Figure 17.2).

Zoning patterns largely reflect existing land uses (Figure 17.3). The railway yards claim a vast tract as 'Special Uses'. The northern commercial precinct is a mix of 'Commercial B' and 'General Industry' zonings. South of Perry Park, a sport and recreational zone, is a residential area interspersed with special use and small commercial zones. The west of the suburb features 'General Industry' and 'Commercial B' zoning bordered by the large special use of the exhibition grounds to the south.

BUSINESS AND LANDUSE DECISION-MAKING

In May 1983, a questionnaire was administered to all private industrial and service establishments in Bowen Hills, save local service outlets such as banks, corner shops and petrol stations. Interviewers were instructed not only to collect information on eligible businesses but also to note the condition of premises and likelihood of traffic congestion. Of 170 establishments approached, 151 (89 per cent) co-operated. The survey considered: first, a profile of land users; second, the level of property ownership; and, third, company plans.

Profile of Landusers

The field census emphasises the orientation of this part of the transition zone to wholesaling as practised by over half the major private establishments (Table 17.1). Within wholesaling, machinery and equipment was by far the biggest category and may well be co-extensive with ASIC 486 - motor vehicle retailing - which also occupied many companies.

Business is essentially young, 44 per cent of firms having set up since 1980. Two-thirds were absent before 1975. Evidently, the transition zone has lost little of its transience. Only about a third of firms commenced in Bowen Hills, the remainder having relocated from elsewhere. The most popular previous locations were the City or suburbs bordering Fortitude Valley: this decentralisation at the micro-level corroborates the 'nursery' function ascribed to inner areas for business development. Firms which entered Bowen Hills generally did so with considerable experience and probably contribute to its economic stability.

Among the 151 enterprises was a total of 2,862 workers. Predictably, firms are small, two-thirds having fewer than 9 workers. The mean employment size is 19. Further, the

Table 17.1:   Firms by Industry Type, Bowen Hills, 1983.

	ASIC Code	Number	Frequency (%)
21-34	**Manufacturing**		
	21 Food, beverages, tobacco	3	2.1
	26 Paper, printing, publishing	7	4.6
	31 Fabricated metals	1	0.7
	33 Other machinery and equipment	5	3.3
	Total	16	10.7
41-42	**Construction**		
	42 Special trades	5	3.3
	Total	5	3.3
47	**Wholesaling**		
	471 General wholesalers	6	4.0
	472 Builders hardware	2	1.3
	473 Machinery and equipment	47	31.1
	474 Minerals, metals and chemicals	2	1.3
	476 Food, drink and tobacco	3	2.0
	477 Textiles and clothing	6	4.0
	478 Household goods	3	2.0
	479 Other specialist wholesalers	10	6.6
	Total	79	52.3
48	**Retailing**		
	485 Household appliances, hardware	7	4.6
	486 Motor vehicles etc.	28	18.5
	489 Other retailers	3	2.0
	Total	38	25.1
51-55	**Transport and Storage**	3	2.0
61-63	**Finance, Property and Business Services**	7	4.6
81-84	**Community Services**	1	0.7
91-94	**Recreation, Personal and Other Services**	2	1.3
	Total	151	100.0

Source: Fieldwork.

distribution is highly positively skewed, one large manufacturer having as many people as all other private enterprise
put together. Where so great a sectoral concentration and
variation exists, special attention is necessary to the situation
and plans of business houses.

Property Status
The majority of firms are branch offices despite the suppo-
sition that, in an area of small business, much could be
locally-owned. Roughly one-third of all firms were in new
premises. Encouraging in terms of vitality, this is a higher
proportion than envisaged in a transition zone. The incidence
of new premises between head and branch offices was virtually the same. Neither type of office is therefore a special
target for property developers or the incentives of local
government.

Tenure patterns underpin the transience of the area.
Only a quarter of firms owned their premises and, among this
group, head offices predominated. Data on leasing practices
were obtained for 88 companies. The model lease is of three
years with the skew towards longer periods. Overall, however, half the leases matured in 1984 or 1985 and relatively
few undertakings were bound beyond 1986. By then, at least
64 of the suburb's 151 businesses will be required (or will
have the opportunity) to review their location.

Business Planning
Accepting the normal caveats about hypothetical questions and
the forecasting ability of respondents in surveys, one can
approach commercial intentions via firms' statements of satisfaction or dissatisfaction with present locations. Satisfaction
apparently stems from proximity to the CBD and the nearby
Brisbane airport. Local road and railway connections, lot
sizes and allegedly low rents further appealed. Many firms
really had no complaints about the suburb. Otherwise, the
chief worries were lack of parking space, noise, traffic
congestion, and inadequate floorspace. Independent observations confirmed these complaints: for example, parking was
judged inadequate outside 52 per cent of establishments.

Business plans were examined via contingency questions.
First, 79 of 151 firms had no plans to alter their location in
any major way. Responses among the other 72 were not
necessarily exclusive such that 30 anticipated expansion in
situ, 23 relocation, 10 branch establishment, and one a reduction of scale. A further 11 were unsure of their plans.

Most changes were planned before 1986. In cases of
relocation, 18 firms could provide a time-frame. Eight were
moving during 1983, four in 1984 and three each in 1985 and
1986. Hence, within three years, Bowen Hills was to lose at
least 15 per cent of its existing business through relocation.
The suburb appears assured of a dynamic future in its functional and land use patterns.

BUSINESS DEVELOPMENT IN URBAN TRANSITION

One way of approaching business planning in the transition zone is to focus on relocating firms since the are likely
to have a marked (and at least initially negative) impact on
the local economy. Discriminant analysis selects variables
important in determining a firm's position on a single re-
location/stability scale. A stepwise analysis adopted the
selection rule of maximising minimum Mahalanobis distance (D
squared) between groups. Prior probability was initially set
at 0.5 but later floated to the ratio of the two groups in the
151 observations. The model with greatest predictive power
from among the variables entered was:

$$Di = -0.76(HEAD) + 0.47(PLOTR) + 0.57(INT6)$$

The first ranking variable was head/branch office status,
followed by interviewers' assessments of the incidence of car
parking congestion, and then the plot ratio. This model
accurately assigned 69 per cent of stable firms and 74 per
cent of relocating ones for an overall efficiency of 69.5 per
cent. This is a reasonable improvement over a random allocation which would offer 50 per cent correctness given prior
probabilities. Yet the outcome explains only about 40 per cent
of the remaining variation in the dependent variable: 46 of
151 cases have been wrongly classified. No meaningful improvement arose from various manipulations possible in discriminant analysis, indicating that a longer survey more
orientated to economic or financial issues may be required if
such models are to be employed in spatial planning. The one
used is obviously biased to the 'push' of an unsatisfactory
transition zone location whereas more influential for relocating
firms could be 'pull' factors of the proposed new site. Their
incorporation would be a first step were discriminant models
reapplied for predictive purposes. Land use recommendations
thus proceed with background information now more detailed
than is usual but inevitably imperfect.

SPATIAL PLANNING FOR BUSINESS DEVELOPMENT

While in Bowen Hills, as in other transition zone areas, a
scenario of abandoned sites and depressed commercial development is not imminent, care is required to ensure that it
is avoided. Despite the suburb's apparent advantages, certain
types of employment have not grown in recent years. The
economic future seems to lie in the three chief functions:
publishing, railway maintenance and small business. Analysis
of the 23 firms planning relocation reveals that their total
full-time employment is 216 which represents 7.6 per cent of
the suburb's private sector workforce (as defined). Yet the
potential for relocation could have been underestimated.
Problems in lease negotiation could increase it or, instead,

302

prompt business closure. The survey did not consider company failure. Among 150 small businesses, one would expect several withdrawals every year because of insolvency, retirement and other factors. Public planning for the transition zone must accommodate such uncertainties. In some respects, they are more problematic than clear-cut evidence that an area is depressed and requires an encompassing solution such as the establishment of an enterprise zone. Policy should identify objectives for an area before considering the methods by which they might be best fulfilled.

Objectives
From the foregoing analysis, key intra-metropolitan roles for the Bowen Hills zone could be to provide:

(a) substantial employment in the two major labour-intensive industries (publishing and railways);

(b) accessibility for business along major transport arteries;

(c) a node of better-class warehousing, retailing and personal services; and

(d) a nursery area involving leased accommodation for entrepreneurs, local marketers and marginally profitable firms.

These possible economic roles require different planning responses and incentives. The first, employment maintenance, would preserve efficient working conditions so that the two major employers are not impeded by local as opposed to wider economic issues (cf. Davies, 1981: 23). No evidence suggests that either the metropolis or the suburb would be well served by their displacement. In each case, avoidance of traffic congestion, and better access for employees (in parking space and public transport) are key needs.

The second point concerning accessibility recognises Bowen Hills' comparative intra-metropolitan advantage in vehicle sales and service. Planning must provide showroom visibility, clear streets, on-site parking, good loading areas and so forth. These elements are also essential to the development of the wholesale-retail-services node. If the suburb is to retain its State branch offices, it will be essential that certain precincts maintain a tidy appearance with good commercial exposure, attractive signs, landscaping, quality architecture and the avoidance of vehicular nuisance. This sector can take particular advantage of Bowen Hills' location and may develop economies of agglomeration. It makes sense to enhance linkages wherever they are facilitative, and factors outlined above which promote company stability should be noted. Also suggested is positive discrimination toward manufacturer's representatives, showrooms and the vehicle industry and some discouragement of non-related operations. The aim in this precinct is to develop a modern, solid business sector in a relatively planned environment with no blight and little dysfunction among adjacent land uses.

The final sector, the nursery, would occupy the 'down market' areas. Planning here would stress the maintenance of cheap, 'no-frills' accommodation with minimal internal control but adequate regulation at the boundaries. Firms would trade low-cost rentals for a relative lack of services: the precinct would probably feature quite high turnover of companies. Accordingly care would have to be taken to control vacancy or blight. In this way a metropolitan authority could move towards 'enterprise zone' conditions without formal legislation. Physical planning stipulations could be immediately relaxed and some economic concessions mooted. These 'nursery' areas, like enterprise zones, could have an experimental role not only to gauge their overall effectiveness in stimulating business, but also to see whether one or other component of the package appeared more useful. Although consultants in Britain have evaluated enterprise zones, more could be known about the effectiveness of individual measures.

Methods

Future development in Bowen Hills could be conducted under alternative auspices. The first might be major public redevelopment, attractive because it is controlled, timely and decisive. It is unlikely because of the cost and because other parts of Brisbane's transition zone are more deserving of attention. Moreover, expensive public intervention should not be a first resort (as it often was in the 1950s and 1960s). The second possibility is major private redevelopment (as has frequently followed public initiative in British enterprise zones). Yet it shares certain problems with its predecessor: in proposing large-scale renewal, it could force a significant number of firms from business and preclude the nursery function outlined above. Given the objectives, major public or private redevelopment could be inappropriate.

Thus for Bowen Hills and certain counterparts elsewhere, non-integrated private redevelopment appears worth considering. It recognises the many physical constraints: fragmented ownership, small lots, narrow streets, some dilapidated structures and old services. Advanced here as a positive planning strategy, it emphasises the need to let market forces act in a relatively unfettered way. Of course, it does not envisage an entirely laissez faire situation since important constraints cannot be ignored. The approach could cause strain if sites became too congested, offered inadequate access and amenity and became too small to cater for reasonable company expansion. Redevelopment proposals would be

304

subject to the standard council requirements of road widening, access, circulation and parking. Bowen Hills presently
offers a reasonable commercial environment by standards of
the Australian transition zone. The aim should be to allow
business to expand if necessary at the expense of other
landuses and so create differentiated commercial environments
which can best exploit comparative advantages.

POSITIVE APPROACHES TO THE TRANSITION ZONE

This chapter has stressed two major themes. First, despite
attention accorded inner city problems in the northern hemisphere during the recent recession, not all transition zones
are depressed or blighted. Their potential as a springboard
for small new business should not be overlooked. Second,
much interest has followed the development in Europe and
North America of enterprise zones. Arguably they are an
economic rather than a spatial solution: they are certainly not
cost-free; and they resemble a blockbusting approach to
urban problems. Where possible, in transition zones showing
at least some economic prospect, first resort should be to the
more traditional tools of the planner sharpened with extra
research. Analyses have been suggested, and recommendations advanced which could be enacted through ordinances or
zoning. Also, it is unnecessary to see enterprise zones as an
'all or nothing' solution: already they vary in application.
This chapter has further proposed 'nursery' areas in which
conditions could be varied to approach or, in certain cases,
replicate those of an 'enterprise zone'.

Performance standards as well as the traditional built
form controls are now favoured in many advanced cities. As
opposed to rigidly defined zones and land use categories,
standards based on productive processes and characteristics
of businesses could play a valuable role in development. Many
industrial and commercial practices have changed considerably
with technological progress (Cardew, 1981: 92): they may no
longer constitute 'nuisances' in respect of embracing residential activity. A far greater regulatory role than in the
past is played by environmental protection agencies whose
evaluations may be much more comprehensive than town
planners' policing of 'nuisance' factors. Some of the key
performance criteria are the generation of traffic, hours of
business, noise, waste disposal and compatibility of processes. These are the issues which should be under discussion in positive economic and physical planning for
business development.

Inner area problems are certainly far worse in older
overseas cities than in Australia. From the United Kingdom,
Davies (1981: 15) warns that the physical environment can
create discontent and deter investment. British urban policy

aims to reduce and, where possible, arrest the decline of inner areas by:

(a) strengthening inner area economies and the prospects for residents by preserving and encouraging the expansion of existing forms and by the attraction of new investment;

(b) improving the physical fabric, enhancing the environment, soliciting new investment and restoring confidence in the future of such areas;

(c) alleviating social problems and providing for those in social need through action by public authorities and community care; and

(d) re-balancing inner areas and the rest of the city region in terms of population and jobs, by enhancing the jobs offered and skills available in inner areas.

Kindred objectives appear in Australian literature. Of increasing relevance, they require thought by various metropolitan authorities which in situations of rapid change might find fully researched and areally-specific policies useful. An approach which stresses positive factors rather than endemic problems has been put forward here in support of local development control planning. If one believes that the struggle against unemployment is worth pursuing, the transition zone warrants reappraisal as an entity which, with further management, could be dynamic and constitute an important urban labour shed.

REFERENCES

Botham, R. and Lloyd, G. (1983) 'The Political Economy of Enterprise Zones', Westminster Bank Quarterly Review, (May) 24-32

Butler, S.M. (1982) Enterprise Zones: Greenlining the Inner Cities, (London: Heinemann), pp. 175

Cardew, R.V. (1981) Government Regulation of Industrial Property Development, [Publication No. 92], Australian Institute of Urban Studies, Canberra, n.c.p.

Davies, H.W.E. (1981) 'The Inner City in Britain', pp. 1-36 in G.G. Schwartz (ed.), Advanced Industrialisation and the Inner Cities, Lexington Books, Lexington

Fagan, R.H. McKay, J. and Linge, G.J.R. (1981) 'Structural Change: The International and National Context', Chapter 1, pp. 1-49 in G.J.R. Linge and J.S. McKay (eds.), Structural Change in Australia: Some Spatial and

Organisational Responses, [Publication HG/15, Department of Human Geography, Research School of Pacific Studies], Australian National University, Canberra

Harris, C.D. and Ullman, E.L. (1945) 'The Nature of Cities', Annals of the American Academy of Political and Social Science, 242, pp. 7-17

Jones, B.G. and Manson, D.M. (1982) 'The Economic Geography of Enterprize Zones: A Critical Analysis', Economic Geography, 58, pp. 329-42

Wadley, D. and Bentley, L. (1981) 'Industrial Restructuring and Metropolitan Planning: Case History of Melbourne', Chapter 8, pp. 237-72 in G.J.R. Linge and J.S. McKay (eds.), Structural Change in Australia: Some Organisational and Spatial Responses, [Publication HG/15, Department of Human Geography, Research School of Pacific Studies], Australian National University, Canberra

Wilde, P. (1986) 'Economic Restructuring and Australia's Changing Role in the World Economic System', in F.E. Ian Hamilton (ed.), Industrialization in Developing and Peripheral Regions, Croom Helm, London

INDEX

312

INDEX

Unskilled work 7-8
US Manufacturing Belt 117-19
US National Academy of
Sciences 15, 22
US Office of Technology
Assessment 263, 269
USSR State Planning
Committee (GOSPLAN)
208, 210-11
US Sunbelt 169, 175-6
Utterbeck, J.M. 262, 269

Varga, G. 202, 207
Vatne, E. 186, 196
Vea, E. 191, 193, 196
Venezuela 85-6, 90, 123
Venture capital 175-8, 263-8
Vernon, R. 240, 257, 260
Virgin Islands (USA) 50-1
Volvo AB 25-44, 253
VUKOV 18-19, 22

Wadley, D. 296, 307
Wages 2, 7-8, 124-6, 161,
172, 232, 251

Walker, D.F. 271, 277, 289,
291
Warnke, T. 280, 290
Water 58, 238
Waterman, R.H. 15, 22
Watts, H.D. 192, 196
Weilenmann, P. 272, 291
Welding 39-44, 226-7
White Plains (USA) 143-4
Wholesaling and distribution
75, 235, 297-300, 303
Wiedersheim-Paul, F. 123-4,
128
Williams, O.E. 180, 182-4, 195
Winter, S.G. 179, 195
Working-life-conditions 5,
7-11, 15, 39-44
Work organisation/tasks 23-6,
32, 39-44, 250, 253

Yakutsk TPC 208, 211
Yamaha 223, 225, 238
Yugoslavia 45, 47, 95, 144

Zoning 296-306